W9-BQM-977

AFRICAN AMERICAN BIOGRAPHY

VOLUME 2
E–J

U·X·L

An Imprint of Gale Research Inc.

AFRICAN AMERICAN BIOGRAPHY

14146 1980
(A)

STAFF

Carol DeKane Nagel, *U•X•L Developmental Editor*
Thomas L. Romig, *U•X•L Publisher*

Amy Marcaccio, *Acquisitions Editor*

Barbara A. Wallace, *Permissions Assistant (Pictures)*
Shanna P. Heilveil, *Production Assistant*
Evi Seoud, *Assistant Production Manager*
Mary Beth Trimper, *Production Director*

Cynthia Baldwin, *Art Director*

Weigl Educational Publishers Limited, *Page and Cover Design and Typesetting*

Library of Congress Cataloging-in-Publication Data

African American biography.
      p. cm. -- (African American reference library)
    Includes index.
    Contents: v. 1. A-D -- v. 2. E-J -- v. 3 K-R -- v. 4 S-Z
    ISBN 0-8103-9234-8 (Set : alk. paper); 0-8103-9235-6 (v. 1); 0-8103-9236-4 (v. 2); 0-8103-9237-2
      (v. 3); 0-8103-9238-0 (v. 4)
    1. Afro-Americans--Biography. I. U•X•L. II. Series.
E185.96.A44 1993
920'.009296073--dc20
[B]
                                                                 93-45651
                                                                CIP

AFRICAN AMERICAN REFERENCE LIBRARY

The **African American Reference Library** fills the need for a comprehensive, curriculum-related reference covering all aspects of African American life and culture. Aimed primarily at middle school and junior high school students, this nine-volume set combines appropriate reading level and fascinating subject matter with quality biographies, statistics, essays, chronologies, document and speech excerpts, and more.

The **African American Reference Library** consists of three separate components:

African American Biography (four volumes) profiles three hundred African Americans, both living and deceased, prominent in their fields, from civil rights to athletics, politics to literature, entertainment to science, religion to the military. A black-and-white portrait accompanies each entry, and a cumulative subject index lists all individuals by field of endeavor.

African American Almanac (three volumes) provides a comprehensive range of historical and current information on African American life and culture. Organized by subject, the volumes contain 270 black-and-white illustrations, a selected bibliography, and a cumulative subject index.

African American Chronology (two volumes) explores significant social, political, economic, cultural, and educational milestones in black history. Arranged by year and then by month and day, the volumes span from 1492 until June 30, 1993, and contain 106 illustrations and maps, extensive cross references, and a cumulative subject index.

Comments and suggestions
We welcome your comments on *African American Biography* as well as your suggestions for topics to be featured in future **African American Reference Library** series. Please write:

Editors, **African American Reference Library,** U•X•L, 835 Penobscot Bldg., Detroit, Michigan 48226-4094; call toll-free: 1-800-877-4253; or fax: 313-961-6348.

CONTENTS

AFRICAN AMERICAN BIOGRAPHY

Volume 1: A-D

Hank Aaron
Kareem Abdul-Jabbar
Ralph David Abernathy
Alvin Ailey
Muhammad Ali
Marian Anderson
Maya Angelou
Louis Armstrong
Molefi Kete Asante
Arthur Ashe
Pearl Bailey
Augusta Baker
Josephine Baker
James Baldwin
Amiri Baraka
Ida B. Wells Barnett
Marguerite Ross Barnett
Marion Barry
Count Basie
Daisy Bates
Kathleen Battle
Harry Belafonte
Chuck Berry
Halle Berry
Mary McLeod Bethune
Dave Bing
Julian Bond
Bobby Bonilla
Arna Bontemps
Riddick Bowe
Ed Bradley
Carol Moseley Braun
Edward W. Brooke III

Gwendolyn Brooks
Claude Brown
H. Rap Brown
James Brown
Ron Brown
Ed Bullins
Grace Bumbry
Ralph Bunche
Yvonne Brathwaite Burke
Octavia E. Butler
Cab Calloway
Roy Campanella
Naomi Campbell
Stokely Carmichael
Benjamin Carson
George Washington Carver
Wilt Chamberlain
Ray Charles
Charles Waddell Chesnutt
Alice Childress
Shirley Chisholm
Joe Clark
Eldridge Cleaver
George Clements
Jewel Plummer Cobb
Johnnetta Betsch Cole
Natalie Cole
Nat "King" Cole
Bessie Coleman
Marva Collins
John Coltrane
Anna J. Cooper
Don Cornelius
Bill Cosby

Elizabeth Cotten
Ellen Craft
Countee Cullen
Angela Davis
Benjamin O. Davis, Sr.
Miles Davis
Ossie Davis
Sammy Davis, Jr.
Juliette Derricotte
Irene Diggs
David Dinkins
Sharon Pratt Dixon
  See Sharon Pratt Kelly
Thomas A. Dorsey
Frederick Douglass
Charles Richard Drew
William Edward Burghardt (W.E.B.) DuBois
Paul Laurence Dunbar
Katherine Dunham

Volume 2: E-J

Marian Wright Edelman
Elleanor Eldridge
Duke Ellington
Effie O'Neal Ellis
Ralph Ellison
Medgar Evers
James Farmer
Louis Farrakhan
Ella Fitzgerald
Aretha Franklin
John Hope Franklin
Mary Hatwood Futrell
Ernest J. Gaines
Marcus Garvey
Arthur Gaston
Henry Louis Gates, Jr.
Zelma Watson George

Althea Gibson
Dizzy Gillespie
Nikki Giovanni
Robin Givens
Danny Glover
Whoopi Goldberg
W. Wilson Goode
Charles Gordone
Berry Gordy, Jr.
Dick Gregory
Angelina Weld Grimké
Bryant Gumbel
Lucille C. Gunning
Clara Hale
Alex Haley
Arsenio Hall
Fannie Lou Hamer
Virginia Hamilton
Hammer
Lionel Hampton
Lorraine Hansberry
The Harlem Globetrotters
Barbara Harris
Marcelite Harris
Patricia Harris
Robert Hayden, Jr.
Dorothy Height
Jimi Hendrix
Matthew Henson
Aileen Hernandez
Anita Hill
Chester Himes
Gregory Hines
Billie Holiday
Benjamin L. Hooks
Lena Horne
Whitney Houston
Langston Hughes

Pauli Murray
Gloria Naylor
Huey Newton
Jessye Norman
Hazel O'Leary
Shaquille O'Neal
Jesse Owens
Satchel Paige
Gordon Parks
Rosa Parks
Sidney Poitier
Adam Clayton Powell, Jr.
Colin Powell
Leontyne Price
Charley Pride
Barbara Gardner Proctor
Richard Pryor
Public Enemy
Lloyd Albert Quarterman
Queen Latifah
Dudley Randall
A. Philip Randolph
William Raspberry
Ishmael Reed
Eslanda Goode Robeson
Paul Robeson
Jackie Robinson
Charlemae Hill Rollins
Diana Ross
Carl T. Rowan
Wilma Rudolph
Bill Russell
Bayard Rustin

Volume 4: S-Z

Edith Sampson
Sonia Sanchez
Dred Scott

Gloria Scott
Bobby Seale
Attalah Shabazz
Ntozake Shange
Al Sharpton
Althea T.L. Simmons
Carole Simpson
Naomi Sims
John Singleton
Bessie Smith
Wesley Snipes
George Stallings, Jr.
Shelby Steele
William Grant Still
Juanita Kidd Stout
Niara Sudarkasa
Henry Ossawa Tanner
Mildred Taylor
Susan Taylor
Susie Baker King Taylor
Mary Church Terrell
Clarence Thomas
Jean Toomer
Jackie Torrence
Toussaint-Louverture
Robert Townsend
William Monroe Trotter
Sojourner Truth
Harriet Tubman
Nat Turner
Mario Van Peebles
Sarah Vaughan
Denmark Vesey
Charleszetta Waddles
Alice Walker
Madame C.J. Walker
Maggie L. Walker
Sippie Wallace

PHOTO CREDITS

The photographs and illustrations appearing in *African American Biography* were received from the following sources:

On the covers: **Schomburg Center for Research in Black Culture, The New York Public Library, Astor, Lenox and Tilden Foundations:** Althea Gibson; **AP/Wide World Photos:** Josephine Baker; **Archive Photos:** Elijah Muhammad.

AP/Wide World Photos: pages 1, 4, 6, 9, 12, 18, 22, 26, 33, 36, 44, 47, 49, 51, 54, 62, 76, 80, 84, 94, 98, 113, 115, 117, 122, 124, 127, 141, 185, 231, 236, 238, 241, 257, 259, 270, 275, 277, 282, 287, 290, 295, 303, 305, 313, 336, 340, 343, 344, 350, 352, 356, 377, 380, 386, 388, 390, 393, 399, 415, 418, 431, 444, 447, 450, 463, 471, 475, 477, 483, 497, 499, 506, 521, 528, 534, 539, 553, 561, 566, 569, 574, 577, 584, 588, 590, 593, 612, 622, 625, 631, 633, 642, 658, 666, 668, 671, 681, 683, 692, 703, 712, 724, 737, 740, 745, 762, 765, 770, 774, 790, 794, 797, 799, 805; **Courtesy of Molefi Kete Asante:** page 24; **Schomburg Center for Research in Black Culture, The New York Public Library, Astor, Lenox and Tilden Foundations:** pages 29, 30, 41, 103, 174, 179, 208, 216, 244, 246, 267, 308, 359, 383, 420, 492, 515, 635, 679, 706, 732, 772; **Courtesy of Belafonte Enterprises:** page 56; **UPI/Bettmann Newsphotos:** pages 59, 199, 360, 434, 459, 468, 578, 637, 756, 777; **U.S. Office of War Information, Prints and Photographs Division, Library of Congress:** page 63; **Ed Haun/Detroit Free Press:** page 66; **UPI/Bettmann:** pages 68, 144, 147, 494, 526, 689, 767; **Reuters/Bettmann:** pages 72, 82, 157, 676; **Harper Brothers:** page 87; **Photograph by Larry McLucas:** page 90; **Courtesy of the United Nations (31216):** page 105; **Raymond W. Smock, Historian:** page 108; **National Education Television:** page 120; **Jazz Institute of Rutgers University:** pages 131, 229; **Photograph by Willard Moore:** page 136; **Courtesy of Shirley Chisholm:** page 139; **Courtesy of Jewel Plummer Cobb:** page 149; **Rick Diamond Photography:** page 151; **The Bettmann Archive:** pages 159, 422; **Courtesy of Marva Collins:** page 162; **Downbeat:** page 164; **Moorland-Spingarn Research Center, Howard University:** pages 167, 328, 543, 647, 708; **Photograph by Marco Sacchi:** page 169; **Photograph by Howard Bingham, Copyright © 1990 Universal City Studios Inc.:** page 172; **American Broadcasting Company:** pages 181, 316, 453; **Photograph by Anthony Barbaoza, © 1988 CBS Records Inc.:** page 187; **Universal

African American Biography

Marian Wright Edelman

Lawyer, children's rights crusader
Born June 6, 1939, Bennettsville, South
   Carolina

"I realize that I am not fighting just for myself and my people in the South, when I fight for freedom and equality. I realize now that I fight for the moral and political health of America as a whole and for her position in the world at large."

R ecognized as a leading spokesperson for the concerns of children, Marian Wright Edelman is the founder and president of the Children's Defense Fund. She has lobbied for new laws, campaigned against teenage pregnancy, and overseen the development of more than 2,000 pages of research on children each year.

Also author of several books, Edelman wrote in *Families in Peril: An Agenda for Social Change*: "As adults we are responsible for meeting the needs of children. It is our moral obligation. We brought about their births and their lives, and they cannot fend for themselves."

Influenced by her father

Edelman was born on June 6, 1939, to Arthur Jerome Wright and Maggie Leola (Bowen) Wright in Bennettsville, South Carolina. Her father was a great influence in her life. He expected his children to get an education and to serve their community, and Edelman did both. Her father believed in black role models and took her to hear prominent blacks whenever they came to town, including Marian Anderson, after whom she was named.

After she graduated from Marlboro Training High School, Edelman's mother and brother, Harry, convinced her to attend Spelman College in Atlanta, Georgia, in 1956. Her outstanding grades earned her a Charles Merrill overseas study/travel grant during her junior year. After spending the first summer at the Sorbonne in Paris, she spent the rest of the academic year at the University of Geneva in Switzerland.

Edelman studied for two months in the Soviet Union during her second semester under a Lisle fellowship. She wanted to visit Russia because of her interest in Tolstoy. After spending so much time traveling, she returned to Spelman College in 1959 a changed person. The civil rights movement was just beginning, and she decided to get involved. In 1960 she participated in one of the largest sit-ins at the Atlanta city hall.

Responded to need for civil rights lawyer

Because civil rights lawyers were so badly needed, Edelman abandoned her intention to pursue graduate work in Russian studies and applied to Yale University's Law School in 1960 and entered as a John Hay Whitney Fellow. She graduated from Yale in 1963, trained for a year in New York, and went to Jackson, Mississippi, as one of the first two interns for the National Association for the Advancement of Colored People (NAACP) Legal Defense and Educational Fund.

Edelman opened her own law office in 1964, although much of her time was spent getting students out of jail. For her trouble she was threatened by dogs, thrown into jail, and even refused entry into the state courthouse on her way to take the Mississippi bar exam. At the age of 26 she became the first black woman to pass the bar in Mississippi. Edelman headed the NAACP Legal Defense and Education Fund in Mississippi from 1964 to 1968.

Moves to Washington

Realizing that the way to make any serious changes in Mississippi would have to be through federal policy, Edelman got a Field Foundation grant to study how to make laws work for the poor and moved to Washington, D.C., in March 1968 to start the Washington Research Project. In July she married Peter Edelman, who had been a Kennedy aide.

In 1971 the Edelmans moved to Boston where he became vice-president of the University of Massachusetts and she became director of the Harvard University Center for Law and Education. Edelman returned weekly to Washington to oversee the activities of the Washington Research Project.

CDF Forms

In 1973 Edelman founded the Washington-based Children's Defense Fund (CDF), a nonprofit child advocacy group. The CDF was designed to provide assistance to children and to make their needs better known. Edelman's devotion to her work caused Senator Edward Kennedy to refer to her as the "101st Senator on children's issues." The Edelmans moved back to Washington in 1979 when Peter re-

ceived a teaching post at the Georgetown University Law Centre.

In 1983 teen pregnancy became a dominant issue with the CDF. Some statistics indicated that 55.5 percent of all black babies were born out of wedlock, many of them to teenage girls, which Edelman realized would create a new generation of blacks living in poverty. The CDF launched a major long-term national campaign to prevent teenage pregnancy.

Edelman's leadership caused the CDF to become one of the country's most active and effective groups concerned with a wide range of children's and family issues. Their mission is to teach the country about children's needs and encourage preventive measures in children before they get sick, drop out of school, suffer early pregnancy or family breakdown, or get into trouble. CDF has become an effective voice in the areas of adolescent pregnancy prevention, child health, education, child care, youth employment, child welfare and mental health, and family support systems.

Edelman is especially proud of the CDF's efforts in the courts. Their legal actions blocked out-of-state placement of hundreds of Louisiana children in Texas institutions, guaranteed access to special education programs for many of Mississippi's children, and represented the interests of children and their families before many federal administrative agencies.

Received numerous awards

Edelman is also the author of several books, including: *Children Out of School in America*, *Portrait of Inequality: Black and White Children in America*, and *School Suspensions: Are They Helping Children?* Her book *Families in*

Marian Wright Edelman

Peril: An Agenda for Social Change was judged a "powerful and necessary document" by *Washington Post* reviewer Jonathan Yardley.

In 1971 Edelman became the first black woman elected to Yale University Corporation, and she served on the board of the Carnegie Council on Children from 1972 to 1977. In 1980 she became the first black and second woman to chair the board of trustees at Spelman College, and she serves on numerous boards. Edelman has received numerous awards in connection with her CDF work, and in 1985 she won the prestigious MacArthur Foundation Prize fellowship.

Elleanor Eldridge

Entrepreneur
Born March 26, 1785, Warwick, Rhode
   Island
Died 1865

Academics still wonder if the story of Elleanor Eldridge is folklore or whether she truly existed. According to the 1838 narrative, *The Memoirs of Elleanor Eldridge*, she was a black entrepreneur who was swindled by unscrupulous white property owners and the local sheriff. Some feel the book was written by Eldridge herself, but others credit the authorship to Frances Whipple Greene. Some accounts seem to suggest that Eldridge actually lived and was not a product of Greene's imagination.

Learns many skills

Eldridge was born on March 26, 1785, in Warwick, Rhode Island, to Robin and Hannah Eldridge. She was the granddaughter of a native African trader, who along with his family, was kidnapped and sold into slavery. They were tempted on board a ship by an American slaver under the ruse that they were about to make a lucrative trade deal. The Congo chieftain did not realize his mistake until the ship set sail.

Eldridge's maternal grandmother was a Native American named Mary Fuller, who purchased her slave husband, Thomas Prophet, by selling a portion of the many acres that her family owned. Eldridge's father was a former slave who won his freedom by volunteering his services for the American Revolution. He was also promised free land, but the government reneged on the deal, and he was forced to work and save for it. When Eldridge was ten, her mother died, and one of her mother's laundry customers, Elleanor Baker, took an interest in her. Baker convinced Eldridge's father to allow the girl to stay with her.

MEMOIRS

OF

ELLEANOR ELDRIDGE.

O that estates, degrees and offices,
Were not derived corruptly! and that clear honor
Were purchased by the merit of the wearer!
How many, then, should cover, that stand bare?
How many be commanded, that command?
How much low peasantry would then be gleaned
From the true seed of honor? and how much honor
Picked from the chaff and ruin of the times,
To be new varnished?—*Merchant of Venice.*

Elleanor Elridge

Eldridge learned many skills from Baker that she would eventually use when she established her own business.

Through hard work, Eldridge managed to save enough to buy a parcel of land and build a home. She learned many trades including managing a dairy, weaving, whitewashing, and wallpapering, and she contracted these skills to do local jobs. After buying a considerable amount of real estate in Warwick, Eldridge wanted to purchase a parcel of land and buildings adjacent to her home. She reached a verbal deal to buy the property for two thousand dollars over a four-year period. She paid five hundred dollars and left to visit relatives in Adams, Massachusetts.

En route she suffered from a bout of typhus fever and was forced to spend a few days recovering in a hotel in Hadley. She was recognized by several of her townspeople who spread the rumor that she was near death. This rumor allowed the man with whom she reached the real estate deal, to acquire illegally her land and possessions. Eldridge recovered from the fever, finished her journey, and returned to find her home taken from her.

She took the matter to court with documented proof that the sale of her property had not been rightfully advertised and conducted. The judge threw out the evidence by insisting that due notice had been given. The only way for Eldridge to get her property back was to buy it. The unrightful owner elevated the original cost of the property and added the cost of storing her personal items to the bill. Eldridge accepted this deal, worked off the debt, and finally regained her life's work.

A groundswell of support

Through the ordeal, Eldridge had the support of numerous friends, both black and white. Her fine reputation in town gained her support among Warwick's local residents in her lawsuit against Warwick's sheriff for improprieties in the sale of her property. In *The Memoirs of Elleanor Eldridge*, one supporter wrote, "Having employed Elleanor Eldridge to work for me, occasionally, during the last sixteen years, at white-washing, painting, papering, &c., I can recommend her, as an honest, industrious, and faithful woman, who has been peculiarly unfortunate in the loss of her property, which she obtained by thirty years of hard labor."

Several others wrote similar messages: "We, the undersigned, having known and employed Elleanor Eldridge to work for us during many years, recommend her as an uncommonly industrious woman—honest and faithful. We think her deserving to hold the property so dearly bought, with the hard labor of thirty years; and worthy a PREMIUM for her untiring perseverance to make herself independent of charity, when sickness, or old age should disable her to pursue her accustomed avocations."

If matters could have been settled by popular support, Eldridge would have regained her property. Since she was a black woman, she was treated differently than a man; if the episode had happened to a white woman, the community would have been up in arms.

It is difficult to say whether or not Eldridge truly existed. Louis Kaplan, editor of the *Dictionary of American Negro Autobiographies*, states that Eldridge wrote *The Memoirs of Elleanor Eldridge*. He found an 1838 entry that is described as "The Story of Negro servant in Rhode Island," and an 1839 description that provides more evidence that Eldridge is the author.

Bert Loewenberg and Ruth Bogin in the book, *Black Women in 19th Century American Life*, closely examined the 1830 census of free blacks in Providence, Rhode Island. Here they found evidence that Eldridge truly existed: "An Elleanor Eldridge...seems clearly to have been the person in question. There can be little doubt of her existence. The volume was certainly written about her, although some fictitious elements cling to the narrative."

Duke Ellington

Bandleader, composer, pianist
Born April 29, 1899, Washington, D.C.
Died May 24, 1974, New York, New York

"The writing and playing of music is a matter of intent.... You can't just throw a paint brush against the wall and call whatever happens art.... I think too strongly in terms of altering my music to fit the performer to be impressed by accidental music."

One of the most outstanding musicians in the history of jazz, Duke Ellington composed well over two thousand pieces during his fifty-five-year career. His works range from songs such as "Take the A-Train," "Sophisticated Lady," and "It Don't Mean a Thing (If You Ain't Got Swing)" to longer works such as *Black, Brown, and Beige* and *Liberian Suite*. They also include sacred music and incidental music for movies and musical comedies.

Most of Ellington's music was written for his own bands, which he led from 1918 until his death. His style as a bandleader brought him the adoration of the public, while his musical innovations brought him the admiration of jazz lovers. He introduced such features as the "jungle-style" use of the growl and plunger, and the use of the human voice as an instrument (by having his soloists sing without words). Jazz critic Ralph Gleason called Ellington the greatest single talent in the history of jazz, and journalist Alistair Cooke said of him, "No one else, in the eighty- or ninety-year history of jazz, created so personal an orchestral sound and so continuously expanded the jazz idiom."

A middle-class upbringing

Ellington acquired the nickname Duke when he was a teenager. It is said to have been given to him because of his elegant and aristocratic manner. As Edward Kennedy Ellington, he was born into a middle-class family, the son of James and Daisy (Kennedy) Ellington. His father made blueprints for the U.S. Navy, but also moonlighted as a butler in order to provide a comfortable and pleasant upbringing for his son and his daughter, Ruth. "I was raised in love," Ellington said, describing the affection showered on him by his devoutly religious parents.

Both of Ellington's parents played the piano, and Ellington was taught to play at an early age—though not with great success. When he was six, he labeled his teacher "Miss Clinkscales" and was the only child to forget his part in her annual piano recital. The following year, "Miss Clinkscales" refused to have him as a pupil because of his passion for experimenting with off-tone chords. Left to his own devices, Ellington showed more talent for drawing than for music. But by the time he was a teenager at Washington's M Street High School, he was taking the piano seriously and was glad to study under the school music teacher, Henry Grant.

When Ellington was fifteen, he took an after-school job in a soda shop, an experience that gave him the idea for "Soda Fountain Rag," his first jazz song. Intent on becoming a musician, he dropped out of school in his senior year and began to play with various jazz groups on an occasional basis. Until the work became regular, he supported himself with a daytime job painting commercial signs.

By 1918 Ellington was in a position to form his own band, which he called the Duke's Serenaders. Although he had a number of bands with different names over the years, it was basically the same band, for he kept many of the same players. This first group featured saxophone player Otto Hardwick, trumpeter Artie Whetsol, and banjoist Elmer Snowden, who were joined the following year by drummer Sonny Greer and banjoist Sterling Conway. Other well-known players who later joined Ellington included Harry Carney, Johnny Hodges, Bubber Miley, Joe Nanton, and Billy Strayhorn.

The year 1918 also launched Ellington's short-lived marriage to Edna Thompson, with whom he was to have one son, the trumpeter Mercer Ellington.

Trail-blazing bandleader

Ellington's band played mostly at local clubs and parties in Washington, but in 1922 he had the chance to play with Wilbur Sweatman's band in New York, and the following year Ellington moved his own band there. They played mainly in Harlem clubs, and in 1927 they began a five-year engagement at the popular Cotton Club. This brought the sound of Ellington's music into every American home, because the performances were broadcast live over the CBS radio network.

It was indeed "Ellington's music" that the public heard—music written by Ellington specifically for his band to play. When composing a piece, he often had a particular player in mind, and he wrote the score to give full rein to that person's style. His compositions were lush and lyrical, often rambling in unexpected places, and they included innovations such as dissonant chords and the use of slurs and mutes to create "jungle sounds." Ellington maintained that he did not write jazz. What he wrote, he said, was "Negro music with very deep African roots."

In the 1930s, Ellington's band made two tours of Europe, where his music had become popular through records of "It Don't Mean a Thing," "Rockin' in Rhythm," and other Ellington hits. The band had also gained fans through its appearance in stage shows and films. In the early 1920s, Ellington had written the revue *Chocolate Kiddies* (which ran for two years in Germany), and in 1929 his band played in the Broadway revue *Show Girl* and the movie *Black and Tan*. The 1930s saw them playing in the films *Check and Double Check* (1930), *She's Got Her Man* (1935), *Murder at the Vanities* (1935), and *Hit Parade* (1937).

Wide-ranging composer

Toward the end of the 1930s Ellington wrote his first longer pieces, such as the miniature concerto "Clarinet Lament," which he composed for clarinetist Barney Bigard. In 1943 he gave the first performance of his *Black, Brown, and Beige,* a jazz symphony that represents the story of African Americans. The piece is arranged in three sections: "Black" is about black people at work and at prayer; "Brown" celebrates black soldiers who fought in the American Revolution; and "Beige" focuses on the African American music of Harlem.

The 1943 premiere performance was conducted by Ellington at Carnegie Hall as the first of a series of annual jazz concerts he organized. The series, which continued until 1955, saw the performance of other works by Ellington, including *New World a-Comin'*, *The Tattooed Bride, Night Creature,* and *Liberian Suite*. The latter was commissioned by the Liberian government to mark Liberia's centenary celebrations in 1947. Ellington received a further honor in 1950 when the world-famous Italian conductor Arturo Toscanini commissioned him to write the jazz symphony *Harlem* for the NBC Symphony Orchestra.

During this period Ellington kept up his theatrical work, writing incidental music for films and musicals, as well as for a production of *Timon of Athens* staged by the Stratford Shakespeare Festival in Ontario, Canada. Meanwhile, he continued to conduct the Duke Ellington Orchestra in settings that ranged from television to churches. Ellington gave his first sacred concert in 1965, when he conducted his orchestra at a solemn jazz concert at Grace Episcopal Cathedral in San Francisco. The performance began with a musical

Duke Ellington

sermon, "In the Beginning God." Ellington gave similar concerts of jazz-style sacred music in New York and other American cities, as well as in France, Spain, and England.

On Ellington's seventieth birthday in 1969, President Richard Nixon invited him to a party at the White House, where Ellington received the Presidential Medal of Freedom. Ellington's other awards include the French Legion of Honor in 1973 and several Grammy Awards. Toward the end of his life he was recommended for a Pulitzer Prize, but the Pulitzer advisory board decided against him. On hearing this, Ellington said, "Fate's been kind to me. Fate doesn't want me to be famous too young."

Effie O'Neal Ellis

Physician
Born June 15, 1913, Hawkinsville, Georgia

W hile she was studying at university, Effie O'Neal Ellis thought about becoming a researcher on parasites and diseases. But after working with the poor, she realized that she could do more for them as a doctor. Ellis rose through the ranks at several hospitals, and eventually became a major national influence in the area of maternal and child care. She travelled across the country, lecturing on prenatal care for mothers and health care for the poor. Along the way she racked up numerous awards and citations, and was the first black woman administrator for the American Medical Association.

Wanted to specialize in research

Ellis was born on June 15, 1913, to Joshua, a successful home builder, and Althea O'Neal in Hawkinsville, Georgia. She received her grade schooling in Atlanta, and obtained a bachelor's degree with honors in biology and chemistry from Spelman College in 1933. She graduated with a master's degree in biology in 1935 at Atlanta University.

Her research work at Atlanta University was so outstanding that she received a study grant to go to Puerto Rico, where she studied diseases and parasites. Although she seriously considered specializing in parasitological research, her work brought her in contact with the health care that was available to the poor. The experience convinced her to switch to medicine so she could more directly help people.

Ellis entered the University of Illinois College of Medicine, where she began demonstrating her remarkable talent for medicine. She finished fifth in her class, and was among only 23 out of 160 students to graduate with honors. During the 1950 to 1951 academic year she served her internship at the University of Illinois Hospital, and the next year she did a residency in pediatrics at Massachusetts College. Ellis received a postdoctoral fellowship to study heart trouble in children at The John Hopkins University School of Medicine from July 1, 1952, to June 30, 1953. Ellis became the hospital staff physician during this period.

While on her fellowship, she met and married Dr. James D. Solomon on March 23, 1953. Solomon was born in 1913, and received his medical degree from Meharry Medical College in Nashville, Tennessee in 1953. He re-

Effie O'Neal Ellis

ceived his doctorate from the University of Illinois. Solomon went to Saint Elizabeth Hospital in Washington, D.C., in 1953. Five years later he was appointed director of the laboratory at Saint Elizabeth's, a position he held until his retirement in 1983. He is currently semiretired from his private practice and works as a consultant.

Ellis became director of medical education and house pediatrician at Provident Hospital in Baltimore, Maryland from 1953 to 1961. From there, she moved to Columbus, Ohio, where she was the director of maternal and child health for the Ohio State Department of Health. Since Ellis was always concerned with the poor, she tried to have a positive impact on policy-making and decisions regarding their welfare by serving in a number of positions for the federal government. She was chairperson for a panel group at the 1969 White House Conference on Food and Nutrition. She served in the Department of Health,

Education and Welfare (HEW) as its first regional commissioner for social and rehabilitation service. She was also regional medical director of the HEW Children's Bureau.

First black to hold AMA executive office

One of the highlights of her career took place in 1970 when was selected to serve in the newly-created post of special assistant for health services to the American Medical Association (AMA). She was the first black woman to hold an administrative or executive office for the AMA. In this position she was a special advisor on child and maternal health matters and health care for the poor. She stayed in this position for five years.

In all of her jobs, Ellis has stressed comprehensive services for maternal and child health. She also believed in family planning as the greatest preventative tool in obtaining better maternal and child health care. She emphasized that family planning should be more than contraceptive measures. She travelled across the country, speaking to community groups, medical organizations, health associations, and other educational audiences on the subject of prenatal care for mothers and health care for the poor.

One of her biggest concerns was preventative health before the baby was born. She believed every mother should be taught family planning, prenatal and postnatal care, nutrition, sanitation, and be given advice on acute and preventative health care.

Ellis is a member of many organizations including: the National Medical Association, American Public Welfare Association, American Association on Mental Deficiency, American Association for Maternal and Child Health, Alpha Omega Alpha, and Delta Sigma Theta sorority. Among her awards and honors, Ellis is an honorary fellow of the School Health Association. She received the prestigious Trailblazer Award from the National Medical Association in 1970.

Ellis currently resides in Chicago.

Ralph Ellison

Novelist
Born March 1, 1914, Oklahoma City,
    Oklahoma

"I was taken very early with a passion to link together all I loved within the Negro community and all those things I felt in the world which lay beyond."

Best-known for writing *Invisible Man*, a book published in 1952 and soon placed on the curriculum in American schools and colleges, Ralph Ellison became famous and won the National Book Award for fiction. His reputation as an original and powerful writer rests almost entirely on *Invisible Man*. The book took him years to write, and almost all his experiences had been built into it in one way or another. Though the book certainly concerns race, *Invisible Man* is far more than just a story about the struggles of a young black man in a hostile society. It is a complex novel, with many levels of meaning, and it brings together both black and white cultural elements, including blues and folklore.

Influenced by books and music

Ralph Waldo Ellison's father, Lewis Ellison, was a construction worker who died when the boy was three; his mother, Ida (Millsap) Ellison, worked as a domestic. Ellison passed his childhood in Oklahoma, where relations between blacks and whites were easier than in states that had known slavery. From early youth he was familiar with both worlds: in his daily life, he was surrounded daily by the vital black community, and he had a white friend, a boy of his own age who shared a common interest in radio.

Ellison also benefited from the books and magazines his mother brought home from the houses in which she worked. She also gave Ellison music records her employers did not want to keep. He consumed these books, magazines, and records avidly. Believing that music would open the door to the exciting world, he learned the trumpet and played in the school band. His ambition was to compose symphonies, so he enrolled as a music student at Tuskegee Institute in Alabama in 1933.

His interest in literature bloomed at Tuskegee

At Tuskegee Ellison's interest in literature flowered. He began by reading such classics as Emily Bronte's *Wuthering Heights* and Thomas Hardy's *Jude the Obscure*. He was facinated by the poetry of T. S. Eliot, especially *The Waste Land*. He wondered why he had "never read anything of equal intensity and sensibility by an American Negro writer." Before long, Ellison was studying a wide range of nineteenth- and twentieth-century writers, absorbing their thought and the underlying meaning of their works.

During Ellison's second year at Tuskegee, he took a course in sociology, but it disappointed him because of the unrealistic picture it gave of American blacks. All the richness of black life was ignored. Where was the music? Where was the vitality? Where were the jokes and banter? The deficits of the sociology course spurred Ellison's creativity, filling him with an urge to find a way of portraying black culture.

Ellison had an opportunity to gain this wider experience sooner than he had expected, because there was a mix-up over his scholarship and he could not afford to stay on at Tuskegee. In 1936 he moved to New York City, which proved to be a turning point in his life.

Received encouragement from professional writers

In New York Ellison at first studied sculpture but soon decided that literature was his true calling. Two days after his arrival in the city, he met black poet Langston Hughes and later came to know black novelist Richard Wright. Both writers were strong influences on the young man, introducing him to the works of contemporary authors and encouraging him to take up writing.

Within two years Ellison was publishing short stories and essays in the *New Masses,* the *Antioch Review,* and other journals. Meanwhile he worked as a researcher and writer on the Federal Writers' Project in New York, and in 1942 he edited the *Negro Quarterly.* Then he was drafted into the armed forces, serving

Ralph Ellison

from 1942 to 1945 in the U.S. Merchant Marine.

Ellison published some stories while he served in the military, and at the end of the war he married Fanny McConnell and received a Rosenwald fellowship. The income enabled him to concentrate on his writing. Though he had been trying to write a war novel, a more impelling theme kept pushing itself forward. Seven years of work on this theme resulted in *Invisible Man.*

Invisible Man made Ellison famous

Presented in a surreal style and using flashbacks to tell most of the story, *Invisible Man* is a cross-cultural masterpiece that is rich in symbolism. In 1965 a group of leading American writers, critics, and editors judged it to be the most distinguished novel published in the previous twenty years.

The story is about a black youth (who is never named), whose naive trust in the goodness of people is gradually shattered. He is dismissed from a Southern college when the administrators object to his behavior. In New York he becomes involved with Communists, then realizes they are using him. At length he realizes that as an individual—as the person he really is—he is invisible to everyone.

The success of *Invisible Man* established Ellison as a writer of note who was eagerly sought in academic circles, abroad as well as at home. During the early 1950s he gave lecture tours in Germany, Austria, and Italy. He then taught at Yale and other universities before joining the faculty of New York University in 1970 as Albert Schweitzer Professor in Humanities. In 1979 he became professor emeritus.

During this active period, Ellison published his second book in 1964, a collection of essays titled *Shadow and Act.* A second collection, *Going to the Territory,* was published in 1986. He was also writing short stories and working on a second novel, excerpts from which have been published in *Quarterly Review of Literature* and in *Noble Savage* and other journals. The story is set in the South, spanning the years from the jazz age to the civil rights movement. Like *Invisible Man,* published more than forty years ago, the second novel involves a search for identity and is concerned with ideologies and culture.

Medgar Evers

Civil rights leader
Born July 2, 1925, Decatur, Mississippi
Died June 12, 1963, Jackson, Mississippi

"Mississippi is part of the United States, and whether the whites like it or not, I don't plan to live here as a parasite. The things I don't like, I will try to change."

The first major civil rights leader to be assassinated in the 1960s, Medgar Evers was secretary of the Mississippi chapter of the National Association for the Advancement of Colored People. He filled his days with protest marches, organized economic boycotts, bailed demonstrators out of jail, and encouraged blacks to sign up to vote.

He and his family were faced with constant death threats, and on June 12, 1963, he was shot in the back. He was thirty-seven years old.

Friend's father was hanged

Evers was born on July 2, 1925, in Decatur, Mississippi, the third of four children of a small farm owner. Growing up in Mississippi Evers experienced racism almost constantly. On his way to school in the first grade, the white students threw things and shouted insults at him and other black children. When he was eleven, the father of one of his close friends was hanged by a group of white men for "talking back" to a white woman.

"They just left him dead at the Decatur fairgrounds," he once said after the incident. "Everyone in town knew it but never [said] a word in public. I went down and saw his bloody clothes. They left those clothes on a fence for about a year. Every Negro in town was supposed to get the message from those clothes and I can see those clothes now in my mind's eye.... But nothing was said in public.

No sermons in church. No news. No protest. It was as though this man just dissolved except for the bloody clothes.... Just before I went into the Army I began wondering how long I could stand it. I used to watch the Saturday night sport of white men trying to run down a Negro with their car, or white gangs coming through town to beat up a Negro."

Evers was determined to get an education, walking a round-trip of twenty-four miles to his high school and home. During World War II he joined the army, where he fought in France and Germany. He was honorably discharged in 1946.

Witnessed lynchings

He returned to Decatur, where he was reunited with his brother, Charlie, who had also fought in the war. The two decided they wanted to vote in the next election, and they registered to vote without running into any trouble. As the election grew nearer, however, whites in the area began threatening their father. When election day finally arrived, they were met at the polling station by an armed white crowd of about 200. The book *Martyrs* recorded Evers's declaration: "All we wanted to be was ordinary citizens. We fought during the war for America and Mississippi was included. Now after the Germans and the Japanese hadn't killed us, it looked as though the white Mississippians would." Rather than confront the hostile group, they turned away and did not vote.

Evers enrolled at Alcorn A & M College in Lorman, Mississippi, in 1948, and he joined the National Association for the Advancement of Colored People (NAACP). He majored in business administration and graduated in 1952. In his senior year he married Myrlie Beasley, a fellow student, and they moved near Evers's hometown, where he found a job selling insurance.

Whenever he visited a black home to sell insurance, he found deplorable living conditions. In 1954 he witnessed another hanging that further hardened him against racism. The hanging took place when he visited his father on his deathbed at the hospital in Union, Mississippi. The sight of his father dying was difficult for Evers, so he took a walk outside the hospital. Earlier that day a black man fought with a white man, and a white mob shot the black man in the leg. The police brought the black to the hospital, but the mob followed, carrying guns, and yelling for the black man. Evers walked into the middle of it. He realized that this was a way of life he and his father endured, and if things didn't change, so would his children.

Home got fire-bombed

Evers quit selling insurance and went to work for the NAACP as a full-time chapter organizer. The first black student to apply to the University of Mississippi Law School, he was not accepted, but he didn't press his case. Within two years he was named state field secretary of the NAACP. In his early thirties, he was one of the most vocal and recognizable NAACP members in the state, always talking about the need to overcome hatred and promote understanding and racial equality.

He relocated his family to the state capital, Jackson, where as the secretary of the Mississippi NAACP Evers worked closely

Medgar Evers

with black church leaders and other civil rights activists. When he began receiving death threats, Evers taught his children to fall on the floor whenever they heard a strange noise outside. When someone threw a firebomb at his home, Evers's wife, Myrlie, was convinced that there were snipers waiting to kill her if she went outside, so she put out the fire with a garden hose.

Despite the threats, Evers continued his work, pressing for blacks to sign up to vote and pushing for a biracial committee to address social concerns in the city. His days were filled with meetings, economic boycotts, marches, prayer vigils, and picket lines. He also bailed out demonstrators arrested by the all-white police force. Evers encouraged blacks to exert whatever strength they could against the system. He said if whites cut off financial credit, then blacks should only buy from other blacks. Tensions throughout the state were very high.

Murdered in cold blood

Just after midnight on June 12, 1963, Evers returned home from a series of NAACP functions. As he left his car, he was shot in the back. His wife and children, who had been waiting up for him, found him bleeding on the doorstep. He was rushed to the hospital, but fifty minutes later he was pronounced dead. On the day of his funeral, thousands of black mourners showed up, and not even the use of beatings and other strong-arm tactics by the police could stop their anger. The NAACP awarded its Springarn medal posthumously to Evers, in recognition of his fight for equal rights.

The governor of Mississippi and several all-white newspapers offered rewards for information about Evers's murderer, but few came forward. An investigation by the Federal Bureau of Investigations (FBI) finally discovered a suspect—Byron de la Beckwith, an outspoken opponent of integration and a founding member of Mississippi's White Citizens Council. A gun found 150 feet from the site of the shooting had Beckwith's fingerprints on it, and several witnesses stated he had been in Evers's neighborhood that night. However, Beckwith said his gun had been stolen a few days before the shooting and that he had been with friends, one of whom was a policeman, sixty miles away from where the incident took place.

Beckwith was tried for Evers's murder in 1964 and again in 1965, but both trials ended in hung juries, so he was freed. After the second trial, Myrlie Evers moved with her children to California. She searched for new evidence to convict Beckwith, and in 1991 he was arrested for a third time on the charge of murdering Evers.

James Farmer

Civil rights leader, union organizer
Born January 12, 1920, Marshall, Texas

"We are fighting not only for our rights and our freedom, we are fighting not only to make our nation safe for the democracy it preaches, we are fighting also to give our whole world a fighting chance for survival.... Some of us may die ... but our war is for life, not death and we will not stop our demands for freedom now.... We will not stop until the heavy weight of centuries of oppression is removed from our backs and like proud men everywhere we can stand tall together again."

B est known as one of the founders of the Congress of Racial Equality, James Farmer played a key role in planning the Freedom Rides that ended segregation on buses and restaurants. He was a pioneer in developing the use of nonviolent direct action as a tactic for fighting racism.

Farmer was a congressional nominee and was one of the first blacks to serve in a high-ranking government position. While in goverment he helped develop the concept of affirmative action, which opened the door for blacks to find new jobs.

Switched his major to religion

Farmer was born on January 12, 1920 in Marshall, Texas. He attended public schools in the South and entered Wiley College at the age of fourteen. He majored in chemistry with the intention of becoming a doctor but changed his major when he discovered that the sight of blood made him sick. He eventually enrolled in the School of Religion at Howard University. Farmer became active in the Christian Youth Movement and the Christian Youth Council of America. He received his Bachelor of Divinity degree in 1941 but refused ordination when he learned he would have to practice in a segregated ministry.

In 1941 Farmer became the race relations secretary for the Fellowship of Reconciliation (FOC), a pacifist group. While living in Chicago, Illinois, he started writing his Provisional Plan for Brotherhood Mobilization. He intended to head a nondemoninational religious organization that would seek social change through nonviolence. The group would use boycotts, noncooperation, picketing, demonstrations, and civil disobedience to achieve its goals.

First sit-in

While Farmer was developing these ideas, he and his friends organized the first civil rights sit-in. A local restaurant refused to serve him when he stopped in for coffee with a white friend. After several such episodes with the owner, Farmer and about twenty-five friends entered the restaurant at dinnertime and seated themselves at the counter and in the booths. The white people were served without a problem, but the blacks were told they would only be served in the basement. After a few minutes the manager realized that none of the white people had touched their meal. They said that they would not eat until their friends had been served. The manager called the police to have them thrown out of his restaurant, but the police had been forewarned and told him they were not breaking any laws. The manager eventually served Farmer and his friends and ended his discriminatory policy.

By 1942 Farmer and his friends were calling themselves the Committee of Racial Equality (CORE). This group undertook other actions that attracted the national attention of the civil rights community. Their nonviolent direct action approach was new to most civil rights groups. In June 1943 it organized nationally under the name National Federation of Committees on Racial Equality, and the next year it was renamed the Congress of Racial Equality (CORE), with Farmer elected as national chairman.

Farmer eventually gave up the leadership because it conflicted with the demands of his other jobs. He worked for the Fellowship of Reconciliation in New York City, and then as a labor organizer.

Throughout the 1950s Farmer was active in several areas of the civil rights movement. In 1958 he was one of a five-man delegation sent to fifteen African countries by the International Confederation of Free Trade Unions. He was a radio and television commentator on programs sponsored by the United Auto Workers in Detroit and served as program director for the National Association for the Advancement of Colored People.

CORE leader

CORE's national directors were white, and it was decided that a black leader should act as spokesperson; in 1961 they chose Farmer. He immediately began planning the Freedom Rides. Although discrimination had been de-

James Farmer

clared unconstitutional years before, blacks riding buses in the South had to ride in the back and sit in segregated waiting areas. CORE decided to send a racially mixed group through seven Southern states, challenging segregation wherever they found it. Farmer and twelve others set out from Washington, D.C., on May 4, 1961. They passed through Virginia, the Carolinas, and Georgia with only a few minor incidents. Farmer left the group before they entered Alabama to attend his father's funeral. While he was away, several riders were beaten and their bus firebombed. A photograph of the burning bus was front-page news across the country, and hundreds volunteered to join the campaign. Over 300 people were trained in nonviolent tactics and sent on buses through Alabama and Mississippi, where most of the riders were arrested. Farmer served time at Parchman State Penitentiary in Mississippi, but the Freedom Rides were eventually successful.

Farmer left CORE in 1966, because he felt the organization was supporting separatist policies and were restricting the activities of whites who had made a significant contribution to the goals of the organization. He intended to head a nationwide literacy program sponsored by the Johnson Administration and funded with a $900,000 grant from the Office of Economic Opportunity (OEO), but the project was canceled because some urban politicians feared it would disrupt the voting patterns that kept them in power.

Entered politics

Farmer taught social welfare courses at Lincoln University for the next two years, then decided to enter politics. He tried to enter the Democratic primary, but the Democrats turned him down. He was then endorsed by the Republicans, who hoped he would at least make a decent showing against Democratic nominee Shirley Chisholm. Farmer was not really a Republican and had endorsed Democratic presidential candidate Hubert Humphrey in the 1968 election.

In 1969, President Richard Nixon appointed Farmer assistant secretary of the Department of Health, Education, and Welfare. Some black leaders thought it inappropriate for a former civil rights leader to serve in a Republican administration, but others defended Farmer, saying blacks should be represented in all political parties. Farmer implemented affirmative action hiring and promotion policies, but he opposed many of the government's policies and resigned in 1970.

Since that time Farmer has lectured, taught, and worked in various capacities on minority, labor, and senior citizen issues, but he has never regained the same prominence he had in the 1960s. In 1977 he became executive director of the Coalition of American Public Employees in Washington, D.C. In 1985 he published his autiobiography, *Lay Bare the Heart*, which documents his role in the civil rights movement.

Louis Farrakhan

Muslim minister
Born May 11, 1933, New York, New York

"Jews see themselves as Jews first. Don't fault me if I love myself and my people first."

Head of the Nation of Islam, Louis Farrakhan takes his place among other controversial Black Muslim leaders, including Elijah Muhammad and Malcolm X. Farrakhan first gained notoriety during the 1984 presidential campaign for his anti-Semitic comments, which he has since downplayed, and moved his group towards overcoming crime and drugs. The Nation of Islam is now welcomed in many black neighborhoods.

Mentored by Malcolm X

Farrakhan was born on May 11, 1933, in New York City. After graduating from high school, he attended Winston-Salem Teachers College and later worked as a calypso singer named Louis X. While also a member of the American Muslim Mission, he was influenced by its leader, Elijah Muhammad, to change his surname to Farrakhan. Farrakhan's mentor, Malcolm X, also belonged to Muhammad's following, but when Malcolm X split with Muhammad over the issue of black separation, Farrakhan remained with the American Muslim Mission. His prior association with Malcolm X, however, made him an outcast.

Farrakhan preached in virtual obscurity until Muhammad died in 1975. Muhammad's sons took over and directed the group towards orthodox, nonracial Islamic practice. Farrakhan followed this direction for three years, then formed his own group, the Nation of Islam. Not affiliated with any other religious groups, Farrakhan turned to such Muslim leaders as Libya's leader Muammar Kaddafi for assistance.

Though still relatively unknown, Farrakhan began to be recognized for his charisma as a speaker and for his personal drive and energy and his success in converting black criminals into good citizens. These converts, known as the Fruit of Islam, would swear off drinking, drugs, and cigarettes, eat one meal a day, and claim their family as their primary means of salvation. Like their leader, who they often accompanied, they were clean-cut and wore bow ties.

Rises to national prominence

During the 1984 presidential campaign, Jesse Jackson, who was seeking the Democratic nomination, asked Farrakhan to help rescue Lieutenant Goodman, an African American pilot shot down over Syria. Jackson thought Farrakhan's knowledge of Arab politicians and Muslim etiquette would prove invaluable. He was not disappointed; the mission was a suc-

cess and both men earned a great deal of media attention.

Farrakhan then threw his support behind Jackson's presidential bid. While hosting one of Jackson's rallies in Chicago, Farrakhan, who was expected to focus his remarks on Jackson, instead promoted his own views, disputing the existence of the prophet Moses, and claiming that the story of the Jews fleeing Egypt only appeared in the Torah. He said black people were the "real Israel," and since Jews, Christians, and Arabs had lived unrighteously, blacks were the only ones to carry the faith. He also cautioned American Jews not to hate or hurt Jackson. "We are ready to talk," he told *Esquire*. "But, if you harm this brother, I warn you in the name of Allah, this will be the last one you harm. We are not making any idle threats. We have no weapons.... If you want to defeat him, defeat him at the polls. We can stand to lose an election, but we cannot stand to lose our brother."

Among those protesting his statements, some even compared Farrakhan to Adolf Hitler. In a March 1984 radio broadcast, Farrakhan rebutted, "The Jews don't like Farrakhan, so they call me Hitler. Well, that's a good name. Hitler was a very great man." He explained that Hitler was able to raise the German nation after its humiliating World War I loss, just as he is trying to raise the blacks from slavery. The comment, nevertheless, stuck with him as a symbol of his anti-Semitism.

Jackson felt it necessary to sever his ties to Farrakhan, explaining to *Newsweek* that Farrakhan's comments were "morally reprehensible and indefensible." Jackson did not completely denounce him, however, because although Farrakhan may have damaged Jackson's political ambitions, his comments brought Jackson into the spotlight—something his twenty years of preaching had been unable to do.

After the rally other African American leaders were called on to denounce Farrakhan, but many refused to do so. Reverend T.J. Jemison, president of the National Baptist Convention, U.S.A., stated, "I cannot disown him because he is a black brother," and African Methodist Episcopalian bishop John Hurst Adams, head of the Congress of National Black Churches, said, "Farrakhan is tapping deep feelings based on 400 years of racism and speaks for many other blacks than just his followers." One of Farrakhan's chief critics was Imam Warith P. Muhammad, leader of the American Muslim Mission, who compared him to Hitler.

Farrakhan ran into further trouble when he called white people "devils." Richard Cohen, a *Washington Post* columnist, labeled Farrakhan a racist, which he denied, calling himself a victim of white bigotry. The more white people criticized him, the higher rose his popularity among the black population.

Formed POWER company

In 1985 Farrakhan branched out into a new business. Believing that African Americans needed a stronger economic base, he founded POWER (People Organized and Working for Economic Rebirth), enlisting blacks to sell health and beauty aids door to door. With a $5 million interest-free loan from Muammar

Louis Farrakhan

Kaddafi to get the company started, Farrakhan contracted five black-owned manufacturers to supply the products for the company, but by the end of 1985, they all pulled out because of the negative publicity from his statements. When he found new suppliers, he refused to identify them. He also toned down his controversial statements to gain credibility. In an interview with *Newsweek* Farrakhan claimed, "We must build a company that is not just a Negro business." He envisioned nonblacks as part of its workforce as well as its customer base.

Farrakhan also explained to *Newsweek* that he would not accept any financial gain from POWER. "If Michael Jordan and other entertainers can sell beer and cigarettes and other commodities that they don't manufacture, why can't I translate the popularity that God is blessing me with into a marketing force second to none, a force that will give black individuals jobs?" Several politicians were happy with Farrakhan's new venture. Charles Hayes, a Democratic congressman from Illinois, assessed, "People need work, and if Minister Farrakhan can help them get that work, then I'm all for it."

Farrakhan's popularity has brought him invitations to speak, with reports of $7,500 per engagement, and his comments still inflame audiences. He has stated he is not anti-Semitic, yet he continues to make apparently anti-semitic remarks, and many claim that he has not fundamentally changed his stance since he said Hitler was a great man. Farrakhan addressed this issue in March 1990 in appearances on five major television shows, his first before the media in four years. On "Prime Time" he was asked that since he referred to white people as devils, why shouldn't white America be scared of him? He replied: "If we are afraid of truth or afraid of justice, then one would be afraid of one who speaks truth or cries out for justice, but if one seeks honest solutions to real problems, and will find that solution in the truth, then there is no need to fear a man who speaks the truth and condemns that which is unjust and wicked."

Targets crime and drugs

Farrakhan further strengthened his role in African American communities by working with a Christian congregation. In Los Angeles, 125 members of the First African Methodist Episcopal (AME) Church went to a nearby mosque to worship with members of the Nation of Islam. The next night the Muslims attended the AME church. The groups focused on what the black community could do together to overcome drugs and crime.

The Nation of Islam also generated good press coverage when they met with the Los Angeles Police Department (LAPD) to talk about a recent police shooting of a young Muslim. "We now have a very positive working relationship with them," said deputy chief William Rathburn, commander of the LAPD's South Bureau, in *Time*. By early 1990 crime in the bureau's area had fallen nearly 17 percent, and a lot of the credit went to the Nation of Islam.

These activities have won respect for Farrakhan and the Nation of Islam. By taking a tough anti-drug stance, the group has been a welcome addition to many black neighborhoods. Farrakhan is being seen as a strong leader willing to stand up to the white hierarchy. Ronald Walters, a Howard University political scientist, said in *Time*, "Supporting Farrakhan has become a way of hitting back at the system and expressing black public opinion."

Ella Fitzgerald

Singer
Born April 25, 1918, Newport News, Virginia

"I love jazz because it's part of me, but I also want to do some other things. I'd probably look silly trying to sing some of these things like some of the younger singers do, but I sing the new material in my way."

J azz singer Ella Fitzgerald has been called "the First Lady of Song," "stupendous," "delightful," "a legend in her own time." Her musical sensibility makes Fitzgerald stand out from other singers. With apparent effortlessness she can subtly reshape a melody while singing it, introducing chord changes and other improvisations. Her flawless phrasing and tremendous sense of rhythm proved her to be a singer with a total mastery of her art. It has been said that with her talent for embellishing the melody, Fitzgerald uses her voice like an instrument.

Won first prize for singing

Fitzgerald's parents were both musically inclined. Her mother had a beautiful soprano voice, and her father loved to play the guitar. When he died soon after she was born, Fitzgerald's mother moved to Yonkers, New York, and it was in this mixed neighborhood that the future singer spent her childhood.

Both at home and at school Ella was steeped in music. At her junior high school she sang in the glee club, and for a while she learned the piano, though the lessons soon became too much for her mother to afford. At home Fitzgerald was surrounded by her mother's records—her mother was a great fan of musical shows—and the two of them spent many happy evenings listening to music and singing along.

Often the young girl danced as well as sang. Her ambition was to be a dancer, and it was as a dancer that she entered the talent contest that changed her life. She was sixteen at the time, and as a result of a "dare" with her girlfriends she committed herself to dancing in the amateur night contest at the Harlem Opera House. But on stage she suddenly panicked and felt unable to move. Since she

couldn't just stand there, she decided to sing one of her favorite songs, "The Object of My Affection." Fitzgerald had often listened to her mother's recording of Connee Boswell singing this song, yet it sounded very different when Fitzgerald performed it—already she was adding her own special touches. She won first prize and had to give three encores.

Hired by Chick Webb to sing at the Savoy

In the following months Fitzgerald entered further competitions, winning them all, and in 1935 she landed her first paying job—a week's appearance with Tiny Bradshaw and his band at the Harlem Opera House. Hard on the heels of this success came an audition with CBS radio and a guest appearance on the Arthur Tracy radio show. But before she could take it up, her mother died. Since Fitzgerald was only seventeen, too young to sign the contract herself, the deal was canceled. Worse still, she was placed in the Riverdale orphanage in Yonkers.

Fitzgerald did not stay long in the orphanage. She continued to enter contests and soon came to the attention of Chick Webb, one of the best-known bandleaders of the day, who hired her to sing with his band at the Savoy Ballroom in Harlem. Since Fitzgerald was still only seventeen, Webb solved the problem of her legal status by adopting her. He and his wife became Fitzgerald's legal guardians.

Fitzgerald was later to say that that her "first singing teacher" was Connee Boswell because of the many Boswell records she listened to during her childhood. Her second teacher was definitely Webb. He helped her

Ella Fitzgerald

polish her style and carefully groomed her performances, telling her to relax and "go with the beat, always the beat." Under his guidance Fitzgerald blossomed, and the band blossomed too. The players seemed to take on a new spirit once she joined them.

Singing scat made her famous

In 1935 Fitzgerald recorded *Love and Kisses* with Chick Webb. Other records soon followed containing such ballads as "Sing Me a Swing Song" and "If You Can't Swing It, You'll Have to Sing It."

Fitzgerald was experimenting with her singing, trying to do with her voice what musicians could do with their instruments. This was how she developed the style called "scat"—a type of improvised singing that uses nonsense syllables instead of words. Fitzgerald's most famous scat song is "A-Tisket, A-Tasket," a swing variation of the nursery rhyme, which she wrote together with Webb.

When the record of the song was released in 1938, it rocketed Fitzgerald to fame. More than a million copies were sold in the first few months. During that excited period Fitzgerald and Webb married, and when they later realized the marriage was unsuitable, Webb—actually Fitzgerald's legal guardian—insisted on having it annulled. Fitzgerald readily agreed.

Webb had been a caring and conscientious guardian to Fitzgerald, and she felt a great loss when he died the following year. However, besides singing with the band, she had been writing songs, so when Webb died, she became the bandleader. She kept it going for the next three years, but she had to dissolve the band in 1942, when the players were drafted into the armed forces to serve in World War II.

New promoter widened her audience

After the war Fitzgerald began her long association with promoter-manager Norman Granz, and from 1946 to 1954 she toured the world with his concert series, "Jazz at the Philharmonic." During this period, Fitzgerald also sang in a jazz combo led by double-bass player Ray Brown, to whom she was married from 1949 to 1953. She and Brown adopted a son, Ray Brown, Jr., and after the marriage ended the boy stayed on with Fitzgerald.

The association with Granz changed the direction of Fitzgerald's career, launching her on the famous songbook project, in which she recorded the songs of Cole Porter, Irving Berlin, and other American songwriters. These records vastly widened her audience. No longer was it mainly jazz enthusiasts who were fans of Fitzgerald. Now millions of music lovers of every type worshipped at her shrine. The series began with *The Cole Porter Songbook,* consisting of two albums containing twenty-six songs from Porter's shows, but by far the most popular was the five-LP *Gershwin Songbook.* Together with *The Best Is Yet to Come,* these are probably Fitzgerald's best-loved albums.

Fitzgerald was also performing at jazz festivals, on television, and at state functions. As she grew older the pace became too much to keep up, and in the 1970s she began to reduce the number of her engagements. As of the early 1990s she was still giving a few performances.

Over the years Fitzgerald's music has brought her many awards and honors, including the American Music Award (1978) and the National Medal of the Arts (1987). Of her more than 200 recordings, 12 have won Grammy awards, and she has been named top female vocalist and most popular female jazz singer time and time again. In 1989 the Society of Singers presented Fitzgerald with its first annual lifetime achievement award. The name given to the award is "the Ella."

Aretha Franklin

Singer
Born March 25, 1942, Memphis, Tennessee

"My heart is still there in gospel music. It never left."

 nown as the "Queen of Soul," Aretha Franklin was one of the first female singers of soul music—the "pop" form of gospel music. A warm and natural performer, Franklin makes the most of the pulsating rhythms, sharing her emotions with her audience. At times she is slow and dreamy, at other times jubilant, matching her mood to the music. Whatever the mood, her singing is always superb. She is considered one of the world's top vocalists, the equivalent in pop and soul music to what Ella Fitzgerald is in jazz.

Started her singing career in a church in Detroit

Aretha Louise Franklin grew up to the sound of gospel music. Her mother was Barbara (Siggers) Franklin, one of the great gospel singers, and her father was Clarence L.V. Franklin, a fiery Baptist preacher and gospeler.

When Franklin was two years old, her father moved the family to Detroit, Michigan, where he became pastor of New Bethel Baptist Church. To this church came many of the leading gospel and blues singers of the day, including Mahalia Jackson, Clara Ward, and Dinah Washington. These singers became friends of the Franklin children, and they helped fill the gap when their mother left home in 1948 and then died a few years later.

At ten Franklin was already an enthusiastic gospel singer, singing with her sisters in local churches as well as in her father's church choir. At home she often sang to the piano, which she had taught herself to play. At the age of twelve, soloing for the first time in her father's church, her passionate singing made a powerful impression. Two years later, also in her father's church, she recorded her first solo record of gospel songs.

Regarding himself as a traveling preacher, Reverend Franklin was often away from home, leaving his children in the care of a housekeeper. When Franklin was fourteen and a student at Northern High School in Detroit, she began to accompany her father on some of his tours. They exposed her to drinking and partying, and at fifteen she became pregnant and the following year dropped out of high school to have the baby. Although this brought an end to Aretha's schooling, it marked a turning point in her musical development. Franklin discovered the blues, listening especially to the songs of Dinah Washington, and she decided to follow in Washington's footsteps, moving on from gospel to popular music. With her father's blessing, Franklin set off for New York City at the age of eighteen, determined to make her way as a blues singer.

Began to ride the crest of success

"This is the best voice I've heard in twenty years!" exclaimed John Hammond of Columbia Records when he first heard Franklin's singing. He gave her a five-year contract with Columbia, and she was soon gaining praise from the critics as well as getting rave reviews at the 1962 Newport Jazz Festival. But the nine long-playing albums Franklin made with Columbia were only moderately successful, partly because of the style that Columbia chose. Rather than taking advantage of Franklin's unique qualities, the records were the usual pop and jazz music, or else they were old Broadway songs.

Franklin married Ted White in 1961, and he replaced Hammond as her manager, but the couple could not leave Columbia Records

Aretha Franklin

until the contract ended. Meanwhile, they did a dreary round of second-rate nightclubs, where Franklin was so nervous that she sang looking at the floor. Although today Franklin is known for her uninhibited singing style, she has always been rather shy, and this was especially obvious when she first started to perform.

When the contract with Columbia ended in 1966, Franklin signed on with Atlantic Records, then a small New York company specializing in rhythm and blues music. Franklin was free to choose her own songs and her own style, which produced immediate results. The first single Franklin recorded for Atlantic, "I Never Loved a Man" (1967), sold a million copies, as did her next four singles; and her first 1967 album, also called *I Never Loved a Man,* sold well over a million copies.

Suddenly Franklin was a star, attracting thousands of fans. When she sang at the Lincoln Center in New York, people leapt to their feet, cheering and applauding even while she was still singing. In the fall she made her first European tour, which also drew cheering crowds, and toward the end of the year she was voted "top female vocalist of 1967." That same year she won the first of her eleven Grammy awards for best female rhythm and blues performance. (She would later win three more Grammy awards in other categories.)

During the next few years, record after record went "gold." Her appeal was not just that she was singing soul music or that she was giving full rein to her magnificent voice. It was also because of her handling of the music—the modulations, the phrasing, the total product she created each time she sang.

Experienced tragedy and triumph

Despite her professionalism, Franklin experienced a drop in popularity in the late 1970s as other styles of music became the rage. During this period, she was going through a bad time emotionally, suffering various personal as well as professional problems. Her marriage failed, and a second marriage, to actor Glynn Turman, also broke up after a few years. In 1979 her father was shot during a burglary. For five years he lay in coma before he died.

Despite the hardships Franklin continued to make records to pay her father's huge hospital bills. Without the success of her earlier years, her career seemed to be fading, but in 1985 she made a comeback with *Who's Zoomin' Who*, followed up with videos and with several best-selling singles. Franklin soared back into popularity as a new generation of fans discovered her wonderful voice.

In recent years she has done more gospel songs, most notably in the dramatic album she made in 1988, *One Lord, One Faith, One Baptism*. Other recent recordings ensure her position as "the Queen of Soul." Among her many honors is one from Detroit, Michigan, which in 1967 named February 16 of that year Aretha Franklin Day.

John Hope Franklin

Historian
Born January 2, 1915, Rentiesville, Oklahoma

"The writing of history reflects the interests, predilections, and even prejudices of a given generation. This means that at the present time there is an urgent need to re-examine our past in terms of our present outlook."

John Hope Franklin has done more than anyone else to retrieve black history from obscurity and put it on record. By doing so, he has helped to correct a situation in which history, as written and taught by whites, had consistently downplayed or totally ignored the African American contribution.

During a career of more than fifty years as historian and professor, Franklin has produced some twenty major works on black history, either as author or editor, and has contributed to numerous journals and magazines. He also has played a pivotal role as general editor of several series of books on black history and biography. These include the "Negro American Biographies and Auto-biographies" series, published by the University of Chicago Press, and the "American History Series" of Harlan Davidson, Inc.

Some of Franklin's works are already regarded as classics. *From Slavery to Freedom: A History of Negro Americans* has long been viewed as the standard text on African American history. It became a leading college textbook soon after its publication in 1947, and since then has gone through many editions.

Like father, like son

Franklin grew up in Tulsa, Oklahoma, where his father Buck Franklin was a prominent lawyer. Buck and his wife, Mollie, had four children, all of whom were set a sterling example by his bravery and integrity. As one of the first black lawyers in Oklahoma, Buck Franklin had to face physical danger as well as racial slurs. When he first set up his prac-

John Hope Franklin

tice in Tulsa in 1921, his office was burned down. Despite this, he went on practicing, and he later became the first African American in Oklahoma to function as a U.S. district court judge, having been appointed master in chancery to hear a case involving an African American church.

With such a father, John Franklin was brought up to pursue his goals, regardless of any barriers placed in his path. His father so objected to segregation that he made a habit of ignoring "whites only" notices, and this confident attitude naturally influenced his children. However, John Franklin's early education was all in segregated schools. He attended Booker T. Washington High School in Tulsa and then, in 1931, enrolled at Fisk University in Nashville, Tennessee.

At Fisk, Franklin majored in history, a subject he found totally fascinating. After graduating with honors in 1935, he took a postgraduate course at Harvard University, which brought him a master's degree in history in 1936. He then taught at Fisk for two years, before returning to Harvard, where he gained his Ph.D. in history in 1941.

In 1940, shortly before gaining his doctorate, Franklin married the librarian Aurelia Whittington, whom he had met as an undergraduate at Fisk. The couple had one son, John Whittington Franklin.

Acclaimed historian

During the next few years, Franklin pursued his career as a history teacher, first in North Carolina and then at Howard University in Washington, D.C., where he was professor of history from 1947 to 1956. While at Howard, he acted as an adviser to the National Association for the Advancement of Colored People (NAACP) and helped prepare the brief that led to the desegregation of public schools in 1954. Thus, the historian himself made history by taking part in this landmark event.

These years also saw the publication of Franklin's first two books: *The Free Negro in North Carolina, 1790–1860* (1943) and *From Slavery to Freedom* (1947). In 1947 he also published *The Civil War Diary of J. T. Ayers.* These books established Franklin's reputation as a historian of considerable insight. *From Slavery to Freedom*, in particular, drew praise for the forthright, yet balanced way in which he handled his subject matter.

Franklin was so well regarded that he was invited to be a visiting professor at Harvard University in 1950; this led to two more visiting professorships—at the University of Wisconsin in 1952–53 and at Cornell University in 1953. Three years later, in 1956, Franklin became the first African American to head a college department in New York State when he was appointed chairman of the Department of History at Brooklyn College of the City University of New York.

That same year, Franklin produced another important work, *The Militant South, 1800–1860*. This study of conditions in the South before the Civil War was a major piece of research, based on original sources. As such, it gave a new understanding of the period and of the militant attitudes that led to the war. A few years later, he followed up with two more books: *Reconstruction After the Civil War* (1961) and *The Emancipation Proclamation* (1963). During this same period, he also found time to research the writings of earlier authors, and he unearthed a number of fascinating journals and personal accounts, which he then edited for publication. Among these was T. W. Higginson's *Army Life in a Black Regiment,* which was published in 1962.

International recognition

Franklin spent the academic year of 1962–63 as a professor at Cambridge University in England, where he held the prestigious position of William Pitt Professor of American History and Institutions. During the year, he lectured in some twenty European universities. This was not the first time Franklin had been invited overseas. He had lectured at Cambridge some years earlier, and in 1960 he had visited Australia to lecture at Australia National University. Over the years, he has made many trips abroad.

Franklin's major appointment came in 1964, when, shortly after his return from Britain, he became professor of history at the University of Chicago. He held this position until 1982, when he moved to Duke University, where he taught for three years before retiring and becoming a professor emeritus in 1985. During these twenty-one years, Franklin had an immense influence on the teaching of history. As a result of his efforts, the contribution of African Americans began to play a far larger role in school curricula, and American history was presented in a more balanced manner, so that much of the pro-white bias was removed. In many ways, Franklin corrected the misrecording of American history, seeing that African Americans were given their rightful place.

Much of this was done through Franklin's own works, for he continued with his writing and research, producing several more books, including *Racial Equality in America* (1976). In 1985 he brought out what many consider to be his major work: *George Washington Williams: A Biography.* This highly acclaimed study of the nineteenth-century black historian was the result of more than forty years of research, in which Franklin followed up leads that took him to Mexico, Central Europe, and Africa, and ended with his discovery of Williams's unmarked grave in Blackpool, England. In a way, the book is a double biography, for it describes much of Franklin's own story as well as that of Williams.

Franklin found that he had much in common with Williams, but whereas he himself gained increasing fame as he grew older, Williams died in obscurity. Franklin attributes this to the prejudices of the times, rather than to his own superiority. He is quick to point out that there have been many African Americans who have been as talented as he—"but they could not get where I have because the white man was not advanced enough to let them." It is this type of comment, this perceptive way of looking at things, that has made John Hope Franklin such an important influence in the study of African American life.

Mary Hatwood Futrell

Educator, president of the National
  Education Association
Born May 24, 1940, Alta Vista, Virginia

"We know that our responsibility is not just to the children of America, but to the children of the world. We know now that the destiny of the American family is intertwined with the destiny of the human family. And we know we can observe that misery or help halt that misery. Let us not be observers."

B ack in tenth grade, Mary Hatwood Futrell worked hard to win the respect of her teachers. She was so impressed with the work her teachers did, she eventually became an educator herself. Wanting to make a bigger difference in the lives of her students, Futrell became an active member of the National Education Association. She rose through the ranks, eventually becoming president in 1983. She held the position for an unprecedented three terms, dramatically increasing membership and taking strong stands on issues such as drug abuse and dropouts.

Rewrites essay six times

Futrell is the daughter of John Ed Calloway and Josephine Hatwood. When she was four years old, her father died. Josephine Hatwood had left school when her parents had died, and she wanted to make sure the same thing did not happen to her children. Although Hatwood wanted to be a nurse, she gave up the idea to work as a domestic for three families and clean churches.

Futrell attended Dunbar Public School in Lynchburg, Virginia, and established a good relationship with her tenth-grade teacher. When Futrell was caught talking too much, her teacher made her write a thousand-word essay on education and its impact on the economy. She was forced to rewrite it with each paragraph beginning with a topic sentence. She had to rewrite it again for grammar. The third time for spelling. The fifth time, it was not neat enough. The sixth time, it was okayed. Her teacher entered it in an essay contest, where it took third place. Futrell said in *Reader's Digest*, "Except for mama, she was the person I most wanted to please in this world."

After graduating, Futrell received a fifteen-hundred-dollar scholarship, which she used toward a B.A. in business education at Virginia State University. She received her M.A. at George Washington University, and later did graduate work at the University of Maryland, the University of Virginia, and Virginia Polytechnic Institute.

Futrell became a teacher of business education in the Alexandria, Virginia, school system. She soon became interested in the National Education Association, a 1.9 million-member organization. As her interest in the NEA increased, she served in various capacities including three years as secretary-treasurer. In 1983 she was elected president and served for six years.

Upon assuming the presidency, Futrell made it known that her top priority was to see that every American child received a quality education. She was committed to educational excellence and spoke out forcefully for teachers and other school employees on what was needed to improve America's schools. "Teachers want to do more than simply teach facts. We want children to be equipped with 'stupid-ity detectors,' so they will know how to raise questions and not simply accept what somebody tells them," she said in *About Time*.

Her monthly essays in *NEA Today* revealed the areas about which she was most concerned. These included: reducing the dropout rate, improving and expanding the Head Start program, child care programs for young families, effective programs to deal with drugs in school, adequate resources, expanded use of computers in teaching, and more funds for college loans. Futrell also worried about NEA membership. The report, *A Nation at Risk*, which focussed on the faults of American education, also had a major impact on her thinking.

In March 1988, Futrell addressed the dropout problem by stating in *NEA Today*; "The thousands of students pushed out of school by in-school discrimination demand and must have relief." She believed that many minority students who were learning English for the first time in high school were being pushed out of the educational system.

Calls for increased drug programs

Futrell was also a firm believer in increasing the number of drug treatment programs. "Nationally, there are now more than six million Americans dependent on drugs, and only 250,000 slots in treatment programs," she stated in *NEA Today* in 1989. Futrell believed there was only so much that could be done for young people already hooked on drugs, since adequate treatment programs did not exist. National programs could be established to convince young people not to do drugs, but there often was no place to send them for help. The problems that Futrell revealed indicated that while politicians said they wanted a national campaign against drug abuse, they were not willing to fully fund it.

Futrell worked with IBM to provide every school in the NEA's Mastery in Learning Project with a personal computer, modem, printer, and an experimental software package called People Sharing Information. The twenty-six schools involved in the program were electronically connected. "Our challenge now is to nurture and expand the relationship we've begun," Futrell wrote in *NEA Today*. "Our challenge is to merge the traditional 3 R's with a new technological three R's. For whether as Resource tools, Research vehicles, or—most importantly—Restructuring mechanisms, computers offer our schools the promise of profound change." Futrell was rightly proud that the NEA cooperated with IBM to take the first steps toward the expanded use of computers in education.

Another issue that Futrell handled successfully was the incredible increase in NEA membership. From September 1983 to September 1988, the NEA added two hundred and fifty thousand members. In November 1989, the NEA announced it had 1.98 million members, making it the largest union in America. Futrell's most ambitious goal was to open the NEA's ranks to all who contribute to the life of the schools and the welfare of students. These included teacher assistants, counsellors, librarians, bus drivers, cafeteria workers, clerical staff, maintenance workers, custodians, and higher education faculty. She successfully moved NEA staff from a conserva-

Mary Hatwood Futrell

tive position to one of reform. "Each time NEA adds a new member, a new advocate is added for America's children, a new voice to speak on behalf of those who cannot vote, a new ally in our struggle for professional compensation," Futrell stated in *NEA Today*.

As membership increased, Futrell lobbied the government for better working conditions and higher wages. With research indicating that no more than half of all teachers stay in the teaching profession, Futrell wanted changes to encourage teachers to stay. She stated that annual salaries should jump from an average of $27,000 to $43,000, red tape must be eliminated, and more support staff were required.

In July 1988, Futrell asked seven thousand NEA delegates to endorse a new initiative for educational reform. She asked all NEA state affiliates to meet with their governors, state school officials, and state legislators to designate at least one school district in every state as a living laboratory for restructuring America's schools. Working with school boards, parents, and civic leaders to develop improved educational programs, the NEA would be a stronger voice for reform.

Many accomplishments

Shortly before stepping down as president on August 31, 1989, Futrell reviewed her accomplishments in a *Black Enterprise* interview: "During the last six years one of my goals reached has been to help the NEA assume a more forceful and more positive position on teachers' union rights. Secondly, we increased union membership from 1.6 million to just under 2 million. Another has been our efforts to bring a higher visibility of teachers into the current talk about changing the curricula of today's schools. In addition, Operation Rescue, our dropout prevention and intervention program, implemented projects in 26 schools in 10 states engaging 15,000 students in enrichment and mastery projects."

After resigning her NEA position, Futrell became a senior fellow and doctoral student at George Washington University, where she took courses on policy studies. She also became the associate director of the Center for the Study of Education and National Development, an organization she describes as "a budding educational think tank, research center and clearinghouse."

Ernest J. Gaines

Writer
Born January 15, 1933, Oscar, Louisiana

"So many of our novels deal only with the great city ghettos.... We've only been living in these ghettos for 75 years or so, but the other 300 years—I think this is worth writing about."

Ernest J. Gaines is best known for his popular novel *The Autobiography of Miss Jane Pittman* (1971), which won two awards and was later made into a television movie. Like Gaines's other books, *Autobiography* focuses on African Americans living in the rural South, a people previously ignored by major novelists.

Gaines has drawn wide praise for his ability to capture the character and speech of the ordinary black people of the South, whom he portrays with strength and compassion. The reviewer J. H. Bryant observed that Gaines's fiction "contains the austere dignity and simplicity of ancient epic." He added, "Gaines may be one of our most gifted story-tellers."

A rural childhood

Gaines's books have their origins in the black culture of Louisiana, where he was born and raised. The son of Manuel and Adrienne (Colar) Gaines, he was born on the plantation where his father worked as a laborer and was raised by an aunt, Augusteen Jefferson. "Aunt Augusteen" had no legs but had overcome her disability so effectively that she was able to look after her young nephew and provide for his needs. The strong aunt character that appears regularly in Gaines's writings is based on Augusteen Jefferson—a religious, older woman, whose selfless efforts make life better for the next generation.

Growing up on the plantation, Gaines was already digging potatoes at fifty cents a day when he was nine years old. His early childhood experiences of working in the fields, fishing in the swamps, and listening to the discussions of his aunt's friends, all provided core material for his writings. His stories are based in an imaginary Louisiana plantation region called Bayonne, which has many similarities to the place he knew as a child.

When Gaines was fifteen he went to live with his mother and stepfather in Vallejo, California, since he could get a better education there. While attending Vallejo Junior College he read avidly. He was disappointed in the books about the South because the characters in them were nothing like the people he had known. He found more in common with such Russian authors as Leo Tolstoy and Ivan Turgenev, because of their understanding of their own peasantry. Reading their works made Gaines see the way he could write about the black people of the American South.

Ernest J. Gaines

Gaines began writing in 1950 and continued his efforts during his two-year military service, from 1953 to 1955. On leaving the army he enrolled at San Francisco State College and in 1956 had some short stories published in *Transfer,* a small San Francisco magazine. He graduated from San Francisco State in 1957 and took a creative writing course at Stanford University during the 1958–59 academic year. Gaines then settled down to write about the South as he knew it. As he later explained, "If the book you want doesn't exist, you try to make it exist."

Professional novelist

It took some years for Gaines to establish himself as a novelist. He wrote a dozen short stories and four novels (only one of which was published) before the success of his second book made him widely known.

His first published novel, *Catherine Carmier* (1964), was set in the era of the civil rights movement yet did not feature the movement prominently. The story centers on Jackson Bradley, the nephew of Aunt Charlotte, who lives on a Bayonne plantation. Jackson has come back to the plantation after gaining an education in California. He falls in love with Catherine, the daughter of a black Creole farmer, who forbids her to associate with darker-skinned people like Jackson. As the story develops, it explores the racial atmosphere within the plantation community and deals with the young couple's clash of loyalties. This strong book, with its undercurrent of despair, did not attract a wide public.

Gaines's second novel, *Of Love and Dust* (1967), had a slightly more hopeful ending. It, too, was a tale of forbidden romance on a Louisiana plantation, and again there was an "aunt" figure, Miss Julie Rand. The story is told by Jim Kelly, a middle-aged plantation worker, who observes the love affairs between the black and white characters as the plot builds up to its explosive conclusion. Although Gaines cannot be classified as a "protest" novelist, he was clearly speaking through this novel to show up the racial and economic conditions in the South.

Riding on the success of *Of Love and Dust,* Gaines brought out a collection of short stories the following year. He then set to work on *The Autobiography of Miss Jane Pittman* (1971), which is undoubtedly his masterpiece. It is an epic work, following the black experience in America from the Civil War to the civil rights movement, as seen and related by Miss Jane Pittman, who is well over a hundred years old. By telling the story in Jane's own voice, *Autobiography* makes history come alive, showing how major national events have affected individual people. As Keith E. Beyerman pointed out, "Jane captures the experiences of those millions of illiterate blacks who never had a chance to tell their own stories."

Autobiography was an immediate success, and its 1974 showing as a television movie starring Cicely Tyson brought Gaines increasing fame. He was much sought-after as a writer-in-residence, a position he took at Denison University in 1971 and at Stanford University in 1981. Since 1983 he has been professor of English at the University of Southwestern Louisiana.

Meanwhile, Gaines has continued with his career as an author, "writing five hours a day, five days a week." In 1971 he published a book for young people, *A Warm Day in November,* and in 1978 he brought out his first urban novel, *In My Father's House.* The main theme of this book is the difficulty of being a black man in America. As Gaines explained, "The blacks who were brought here as slaves were prevented from becoming the men they could be.… A man can speak up, he can do things to protect himself, his home and his family, but the slaves could never do that."

Gaines returned to his familiar plantation setting with his next book, *A Gathering of Old Men* (1983), a story of a group of aging African Americans who take a valiant stand against injustice. Like his earlier works, *Gathering* contains strong, convincing characters. In total, Gaines's novels have greatly enriched American literature with a powerful infusion of black culture and history. While telling gripping stories, they explore major themes that are relevant to all Americans, and at the same time give a vivid picture of black rural life in the South.

Marcus Garvey

Political leader
Born August 17, 1887, St. Ann's Bay, Jamaica
Died June 10, 1940, London, England

"One God! One Aim! One Destiny!"

eplorable working and living conditions of blacks around the world inspired Marcus Garvey to begin a one-man campaign to raise their status. Best known as the founder of the United Negro Improvement Association (UNIA) and as a proponent of black nationalism, he hoped the UNIA would build a unified African nation through commerce and education. He said Africa was for the Africans and urged blacks to look to the motherland, where a black king would soon be crowned.

At the height of his popularity, his organization numbered almost one million and owned a variety of businesses including grocery stores and a shipping line. Garvey's policies of black and white segregation caused problems with other black leaders, and the U.S. State Department eventually had him deported.

Although his success was short-lived, Garvey has become a symbol of black nationalism and inspired many of the leaders of the civil rights movement of the 1960s.

Motivated to improve living conditions

Garvey, the youngest of eleven children, was born in St. Ann's Bay, Jamaica, on August 17, 1887. Since his family was poor, he apprenticed in the printing trade, where he developed his writing skills. In 1907 he participated in a printer's strike, which motivated him toward politics. About four years later he joined the migration of many Jamaicans seeking a better life in Central and South America. Garvey lived in Costa Rica, where he wrote for publications that documented the terrible working conditions blacks faced. He also tried unsuccessfully to convince the British government

to provide colonial protection for West Indians.

In 1912 Garvey returned to Jamaica. He realized the island offered few opportunities for a young black politician, so he traveled to London later that year to meet with black laborers, intellectuals, and businessmen who also suffered from racism. The most important of those he met was Duse Mohammed Ali, a Sundanese-Egyptian actor, journalist, and nationalist. Garvey began working for Ali's publication, the *African Times and Oriental Review*, which allowed him to understand African business and the proud moments of Africa's ancestral past. He also read *Up From Slavery*, a book about American race relations, which inspired him to become a "race leader."

Formed United Negro Improvement Association

In 1914 Garvey returned to Jamaica with a plan to create the United Negro Improvement Association (UNIA) and its coordinating body, the African Communities League. On August 1 Garvey and a few of his associates officially launched the organization. His main aim was to establish black educational institutions, which would allow blacks to gain economic control of their lives. Most black middle-class Jamaicans were indifferent to his ideas, so he wrote to Booker T. Washington in New York city for assistance. Washington's ideas paralleled some of Garvey's, but he died before Garvey arrived.

Garvey arrived penniless and unknown in New York in 1916. His first speeches were ignored, and he began to realize that instead

Marcus Garvey

of reforming the current system, a revolutionary plan was needed. He began endorsing a broad economic plan for private business and industry. By 1918, black migration, racial violence, and continuing segregation helped to promote Garvey's ideas. UNIA's economic strategy and its publication, *Negro World*, attracted thousands of supporters. The success convinced Garvey to move his headquarters from Jamaica to New York.

Planned black economic power

The first UNIA convention took place on August 1, 1920, and featured a parade that stretched for miles along Lennox Avenue in Harlem. Later that evening Garvey spoke before 25,000 people at Madison Square Garden. He announced his plans to form an African nation-state and called upon blacks to find their "own place in the sun." One of the highlights of the week-long convention was the adoption of the Declaration of the Rights of the Negro Peoples of the World, containing a bill of rights that proclaimed the equality of the black race and included resolutions for creating independent legal and educational systems.

Garvey established several business ventures, including the Negro Factories Corporation, a restaurant, a millinery, a publishing house, and a chain of cooperative grocery stores. He also tried to create a shipping fleet that he hoped would give blacks political power and bring them to the forefront of worldwide trade. He sold $5 shares through the mail, which allowed him to buy three ships to start the Black Star Shipping Line (BSL). This company helped Garvey to continue to grow in popularity as a champion of Pan-Africanism. He also introduced a plan to transfer his headquarters to Monrovia, Liberia.

Despite his popularity, Garvey was criticized by blacks and whites as well as by religious organizations. Many began to fear Garvey was leading his supporters towards radical black power. In 1919 the U.S. State Department investigated his BSL operation but failed to find any evidence of wrongdoing. Still, they pursued a plan for his eventual deportation. Black leaders such as W.E.B. Du Bois, cofounder of the National Association for the Advancement of Colored People (NAACP), rejected Garvey's economic and segregationist policies.

Popularity faded

Over time, the UNIA's popularity began to fade. When Garvey visited Central America in 1921, the State Department denied him a visa, which delayed his reentry into the United

States by several months. A year later he was convicted of mail fraud. He was released on bail and tried unsuccessfully to rescue BSL from financial collapse. The same year he met with the acting Imperial Wizard of the Ku Klux Klan (KKK) and said the UNIA and the KKK shared a similar policy of racial separation. The statement outraged many in the black community. His lobbying for a unified African Orthodox Church left him isolated from many black churches.

In 1924 Garvey was unable to defend himself against charges of mail fraud and he served six months in jail before posting $25,000 bail. The next year he launched a new shipping fleet, called Black Cross Navigation and Trading Company, but it soon folded. He also unsuccessfully used UNIA to found an independent Liberian republic. In 1925 Garvey lost his appeal to the Supreme Court and was jailed in an Atlanta penitentiary. After serving two years, he was released and deported to Jamaica.

Garvey entered Jamaican politics in 1927, forming the People's Political Party. UNIA's convention in Kingston, Jamaica, during 1929 helped renew the organization, but it would never again attract the huge following it once enjoyed. Garvey moved the headquarters to Jamaica, causing many of its American members to quit. In 1935 Garvey was faced with political defeat and financial problems so he moved to London, England. Britons cared little for his ideas, so he began traveling to Toronto, Canada, to attend conventions. He eventually established the School of African Philosophy in that city. After a long period of failing health, he suffered a stroke in 1940 and died in June of that year. Although he had only limited success during his lifetime, Garvey became an international symbol of black freedom and eventually inspired a new generation of blacks to seek equality.

Arthur Gaston

Entrepreneur
Born July 4, 1892, Demopolis, Alabama

E ven when he was a child, Arthur Gaston displayed entrepreneurial skills that would one day make him the richest black man in America. He charged his friends whatever they had— usually pins and buttons—to swing in his grandparents' yard. In 1932, at a time when white insurance companies ignored blacks, Gaston founded Booker T. Washington (BTW) Insurance Company. Today the company has assets of almost $40 million. Leading a group of investors in 1957, Gaston also started Citizens Federal Savings Bank, a savings and loan association. Bank deposits now exceed $72 million. Besides these ventures, Gaston has also launched or acquired construction companies, business colleges, funeral homes, and radio stations, and he practices philanthropy, helping senior citizens and young adults.

Entrepreneurial from his childhood

Gaston was born in the log cabin his grandparents built in Demopolis, Alabama, in 1892. His father died while he was a baby, and his mother moved to Birmingham in 1900 to become a cook. Gaston enrolled at Carrie Tuggle

Institute and held a variety of odd jobs. He sold subscriptions for a black newspaper, the *Birmingham Reporter,* and did so well that the owner lined up a post office job for him in Mobile. When he arrived in Mobile, he found there was no such job and became a bellhop at Battle House Hotel. He made so much money that when the post office job became available, he turned it down.

With the onset of World War I, Gaston joined the military, believing there was more opportunity in the armed forces. He was eventually promoted to sergeant and served with distinction in France as part of an all-black unit, the 317th Ammunition Train of the 92nd Division. When the war ended, Gaston was disappointed to find that blacks were still treated with second class status despite their war efforts. "The black soldiers stayed in their place during the war," Gaston told *Black Enterprise.* "And they had Dr. [Robert R.] Moton of Tuskegee speak to the black soldiers, just before leaving Europe. We were looking for equal rights back then. We were all prepared for it. But it dampened our spirits when Dr. Moton advised us to stay in our place. But I was a follower of Booker T. Washington, and I took his advice. I stayed in my place."

Gaston returned to Birmingham and found a job with the Tennessee Coal and Iron (TCI) Company for $3.10 a day, a good wage in those days. He made extra money by selling box lunches, which were prepared by his mother, to his co-workers. Since Gaston was very frugal, he used to lend money at the rate of twenty-five cents on the dollar every two weeks. He also operated a popcorn and peanut stand in his spare time.

Arthur Gaston

Gaston noticed that whenever a preacher stopped by the plant asking for donations for the burial of a black person, most of his co-workers would chip in. Gaston thought they might be willing to start their own burial society. He got lots of encouragement, but very few were willing to contribute. When the first member died, there was only thirty dollars in the account to pay for a hundred dollar funeral. Gaston managed to get the woman buried on credit, but the future of the society was in doubt. Finally, Rev. S.H. Ravizee of Hopewell Baptist Church refused to take any more collections for burials and told his congregation to support Gaston.

Bailed King out of jail

In 1923 the burial society soon acquired the mortuary that became the home of Smith & Gaston Funeral Directors. Nine years later it was incorporated as Booker T. Washington Burial Insurance Company. Gaston continued to diversify his interests, and in 1939 he started BTW Business College to train black clerical workers. In 1947 he purchased New Grace Hill Cemeteries Inc., and seven years later he opened the Gaston Motel in downtown Birmingham for black travelers, who were banned from white-only accommodations.

Gaston made further acquisitions and established more companies through the 1950s and 1960s. He began Vulcan Realty and Investment Company in 1955, Citizens Federal Savings and Loan Association in 1957, opened the A.G. Gaston Home for senior citizens in 1963, and established the A.G. Gaston Boys and Girls Club in 1966.

The entrepreneur also made substantial contributions to the civil rights movement. In 1957, when blacks in Tuskegee staged an economic boycott to gain voting rights, white banks put pressure on anyone who had outstanding mortgages or business loans. Gaston promised to advance mortgage money to anyone being pressured. He also provided lodging for leaders like Dr. Martin Luther King, Jr., and paid their bail when they were arrested for marching.

Although some said Gaston should have been at the forefront of the demonstrations, he played a key role in furthering discussions between black activists and white businessmen. When other cities were filled with race riots in the late 1960s, Birmingham managed to avoid much of this unrest, partly because of Gaston's biracial ties.

As word of Gaston's wealth spread, he and his wife, Minnie, were the victims of a kidnapping attempt in 1976. A late-night intruder assaulted them in their home and drove a handcuffed Gaston around the city for hours before being apprehended by the police.

In 1987 Gaston created an employee stock option plan (ESOP) and sold his parent company, BTW Insurance Company, to his employees for $3.5 million, a fraction of its estimated $34 million in assets. Bettye L. Clay, an executive assistant who had been with the company for thirty years, told a *Black Enterprise* interviewer, "Those of us who have seen this company grow over the years feel our loyalty and dedication have paid off."

Over the years Gaston has received recognition nationally and abroad. He has been honored by the U.S. Department of Commerce, the U.S. Small Business Administration, and the Chamber of Commerce of the United States. Although his formal education ended with a tenth grade completion certificate, Gaston has more than ten honorary doctorates, including degrees conferred by Tuskegee University and Monrovia College and Industrial Institute in Liberia. In 1992 *Black Enterprise* named him the Entrepreneur of the Century.

Gaston told *Black Enterprise* his fondest business ventures were his purchase of the rhythm and blues radio station WENN-FM, and the gospel station WAGG-AM. Both stations have received consistently high ratings among Birmingham listeners, both black and white.

BTW Insurance president Louis J. Willie, who has been with Gaston since 1952, credits Gaston for teaching him how to employ his education in the business world. "He told me that with my education—I was the only black person in my M.B.A. class at the University of Michigan— and with his practical skills, we could really build something," Willie told *Black Enterprise*. "Dr. Gaston put into practice all that I learned in school. He is a genius of psychology, someone who knows what makes people tick, and how to get the best out of them."

Henry Louis Gates, Jr.

Literary scholar, professor, critic
Born September 16, 1950, Keyser, West
  Virginia

"I find the lack of knowledge about black people that black people have is distressing. What I think of as intellectual racism—the idea that blacks are innately inferior—will be countered if each of us is an authentic scholar."

One of America's leading academics, Henry Louis Gates, Jr., has long been pressing for changes in the educational system so that school curricula take a multicultural approach, with in-depth studies of non-Western as well as Western cultures. In particular, Gates has been at the forefront of the movement to get African American studies programs established in American universities and colleges.

To promote the study of African American literature, Gates has unearthed a large number of stories, poems, and autobiographies that had previously been ignored. His passion for finding long-lost African American writings caused the writer Maya Angelou to call

him "a wonderful mixture of Alex Haley and Sherlock Holmes." By 1990 Gates had collected twelve thousand short stories, eighteen thousand poems, and forty-two thousand reviews and notices—all written by black Americans between 1929 and 1940. As he continues to retrieve the writings of formerly overlooked black writers, the great wealth of African American literature is at last being widely recognized.

Early influences

Gates is the son of Pauline (Coleman) Gates and Henry Louis Gates, Sr., a paper-mill loader. He grew up in the village of Piedmont, West Virginia, where he attended integrated schools. The majority of students there were white, but Gates recalls no racism at school. His worst experience of the blindest form of racism came after fracturing his hip at the age of fourteen. When the doctor who examined him learned that this black teenager wanted to be a doctor like himself, he told Gates's mother that the boy's problems were psychosomatic—Gates was clearly an overachiever and that was why he thought there was something wrong with his leg. Because of this shocking misdiagnosis, Gates's right leg is more than two inches shorter than his left.

Despite the doctor's putdown, Gates remained ambitious and after a year at junior college he enrolled at Yale University in 1969. The following year he won two fellowships that allowed him to take leave from his studies to go to Africa, where he worked as a general anesthetist in the Tanzanian village of Kilimatinde. Three years later, after graduating summa cum laude from Yale with a B.A.

in history, Gates won a scholarship to study in England at Cambridge University's Clare College.

At Cambridge, Gates met the Nigerian playwright and Nobel laureate-to-be Wole Soyinka, who fascinated him with tales of the mythology of the Yoruba people of Nigeria and inspired him to study African American literature by looking at its roots in Africa and the Caribbean. After graduating with an M.A. from Cambridge in 1974, Gates stayed on to study for a doctorate in literature. Meanwhile he also took several jobs. He was staff correspondent at *Time* magazine's London bureau (1973–75) and then, on returning to the United States, was public relations representative for American Cyanamid Company (1975) and a lecturer at Yale University (1976-79). In 1979, having completed his thesis, Gates obtained his Ph.D. from Cambridge—the first African American to do so in the university's eight-hundred-year history.

Champion of Afro-American literature

In 1979 Gates was offered a permanent appointment at Yale University, where besides teaching in the English department he directed a course of African American studies. Within a year he had established the Black Periodical Literature Project, which involved collecting and publishing unknown writings by African Americans.

Browsing through a bookstore one day, Gates came across a copy of Harriet E. Wilson's novel *Our Nig, or Sketches from the Life of a Free Black* (1859). Literary critics had always assumed that Harriet Wilson was

Henry Louis Gates, Jr.

the pseudonym of a white man, but Gates's research proved that Wilson was in fact a black woman, making her book the earliest known novel written by an African American. When Gates published a new edition of the book in 1983, it brought him wide attention, adding to the prestige he had gained two years earlier on being awarded a $150,000 "genius" grant from the McArthur Foundation for his critical essays on black literature.

Though still only in his early thirties, Gates was already recognized as a leading African American scholar. In addition to his many essays and articles, he edited several books of literary criticism, most notably the controversial *Black Literature and Literary Theory* (1984), in which he called for a more widespread study of works written by African Americans. Gates also compiled the thirty-volume *Schomburg Library of Nineteenth-Century Black Women Writers,* which was published in 1988. The *Norton Anthology of*

Afro-American Literature was another mammoth work that he compiled and edited.

Gates has written several books of his own, the most important being *The Signifying Monkey: Towards a Theory of Afro-American Literary Criticism* (1988), which won the American Book Award. In this book, Gates harks back to the Nigerian origins of "signifying" (a tradition of playing on words) and shows how the practice has been an element in African American culture. In 1990 he helped defend the rap group 2 Live Crew against charges of obscenity by explaining to the jurors that rapping was a modern form of signifying. The words of the group's song, he said, were not a call to violence; they were simply a joke, a parody, in the African American tradition of signifying.

One of Gates's most recent books is *Loose Canons: Notes on the Culture Wars* (1992). Gates has been embroiled in a number of academic disputes because of his outspoken cricitism of the educational system. He feels that American education has been guilty of racism in the way it has failed to recognize black cultural achievements. Yet he also considers it racist when black schools concentrate single-mindedly on African American culture, ignoring the achievements of others. He believes that education should be broad-based and open-minded, taking in all points of view. Nor does Gates go along with the idea that only blacks can teach or write about black culture. "It's as ridiculous as if someone said I couldn't appreciate Shakespeare because I'm not Anglo-Saxon," he says. "I think it's vulgar and racist whether it comes out of a black mouth or a white mouth."

Although such comments have raised hackles among blacks as well as whites, Gates has remained one of the most sought-after academics. After ten years at Yale, he moved to Cornell University, where he taught from 1985 to 1990. He then spent a year at Duke University before accepting his present position at Harvard University, where he is W. E. B. Du Bois Professor of the Humanities as well as chairman of the Department of Afro-American Studies. Gates is married to artist Sharon Adams and has two daughters who are being raised with multicultural attitudes while being made fully aware of the richness of the black cultural heritage.

Zelma Watson George

Sociologist, musicologist
Born December 8, 1903, Hearne, Texas

"Your personal integrity is all you've got.... It was just something that, to be honest, I had to do."

Sociologist, musicologist, educator, administrator, actress, and lecturer Zelma Watson George is best known for her service on numerous volunteer boards ranging from women's issues to religion to civil rights, and on the national stage for presidential committees and as a delegate to the United Nations.

Began schooling at home

George was born on December 8, 1903, in Hearne, Texas, to Samuel and Lena Watson.

She and her five siblings were taught at home by their mother until the sixth grade in a classroom that included other children of the same age to create a spirit of competition. Occasionally her father would teach mathematics and a few other courses.

Since her father was a Baptist minister, the family moved to several pastorates. When they moved to Topeka, Kansas, George attended high school and had her first taste of an integrated school. The white counselor advised her against applying to the University of Chicago, which only made her more determined. The university accepted her enrollment, but the dormitory refused her housing because of her race. Other obstacles followed. She was refused membership in the choir because her voice was "too good," and when she appealed the decision, she learned that the chaplain cast the deciding vote against her, contending that she would be too distracting for the congregation. When she tried out for women's basketball, the others decided to play football instead. They tackled her so hard that her knee was permanently injured. She decided to take swimming class as therapy for her knee, but everybody got out of the pool when she arrived, and one student said, "I don't swim with niggers." Nevertheless, George says her time at the university was one of the best times of her life. She loved the library and its quiet study halls and would sit under the trees reading her textbooks.

After graduating she first became a social worker for the Associated Charities of Evanston, Illinois, then a probation officer for juvenile court in Chicago. In the evenings, George studied organ at Northwestern University, and later she received a certificate for voice study at the American Conservatory of Music in Chicago. She also volunteered for several organizations, especially the Girl Scouts.

In 1932 George became dean of women and director of personnel administration at Tennessee Agricultural and Industrial State College in Nashville, where she developed materials for her freshman orientation course. Her volunteer work included establishing a Girl Scout troop, which would have been the South's first black troop but George was unable to get her unit invested. She also became chapter president of the Fellowship of Reconciliation and helped them accomplish important social and civic educational programs in the Nashville area.

Developed community center

In 1938 George married Baxter Duke, a young minister she knew when both were teenagers in Topeka, Kansas. For the five years this marriage lasted, she performed the usual duties of a minister's wife and also developed the Avalon Community Center, a mission-type community center that provided in-service training and personal guidance. At this same time George began work for a Ph.D. at the University of Southern California in the School of Education. Her plan to comprehensively study Negro music and its sociological impact was implemented when George received a two-year Rockefeller Foundation grant, enabling her to do extensive research across the country.

George moved to Cleveland, Ohio, after marrying her second husband, Clayborne

Art Music by Negro Composers or Based on Negro Thematic Material," catalogued 12,000 titles by or inspired by black Americans.

Her musical activity included her highly regarded title role in Gian-Carlo Menotti's opera *The Medium* in 1949 at the Karamu Theatre in Cleveland, which she performed on Broadway in New York in 1950. She also sang the lead role in the Cleveland Play House for Menotti's *The Consul* in 1951 and Kurt Weill's *Threepenny* in 1955.

Contributed on the national level

In 1956 George was appointed by Secretary of Defense Charles E. Wilson for a three-year term to the Defense Advisory Committee on Women in the Armed Services. The next year Vice-President Richard Nixon asked her to participate in the Minority Youth Training Incentives Conference. In 1958 she became a member of the Washington Conference on the Community's Responsibility for the Development of Minority Potential. Later that year President Dwight D. Eisenhower appointed her to the President's Committee to plan the 1960 White House Conference on Children and Youth. In 1959 George received a State Department grant for a six-month lecture tour of thirteen countries in the Far East, Southeast Asia, Europe, and Africa. In 1960 she was named an alternate to the U.S. delegation to the Fifteenth General Assembly of the United Nations, where she represented her country on the Economics and Finance Committee. After her appointment, George became a highly sought speaker and lecturer. She eventually lectured full time under for the Danforth Foundation and the W. Colston Leigh Bureau;

Zelma Watson George

George, a highly respected lawyer and chairman of the Civil Service Commission. She continued to combine several careers with volunteer work, serving on the boards of the YWCA, Council of Church Women, Girl Scouts, Conference of Christians and Jews, the Council on Human Relations, the League of Women Voters, the Central Areas Community Council, Karamu, the Association of National Scholarships, the Phyllis Wheatley Association, the Cleveland Council on World Affairs, the United Nations Board, and many others.

Educational credentials include her master's degree in personnel administration in 1943 from New York University, graduate courses in radio and television at Western Reserve University during 1947–48, and her Ph.D. in sociology and intercultural relations in 1954 from New York University. Her dissertation, "A Guide to Negro Music: An Annotated Bibliography of Negro Folk Music and between 1964 and 1967 George visited fifty-nine colleges as a Danforth visiting lecturer.

From 1966 to 1974 she served as executive director of the new Cleveland Jobs Corps Centre for Women, a residential vocational training program for young women from low-income backgrounds who had dropped out of school, and during the 1980s she taught at Cuyahoga Community College.

Now in her eighties, George is still sought for speaking engagements and continues to serve on some community and national boards.

Althea Gibson

Athlete
Born August 25, 1927, Silver, South
 Carolina

"I hope that I have accomplished just one thing: that I have been a credit to tennis and my country."

The first black female tennis player ever to compete and win at Wimbledon and Forest Hills, Althea Gibson grew up on the streets of Harlem. She skipped school, was fired from several jobs, and lived with her family in cramped quarters.

But when she was spotted playing tennis in a city court, Gibson's future changed for the better. After honing her talents, she won tournaments in Sweden, Germany, France, England, Italy, and Egypt. Gibson ushered in a new age for black women tennis players and remains a role model for many of today's stars.

Skipped school frequently

Gibson was born on August 25, 1927, in Silver, South Carolina, to Daniel and Annie Gibson. The family eventually moved to New York, where she was raised in an apartment in Harlem. Living in a ghetto was difficult for Gibson, and she often skipped school, but she managed to complete junior high school in 1941.

When she was promoted to Yorkville Trade School, Gibson requested a transfer to a downtown school her friends attended, but the school board turned down her request. Gibson was so disappointed she began skipping school again. She was eventually sent to the Society for the Prevention of Cruelty to Children, a place for troubled and homeless children. She got along well with the social workers, who told her if she did not stop skipping school, the Society was going to be her new home.

Began playing tennis

Gibson requested that she be given working papers on condition that she attend night school for a set number of hours per week. She worked at several jobs, including a position as mail clerk at the New York School of Social Work. She liked this job but was fired after six weeks for skipping work and watching movies.

Gibson's self-esteem was at a low point, but it improved after she discussed her situation with boxer Sugar Ray Robinson and his wife, Edna. She had met the couple while still a student of the trade school. They encouraged her to complete her high school education so she could get a good job.

Having a variety of jobs didn't keep her off the streets, and when Welfare Department

Althea Gibson

personnel noticed her, they made arrangements for Gibson to live in a less crowded home and helped her look for work. In her spare time, she played in local tennis games sponsored by the Police Athletic League.

Spotted playing tennis

While playing tennis one day she was spotted by Buddy Walker, a musician who also worked for the city recreation department in the summer. He bought Gibson a second-hand racket and challenged her to a few sets at the New York Cosmopolitan Club with professional Fred Johnson. Gibson's performance was judged above average, and club members provided a junior membership for her. Johnson taught her the basics of tennis.

Within a year of lessons Gibson won her first tournament—the girls' singles in the New York State Open Championship in 1942. Cosmopolitan Club members sent her to the American Tennis Association's (ATA) national

girls' championship, a predominately black competition at Lincoln University in Pennsylvania. Gibson reached the finals but lost to Nina Davis. The defeat caused her to work even harder, but with the advent of World War II, the ATA canceled the national championship due to travel restrictions. The tournament resumed in 1944, and Gibson won the girls' singles in 1944 and 1945.

Mentored by ATA leaders

When she turned eighteen Gibson was eligible for the women's singles and played at Wilberforce College in Ohio. She lost to Roumania Peters, a teacher at Tuskegee Institute, but Hubert Eaton of Wilmington, North Carolina, and Robert W. Johnson of Lynchburg, both ATA leaders, recognized her potential and offered to feed, clothe, and educate Gibson at their own expense. During the school year she lived with Eaton's family, attended high school, practiced on their private court, and during the summer received intensive training from Johnson.

Gibson did well in school and finished tenth in her class, then was awarded a scholarship to Florida Agricultural and Mechanical College in Tallahassee. At college she focused on her studies, continued to build her tennis skills, and accepted invitations to play in Eastern and national indoor championships.

Gibson yearned for an invitation from the United States Lawn Tennis Association to play in the prestigious summer grass court tournament at Forest Hills, Long Island. Alice Marble, a white tennis player, also hoped Gibson would be invited. When Gibson received no invitation, Marble blasted the association in the July 1950 issue of *American Lawn Tennis* magazine for not letting Gibson play.

When the article was published, doors began opening for Gibson. She was accepted to play in the Eastern Grass Court Championship, and after defeating one player, she was eliminated by Helen Pastall. She reached the quarterfinals in the National Clay Courts Championships at Chicago, where Doris Hart beat her 6–2, 6–3.

Won at Wimbledon and Forest Hills

Gibson was accepted into the United States Lawn Tennis Association. At the national championship tournament, she easily won her first round match against Great Britain's Barbara Knapp, but she lost to Louise Brough, Wimbledon champion and former United States champion. Gibson became the first black to play major lawn tennis, but it took seven years for her to win the nation's tennis championship at Forest Hills.

Gibson put tennis on hold for awhile after graduating from Florida A&M with a degree in physical education. She joined the physical education department faculty of Lincoln University in Jefferson City, Missouri, where she taught for two years. She returned to the game as a dominant force. She won sixteen out of eighteen tournaments around the world.

In 1957 Gibson became the first black woman to compete and to win at Wimbledon and Forest Hills. She faced Darlene Hard at Wimbledon and won the singles match 6–3, 6–2. She later teamed with Hard to win the doubles championship. At Forest Hills, Gibson emerged victorious over Louise Brough, 6–3,

6–2. The next year she returned to Wimbledon and defeated Britain's Angela Mortimer 8–6, 6–2 in singles. Paired with Maria Bueno of Brazil in doubles, Gibson beat Margaret Gaborn du Pont and Margaret Varner 6–3, 7–5.

Shortly afterwards Gibson retired from tennis, and after trying several activities, eventually turned to golf. She played in several tournaments from 1963 to 1967. Gibson's career in sports did not make her wealthy, but she opened the door for many black athletes to follow in her footsteps.

Dizzy Gillespie

Trumpeter, bandleader
Born October 21, 1917, Cheraw, South
  Carolina
Died January 6, 1993, Englewood, New
  Jersey

"We had a special way of phrasing. Not only did we change harmonic structure, but we changed rhythmic structure."

Dizzie Gillespie was a brilliant virtuoso on the trumpet, famed for his harmonic and rhythmic experiments. Together with saxophonist Charlie Parker, he created the style of jazz known as bebop, or bop, which emerged during the 1940s. As Gillespie described it, "We'd take the chord structures of various standard and pop tunes and create new chords, melodies, and songs from them." Gillespie also adapted Latin American rhythms to jazz, setting a fashion for Afro-

Cuban jazz in the 1950s. He was always open to new influences in his music.

A born performer who made his audiences feel part of the show, Gillespie gained his nickname Dizzy from his habit of clowning onstage, or breaking into a dance. Long before the "hippie" era, he wore eccentric costumes, topped off by a beret and dark glasses. His trademark was his upturned trumpet—the result of an accident at a party when one of the guests sat on his trumpet, bending the bell to a forty-five-degree angle. Gillespie so liked the muted sound it made that from then on he had the bells of his trumpets set at the same angle. In the summer of 1993, a few months after Gillespie's death, one of these bent trumpets was sold for more than fifty-thousand dollars at a Sotheby's auction in New York.

The young trumpeter

Born John Birks Gillespie, Dizzy was the youngest of the nine children of James and Lottie Gillespie. His father, who was a bricklayer and part-time musician, insisted that all the children learn the piano. As a result, Gillespie had a basic grounding in music from an early age. At his elementary school he joined the band, hoping to learn the trombone, but his arms were not long enough to do the slides, so he took up the trumpet instead. His trumpet playing gained him a scholarship to Laurinberg Technical Institute in North Carolina, where he studied both trumpet and piano.

In 1935 Gillespie's family moved to Philadelphia, where he landed a spot with the Frankie Fairfax Band. Moving to New York two years later, he soon attracted attention in jazz circles. Already he was developing his own style, playing at great speed and using new rhythms and chord changes. At first much of Gillespie's playing was at informal all-night jam sessions, for he had no regular job, but within a year he was hired for a European tour by the Teddy Hill Orchestra. Gillespie's first recordings were made with the Teddy Hill Orchestra.

The birth of bebop

Between 1939 and 1943 Gillespie played with some of the most famous big bands of the day, including the Cab Calloway Orchestra (1939–41) and the Earl Hines Orchestra (1942–43). He became one of the most sought-after jazz trumpeters in New York and was also known as a composer. His famous song "A Night in Tunisia" was written around this time. As bebop gradually became popular, various bandleaders asked him to compose numbers for them.

Bebop emerged early in the 1940s during the after-hours jam sessions that Gillespie took part in with Charlie Parker and a handful of other musicians. They would stay on after the clubs closed and and let loose their musical talents in impromptu playing, which often lasted right through until morning. The New York clubs most associated with the birth of bebop are Monroe's Uptown House and the famous Minton's Playhouse in Harlem.

Like Gillespie, Parker was a member of Earl Hines's band, and both moved to the band that Billy Eckstine formed in 1943. But within a few months Gillespie left to lead his own quintet, and early in 1944 his group secured a regular spot at the Onyx Club, which had recently opened on 52nd Street. At last

Gillespie was in a position to play bebop full-time. "The opening of the Onyx Club represented the birth of the bebop era," he wrote in his autobiography, *To Be or Not ... to Bop* (1979). "In our long sojourn on 52nd Street we spread our message to a much wider audience."

The stint at the Onyx Club also saw the naming of bebop, as Gillespie explained in his book: "We played a lot of original tunes that didn't have titles. We just wrote an introduction and a first chorus. I'd say, 'Dee-da-pa-dan-de-bop...' and we'd just go into it. People, they'd wanna ask for one of those numbers and didn't know the name, would ask for bebop."

As well as playing with his quintet, Gillespie formed his own big band, with which he toured widely in the late 1940s. In 1947 the band gave a concert in Carnegie Hall—a landmark event in that it signaled the recognition

of bebop as an established jazz form. Another landmark was the dazzling performance of Gillespie's quintet at Massey Hall in Toronto, Canada. The recording of this concert, *Jazz at Massey Hall* (1953), has become a classic.

During this period Gillespie was also developing Afro-Cuban jazz, in collaboration with the Cuban percussionist Chano Pozo. Popularizing such numbers as "Cubana Be, Cubana Bop" and "Tin Tin Deo," the Gillespie band made a successful tour of Europe, with Pozo on drums, in 1948.

Upward and onward

During the 1950s Gillespie became a regular performer in the "Jazz at the Philharmonic" concert tours, and in 1956 the U.S. State Department commissioned him to tour Africa, the Middle East, and Asia. This was followed by a similar tour in South America. These tours proved to be a two-way street, for besides introducing bebop to far-distant communites, Gillespie absorbed the music of those same communities and incorporated their styles in his works. Like all great artists, he was constantly innovating and was always open to new ideas.

In the 1960s Gillespie gradually turned away from pure bebop as he included other influences in his music. He remained open to new styles during the 1970s and 1980s, when his band became a training ground for younger musicians. As Gillespie grew older, he kept up his busy schedule, performing regularly at jazz festivals and in concert halls, and touring for as much as nine months each year. In 1989, when he was seventy-two, he gave about three hundred concerts in twenty-seven countries

Dizzy Gillespie

and in a hundred cities throughout the United States, as well as recording four albums.

Honors were showered upon Gillespie during his later years. These ranged from being named a regent professor at the University of California, Los Angeles, to being inaugurated as a tribal chief in Nigeria. One of the most appreciated honors was the National Medal of Arts, which was presented to Gillespie by President George Bush in 1989 "for his trail-blazing work as a musician who helped elevate jazz to an art form of the first rank, and for sharing his gift with listeners around the world." That same year he also received a Grammy Lifetime Achievement Award.

Nikki Giovanni

Poet
Born June 7, 1943, Knoxville, Tennessee

"My family on my grandmother's side are fighters. My family on my father's side are survivors. I'm a revolutionist. It's only logical."

A well-known, successful poet committed to her people, Nikki Giovanni burst on the scene in the 1960s as a revolutionary poet fiercely promoting black rights. Though she has since widened her scope, her profound pride in her black heritage remains an underlying theme throughout her work, which includes more than a dozen volumes of poetry as well as some prose collections. There are also three books for children, *Spin a Soft Black Song* (1971), *Ego Tripping and Other Poems for Young People* (1973), and *Vacation Time* (1980).

In her poetry as in her life, Giovanni has taken an independent approach, ever willing to experiment and try something new. Many of her poems use the rhythms of jazz and blues, and she has made recordings of some of her poetry, reciting the verses against a background of gospel music. To date, she has produced six albums. She has also written a witty and outspoken collection of autobiographical essays, *Gemini* (1971), which gives a fascinating glimpse of the person behind the poetry.

Learned pride from her grandmother

In a poem about her childhood, Nikki Giovanni wrote, "Black love is Black wealth." In this sense, she had a rich and happy childhood, for although her parents could seldom afford luxuries, she was surrounded by love in her closely knit family. Both her parents were college graduates; her father, Jones Giovanni, was a probation officer; her mother, Yolande (Watson) Giovanni, was a social worker. Giovanni's full name is Yolande Cornelia Giovanni; she was nicknamed Nikki by her sister Gary.

During her childhood, her family lived in a mainly black suburb of Cincinnati, Ohio, and she attended school through eighth grade. Then she stayed with her grandmother while attending Austin High School in Knoxville. Giovanni's grandmother, a woman of powerful character and a strong influence on the teenage girl, taught her to speak out about things that were important to her. Her grandmother's intolerance for white people and proud sense of race were also strong influences, teaching Giovanni to place great value on being a part of the black culture and to see herself as having a responsibility to fellow blacks. Clearly, the seeds of her future activism were sown during those years she was with her grandmother.

Giovanni's independent spirit showed itself soon after she enrolled at Fisk University at the age of seventeen. Believing it important to be with her family at Thanksgiving, she left the campus without permission to spend the weekend with her grandparents. As a result she was "released" from the university after her first semester. Four years later she returned to Fisk and from 1964 to 1967 studied for her B.A., graduating with honors just a month before her grandmother died.

Wrote poetry with a purpose

During Giovanni's years at Fisk, she was a well-known figure on campus. Early on she rallied 200 students to demand that the Fisk chapter of the Student Nonviolent Coordinating Committee (SNCC) be restored. The demonstration was a success.

Giovanni's activism continued when she left Fisk. After an unsatisfactory nine months at the University of Pennsylvania's School of Social Work, she became deeply involved in the black rights movement. Her aim was to use poetry and prose to give African Americans a sense of awareness and pride and to spur people to action. This was the thrust of the two books of poems she published in 1968, *Black Feeling, Black Talk* and *Black Judgement*.

With these books, Giovanni gained national attention as an eloquent voice in the struggle for black rights. *Black Judgement* sold 6,000 copies in the first three months—a phenomenal success for a book of poems. Giovanni was suddenly in great demand as a lecturer and speaker, and in 1969 she accepted the position of associate professor of English at Rutgers University in New Jersey. Although only in her mid-twenties, she was recognized as one of the leading figures of the new black poetry.

During the summer of 1969, Giovanni asserted her individuality in a different way—by giving birth to a son, Thomas. As she later explained, "I had a baby at 25 because I *wanted* to have a baby and could *afford* to have a baby. I did not get married because I didn't *want* to get married and could *afford* not to get married."

Brought her poetry to young and old

After the birth of her son, Giovanni's poetry became warmer in tone, concerned less with revolution and more with such themes as family love and with the nature of poetry itself. She formed her own publishing cooperative in 1970 and the following year published the first of her books for children, *Spin a Soft Black Song,* a collection of poems written for her son.

Giovanni had always seen it as her mission to write for black people, about black people, and to talk directly to black people in her poetry, and she found a new way of doing so when she thought of recording her poems against a background of gospel music. Her first album, *Truth Is on Its Way* (1971), was a

Nikki Giovanni

success with the older generation as well as with the young. As she later explained, she had wanted it to be something that her grandmother would have enjoyed listening to. The album sold more than 100,000 copies, reaching a wide audience among whites as well as blacks.

Giovanni used a variety of media to reach as wide an audience as possible. As well as publishing more books, she read her poems on television and appeared on television talk shows, and she made some audio and video tapes in which she discussed poetry and black issues with other poets.

Her 1973 collection of poems, *My House*, was chosen by the American Library Association as one of the year's best books for young adults. Like so much of Giovanni's work, *My House* stresses the importance of family love. Giovanni feels very strongly that a good family spirit, with supportive and loving relationships, is essential in order to build successful black communities. This personal and thought-

ful tone was continued in *The Women and the Men* (1975) and *Cotton Candy on a Rainy Day* (1978). Then, in 1983, Giovanni returned to poems that were more political in tone, with her collection *Those Who Ride the Night Winds*.

Since 1985 Giovanni has taught creative writing at Mount St. Joseph on the Ohio. She has received numerous honorary degrees and other tributes, notably the television film, *Spirit to Spirit: The Poetry of Nikki Giovanni*, which aired on PBS in 1986.

When asked how she reconciles her established position today with the activist she was in her twenties, Giovanni has no difficulty explaining. "One winds down," she remarked. "We've touched on every sore that anybody in the world ever had and I think we ought to do some healing. I'm not downgrading anger, but how long can you stay angry?"

Robin Givens

Actress
Born 1965, New York, New York

"As a young actress in Hollywood, I hope that some little girl looks at me and says: 'She's doing it. I can do it.' Often that possibility is what keeps me going when I'm tired and frustrated, when I feel like the injustices of the world have taken their toll on me."

As the former wife of heavyweight boxing champion Mike Tyson, Robin Givens has attracted more media attention than most young actresses. But very little of it has been favorable. Givens sued Tyson for divorce in 1988 on the grounds of physical abuse, saying that he had assaulted her. In the highly publicized divorce proceedings, she was usually portrayed as an unprincipled gold digger who was almost certainly a liar.

Her accusations were taken more seriously after her divorce, when Tyson was convicted of raping another woman. His conviction brought Givens more sympathetic treatment from both the press and the public at large, along with serious consideration of her abilities as an actress. She has played a range of roles, from struggling ghetto dweller to confident corporate executive.

A privileged upbringing

One of the reasons for the bad press Givens so often received is that she has tended to make enemies more easily than friends. Her privileged upbringing gave her a superior manner that turned off many of her contemporaries. Givens's parents were well-to-do, middle-class people. Her father, Reuben Givens, was an artist, and her mother, Ruth Roper, a business executive. They divorced when Givens was two years old, and she was brought up by her mother, who sent her to exclusive private schools in New Rochelle, New York, and then to the prestigious Sarah Lawrence College in Bronxville, New York.

Givens regularly had good grades in her schoolwork and also took weekend classes in dance, music, and theater arts. An exceptionally pretty girl, she had her first modeling and acting jobs while still a teenager. Yet her classmates did not admire her success. As one of them told *Sports Illustrated,* "Robin didn't

have any friends at Sarah Lawrence. She made her presence known, but she rubbed everybody the wrong way. At our graduation, they called her name and she was booed."

After receiving her B.A. from Sarah Lawrence in 1984, Givens enrolled at Harvard University's medical school with the intention of training to be a doctor. But she dropped out within less than a year in order to work full time as an actress. Her first major role was in the television series "Head of the Class" on ABC-TV. As Darlene, the intelligent but snobby student, Givens soon became a familiar figure to American television viewers.

Givens gained further celebrity when she began to date such stars as comedian Eddie Murphy and Chicago Bulls basketball player Michael Jordan. Boxing champion Mike Tyson said he fell for Givens the first time he saw her on television, and for four months he tried to persuade her to go out with him.

A stormy marriage

Mike Tyson had spent much of his youth in a reform school and was known to be a tough character. Givens was so scared of meeting him that in 1987, when she had her first date with him, she brought along her mother, her sister, and two publicists.

Within two months Givens was deeply in love with Tyson, though she already had personal experience of his violent nature. She found it out the first time he took her to his apartment: "He just picked me up and carried me to 41st Street, where he lived. I didn't want to go…. When I wanted to leave, Michael hit me in the back of the head. It felt like my head would come off."

By Tyson's account, Givens often did some hitting too. Later the same year he told *Sports Illustrated,* "We fight all the time. She thinks she is so much better than me, just because she has had an education.… It may be true, but I hate the way she goes about telling me. I retaliate by telling her I am the heavyweight champion and she should know her place. Man, she really gets into a temper at that and comes at me."

Despite their quarrels, Givens and Tyson were married in February 1988 and to begin with all seemed to go well. Givens repeatedly said how happy she was and in May she announced that she was pregnant. But the following month she had a miscarriage, and soon rumors began to circulate about problems within the marriage—that Tyson had crashed his car because Givens was hitting him at the time, and that on vacation in the Bahamas he struck Givens and her friend, tennis player Lori McNeil.

In September 1988, when the couple appeared on the television program "20/20," Givens told interviewer Barbara Walters that her marriage was "torture, pure hell, worse than anything I could imagine." Meanwhile, Tyson, who was sedated with pacifying drugs, sat glassily beside her saying nothing. But two weeks later, according to Givens, he woke her in the middle of the night by hitting her violently on the head and body. She fled their mansion and subsequently filed for divorce.

The divorce proceedings were very ugly, with Tyson launching a countersuit in an attempt to get the marriage annulled. He alleged that Givens had made him marry her by pretending to be pregnant. The media had a field

Robin Givens

day, collecting gossip from friends and enemies, and reporting every detail, including Tyson's tirade against Givens: "Not only did she want to take my money, but she wanted to ruin me, embarrass me, take my manhood, and humiliate me on television so that no woman would ever want me again." At the end of it all, Givens did indeed get much of Tyson's money. When the divorce was granted in 1989 she came away with a seven-figure financial settlement.

Film and television actress

Soon after the divorce, the public had the opportunity to see Givens in two television movies which had been filmed previously: *The Penthouse* and Oprah Winfrey's *Women of Brewster Place.* Both were shown in 1989 when Givens was trying to keep a low profile to escape the unwelcome attention of the media. However, in 1990 she agreed to a long interview with an *Ebony* magazine journalist, who wrote a sympathetic article portraying Givens as thoroughly honest and convincing.

Givens's acting career continued with a challenging role in her first feature film, *A Rage in Harlem* (1991), in which she played Imabelle, a struggling ghetto dweller who falls for an accountant. She followed up in 1992 with the short-lived television series "Angel Street," about two women detectives. She also had a supporting role in Eddie Murphy's comedy *Boomerang,* in which she played Jacqueline, a high-powered executive.

Meanwhile, in 1990, Givens formed her own production company, Never Blue Productions. Her aim is to expand the number of parts available to black actresses. In this, as in her acting, she sees herself as a role model: "As a young actress in Hollywood, I hope that some little girl looks at me and says: 'She's doing it. I can do it.' Often that possibility is what keeps me going when I'm tired and frustrated, when I feel like the injustices of the world have taken their toll on me. If I don't do my part, then the dream has died."

Danny Glover

Actor
Born 1948, Georgia

"I have to be careful about the parts I take. Given how this industry has dealt with people like me, the parts I take have to be political choices."

ildly successful co-star of *Lethal Weapon*, Danny Glover originally in-

tended to be an economist. After he discovered and fell in love with the theater, he eventually succeeded to get roles in large-scale movie productions, such as *Places in the Heart, The Color Purple*, and *Lethal Weapon 1* and *2*.

In an industry that has not been historically wide open to black actors, Glover has the reputation of being one of the most versatile and respected actors in the business. Coupled with his talent is a desire to be a role model for black people trying to become actors.

Changed major from economics to acting

Glover was born in rural Georgia, raised in San Francisco, California, and became interested in acting while attending San Francisco State University in the late 1960s. He had planned to become an economist, but soon found himself drawn to acting. He began with roles in college plays written by Amiri Baraka, who traveled to San Francisco to stage new theater productions aiming for a new start in black arts. Glover enjoyed playing activist roles in these plays, because he felt he was making a statement on the way in which he wanted to live his life.

Since he enjoyed drama so much, Glover changed his major to acting. He also became interested in political activism and joined the African Liberation Support Committee. After graduating in the late 1960s, he continued his activism by working as an evaluator of community programs for the Mayor's Office in San Francisco. He continued to act in local theater and eventually decided to become an actor.

Danny Glover

Glover studied at the American Conservatory of Theater and the Black Box Theater Company, working nights as a taxi driver. He appeared in South African anti-apartheid playwright Athol Fugard's "The Island and Sizwe Bansi Is Dead" at the Eureka Theater in San Franciso and the Los Angeles Actors Theater. He appeared later at New York City's Roundabout Theater in Fugard's "The Blood Knot."

Discovered by a movie director

In 1982 Glover's career began to take off because of his performance in Fugard's "Master Harold ...and the Boys," which premiered at the Yale Repertory Theater in New Haven, Connecticut, and eventually opened on Broadway in New York. Glover's performance won him a Theatre World Award as one of the most promising actors of that year.

Film director Robert Benton saw Glover in "Master Harold" and cast him in the role of Mose in his 1984 movie, *Places in the Heart.*

Although Mose was intended to be an older man, Benton was so impressed with Glover's reading for the part that he had the script rewritten. Glover portrayed a black hobo-farmer who helps save the farm of a Southern white widow, played by Sally Field. Glover managed to draw upon the years he spent as a youth on his grandparents' farm in Georgia. He was even more influenced by his mother's death in an automobile accident a few days before he began work on the film. In *Films in Review,* Glover stated that his mother "was with me in so many ways. I mean, she was there when I gave the handkerchief to Sally. I think as actors, we probably would have found ways to get what we wanted, but what happened with my mother gave us the thrust. At a time I was mourning, it gave me strength."

Starred with Whoopi Goldberg in *The Color Purple*

Places in the Heart was nominated for best picture and helped Glover land a role in *Witness* (which also received a best picture nomination). This movie provided Glover with the chance to play a completely different character—an ex-police officer turned murderer. Later that year Glover appeared in the acclaimed western *Silverado.* He played the role of Malachi, a black cowboy-hero. Glover once said that feedback from the role, especially by children, convinced him of the importance of being a black actor.

In 1986 Glover appeared in *The Color Purple* in a role that was complex and controversial. He played Mister, a Southern black widower who marries a young woman, Celie (Whoopi Goldberg). Mister separates Celie from her sister and intercepts and hides her letters for many years. He is an abusive husband who exploits Celie ruthlessly, openly carrying on a love affair with a sultry blues singer named Shug. Some criticized Glover's character for projecting a negative image of black men as violent and insensitive. But Glover maintained the character accurately depicted life in the early 1900s. He told *People* magazine that "Mister was an adequate representation of one particular story. He's a product of his past and his present and I think we showed that he has some capabilities for changing." His performance received many favorable reviews. Donald Bogle in *Blacks in American Films and Television* wrote, Glover "gave a tightly drawn, highly-charged performance of a man who's been both brute and simp." Janet Maslin in the *New York Times* said that Glover "somehow makes a very sympathetic villain."

Scored biggest hit of the year with *Lethal Weapon*

The next year Glover made the biggest movie hit of the year co-starring with Mel Gibson in *Lethal Weapon*. Glover portrayed Roger Murtaugh, a homicide detective and dedicated family man, whose partner is a reckless, daredevil officer named Martin Riggs (Gibson). Glover's stable character is the exact opposite of Gibson's character. The two worked well together and helped make the movie at success, not only at the box office but also with the critics. Two years later they combined for *Lethal Weapon 2*, which was just as successful.

In 1990 Glover starred in the Charles Burnett film *To Sleep with Anger*. Although it received little attention, many critics said it was Glover's best work to date. He played a superstitious and manipulative man from the Deep South paying a visit to old friends, now a middle class black family in Los Angeles. His character slowly works to stir up trouble within the family, which eventually comes to a head. David Ansen in *Newsweek* wrote, "Glover, in what may be the best role of his film career, makes (his character) an unforgivable trickster, both frightening and a little pathetic."

Throughout his career Glover has been aware of his responsibility to serve as a role model for blacks. He once told an interviewer for *Jet* magazine that "I've always felt my experience as an artist is inseparable from what happens with the overall body of black people.... My sitting here now is the result of people, black people and people of good conscience in particular, fighting a struggle in the real world, changing the real attitudes and the real social situation."

Glover still lives in his hometown of San Francisco in a house in the Haight-Ashbury district he purchased years ago.

Whoopi Goldberg

Actress
Born November 13, 1949, New York City, New York

"Everywhere I go, I see incidents, or I meet someone who sticks in my mind. And people tell me stories. Then I develop a character and try it on different audiences until I get what I want right in my head."

Famous film and television star Whoopi Goldberg is known mostly as a comedienne, yet the characters she plays are often sad creatures, awkward misfits and outcasts from society. But they are far from pitiful. So sympathetically does Goldberg draw her characters that they arouse admiration as well as amusement. There is a serious message behind much of her humor, so that even while she is provoking laughter, she can be making a stinging point about society. She has said that she wants to make people think as well as laugh.

Knew from childhood that she wanted to act

Abandoned by her father, Goldberg and her brother were raised by their mother in a New York housing project, where they spent much of their childhood wishing that they were rich or that they were white—or were anything that would allow them to escape from the problems of everyday life.

Goldberg coped through laughter. Even now it is difficult to get her to talk seriously about her background, and for many years she kept her real name secret. She claims to be half Jewish and half Catholic and has given the following explanation of how she chose her stage name: "It was a joke. First it was Whoopi Cushion. Then it was French, like Whoopi Cushon. My mother said, 'Nobody's gonna respect you with a name like that.' So I put Goldberg on it. Goldberg's a part of my family somewhere and that's all I can say about it."

Her real name is Caryn Johnson, and her first teachers were the nuns at the parish school of St. Columba Church on West 25th Street. Her first stage appearance was at Helena Rubenstein Children's Theater at the Hudson Guild on West 26th Street, where she performed in plays from the age of eight. Even then Goldberg knew she wanted to be an actress, but there were several hurdles in her way, including the fact that she suffered from dyslexia and had difficulty learning to read. As a teenager she dropped out of high school and started using drugs, but eventually she managed to break free, having asked herself, "Am I going to keep doing drugs and kill myself or figure out what I'm going to do with my life?"

For a time she took part in student protests and civil rights marches and even worked as a counselor at a summer camp. Then, in the early 1970s Goldberg managed to get work in the chorus of the Broadway productions of "Hair," "Jesus Christ Superstar," and "Pippin." She also had a brief marriage and gave birth to a daughter, Alexandrea Martin. Yet her true career only began in 1974 after she moved with her daughter to San Diego, California.

Launched career with one-person show, "The Spook Show"

In San Diego Goldberg teamed up with comic actor Don Victor, presenting two-character shows on the West Coast. The act became a one-character show when Victor failed to turn up in San Francisco, which is when Goldberg found out she could hold an audience as a solo performer—the type of act in which she would later excel.

She settled in Berkeley and joined the Blake Street Hawkeyes, an experimental theater group that provided valuable acting experience over the next few years. Since the theater did not bring in much money, Goldberg had to rely on welfare when she couldn't find other work. Taking whatever jobs she could get, she acquired experience being a brick-layer and applying makeup to the corpses in a mortuary.

In 1983 Goldberg opened the one-person show that launched her as a comic character actress. Titled "The Spook Show" (and also called "A Broad Abroad" and "Whoopi Goldberg Variations"), the show toured the United States and Europe during 1983–84, and it was produced on Broadway to great acclaim in 1984–85. Goldberg acted all the parts, exhibiting wit and pathos for the vari-ous roles. One of the most affecting portrayals was of a nine-year-old black girl who longed to be white. The little girl covers her tight braids in a white skirt, pretending she has long

Whoopi Goldberg

blond hair, while she explains: "I told my mother I don't want to be black no more. You have to have blond hair to be on *Love Boat.*"

From comedy to Comic Relief

The success of *The Spook Show* opened the way to films, though Goldberg's first film was not a comedy. Steven Spielberg cast her as the battered wife Celie in his movie *The Color Purple* (1985). Goldberg's sensitive perform-ance won her a Golden Globe Award and the NAACP Image Award, as well as an Acad-emy Award nomination.

During the next five years Goldberg played in a succession of films: *Jumpin' Jack Flash, Burglar, Fatal Beauty, The Telephone, Homer and Eddie, Clara's Heart,* and *Beverly Hills Brats.* Some of these movies were far from successful, but her performance in the highly successful movie *Ghost* (1990) won her an Academy Award as best supporting actress. More in demand than ever, she ap-peared in further films, including the hilarious *Sister Act* (1992), for which she won the Peo-ple's Choice Awards in 1993 as best actress.

Goldberg has also worked in television. In 1990 she starred with Jean Stapleton in the situation comedy "Bagdad Café," in which she played the hot-hearted but soft-headed owner of the café. She has been a member of the crew in "Star Trek: The Next Generation," and has been the star of such shows as "Whoopi and Robin." One of her numerous guest appearances, on "Moonlighting," earned her an Emmy award nomination.

A very public figure, Goldberg endures criticism from members of the black commu-nity for dating white men and for her two-year marriage to Dutch cameraman David Claessen in the 1980s. Her performance in *The Color Purple* drew criticism from some black viewers because of the way she portrayed Celie and because of the language she used. Even her comedy acts can cause offense when she sounds off about sex or drugs or race or exposes the truth about anything people would rather not know.

But none of the criticism prevents Goldberg from carrying on in the direction she means to go. One of her aims has always been to correct the ills of society. As a student she often campaigned for causes she believed in, and as an actress she campaigns through the characters she creates. In her thrust to make the world a better place, she has helped organize the Comic Relief benefit shows, which have raised millions of dollars for the homeless.

W. Wilson Goode

Former mayor of Philadelphia
Born August 19, 1938, Seaboard, North
  Carolina

"I've had a charmed life as mayor because I've learned the arts of compromise and negotiation. I will run again. There's work here that has to be done and that cannot be finished in this term. We have to rebuild that neighborhood."

The life of W. Wilson Goode is a classic American success story. Born in a wooden shack and raised in poverty, Goode rose to public prominence as the executive director of the Philadelphia Council for Community Advancement, a non-profit organization established to help neighborhood groups and to promote housing projects. His administrative abilities were rewarded when he was appointed head of the Pennsylvania Public Utility Commission. After serving as Philadelphia's first African American managing director, Goode became the city's mayor for two terms and won accolades for his deft decisions and articulate stances.

Raised in poverty

Goode was born in a shack just outside of Seaboard, North Carolina, to Albert and Rozella Goode. The family lived in poverty, but believed that hard work and determination would see them through the tough times. Goode received his early education in a succession of one-room schools. When he turned fifteen, his parents relocated to a black working-class area of Philadelphia, hoping to find better employment.

After graduating from John Bartram High School, Goode attended Morgan State University and graduated in 1961 with a B.A. degree. While at the university he enrolled in the Reserve Officers Training Corps, which lead to a tour of duty in 1961–62 with the United States Army.

Returning to civilian life, Goode held a variety of jobs including probation officer, supervisor of a building maintenance firm, and insurance claims adjuster. He became interested in community and church activities, and he attended courses at Wharton School at the University of Pennsylvania, where he received his master of public administration degree in 1968.

The next year Goode became executive director of the Philadelphia Council for Community Advancement, a non-profit organization that helped neighborhood groups and promoted housing construction. The position enabled him to establish contacts that would later become the basis of his political support. In 1969, he was one of five finalists in the Jaycees Philadelphia community awards, and in 1972 the Jaycees named him outstanding young leader of the year.

Six years later, Governor Milton J. Shapp appointed Goode head of the three-member Pennsylvania Utility Commission, an influential body that oversees the state's utility rates. After the March 28, 1979, disaster at the Three Mile Island nuclear generating station, Goode conducted an investigation into the incident and suspended a rate hike recently granted to the Metropolitan Edison Company, which owned the plant.

City's first black managing director

In early 1980 Philadelphia Mayor William J. Green appointed Goode the city's managing director. He was the first African American to hold the position. Many skeptics thought the appointment was made by Green simply to garner support from the black community. Although this may contain some truth, there was no doubting the credentials Goode had for the job. He had established a reputation as an excellent administrator with a solid backing from the community.

Goode worked seven days a week, held neighborhood meetings about city problems,

W. Wilson Goode

and adopted strategies to streamline city hall operations. He became a popular figure in the city as he could be seen riding garbage trucks to monitor the progress of sanitation workers and participating in neighborhood clean-ups. As the November 1983 mayoral elections approached, Goode's name was mentioned, since Green announced he would not be seeking a second term.

Goode decided to seek the mayor's chair, and his main opponent for the Democratic nomination was Frank Rizzo, a former mayor who was defeated by Green. Goode campaigned like a veteran—greeting rush-hour commuters, making appearances on downtown streets and at public functions, and waving to people from his motorcade. He gathered endorsements from all but two of sixty-nine Democratic ward leaders and from most of the city's major labor unions.

Rizzo tried unsuccessfully to link Goode to police corruption. He tried to joke about

Goode's absentmindedness when he forgot the names of his children during an interview. On May 17, 1983, Goode swept 98 percent of the black vote and about 23 percent of the white vote in the primary. He defeated Rizzo by a margin of 53 to 46 percent or 59,000 votes.

With Democrats traditionally outnumbering Republicans five to one in the city, the mayoral election turned out to be anti-climatic. Goode's two main rivals, Republican John J. Egan, Jr., and independent Thomas A. Leonard split the opposition vote. On November 8, 1983, Goode received 55 percent of the vote—including 27 percent of the white vote—to Egan's 37 percent and Leonard's 8 percent.

Goode's highest priority as mayor was to revive the ideals established by the city's founder, William Penn, more than three hundred years earlier. He spoke about the need for jobs, affordable housing, cleaner streets, a more accessible city hall, new contracts for city employees, a more efficient garbage disposal system, and improved relations between the city council and mayor.

A positive response

In an attempt to address the problems of the city's sagging industrial base and inner city poverty, Goode appointed a new six-member cabinet that was equally divided among men and women. He recruited local businesspeople to take part in talks designed to encourage new investors to the city. Residents became dazzled by his accomplishments, and some journalists referred to him as "Wilson Too Goode."

Goode's toughest political challenge came in 1985 when he faced members of MOVE, a militant radical movement. On May 12, police surrounded a heavily fortified MOVE house, and early the next day a gunfight ensued as they unsuccessfully tried to arrest group members. After several more unsuccessful attempts, Goode approved a plan to drop a bag of water-based gel explosive on the roof to destroy a bunker-like fortification. The police dropped the bomb, and the results were disastrous. By the time firemen moved into the area, a blazing inferno had erupted. When the damage was finally tallied, sixty-one buildings were destroyed, two hundred people were left homeless, and an estimated $8 million in property damage had been caused. Authorities found the bodies of eleven people, including four children, in the rubble of the MOVE house.

Accepting full responsibility for the debacle, Goode stated he would rebuild the neighborhood as soon as possible. His pledges seemed to satisfy most residents: Local polls indicated that as many as 71 percent approved of his actions. During the 1987 mayoral race, Rizzo ran for his old job, blasting Goode for the role he played in the fire bombing. He appealed to his core constituency of white ethnic voters, and he almost succeeded. Goode still maintained 20 percent of the white vote and 98 percent of the black vote to win the Democratic nomination, 51 percent to 49. He easily won reelection against his Republican challenger.

During his second term in office, Goode suffered from heart problems and was forced to cut back on his fourteen-hour-a-day, seven-days-a-week work schedule. Since law prohibited Goode from seeking a third consecutive term, he retired from politics in 1992. His intentions are to teach and write a book about his administration to help other government leaders.

Charles Gordone

Playwright, actor, director
Born October 12, 1925, Cleveland, Ohio

"Charles Gordone is the most astonishing new American playwright to come along since Edward Albee."—Walter Kerr

In 1970 when Charles Gordone was awarded the Pulitzer Prize for his play *No Place to Be Somebody*, he became the first black playwright to win that award. The play was the first ever to win the Pulitzer before it moved to Broadway.

Gordone had taken up writing plays when he had difficulty getting work as an actor. As he explained in the *New York Times,* "At the time I moved into acting seriously, here in New York, there were damned few jobs in the profession for anybody, black or white. I turned to writing out of expediency. I love the theater and I had to do something to stay in it." Despite this disclaimer, Gordone has had a successful career in the theater, where besides working as an actor, he has directed some twenty-five plays.

Work in the theater

Like the hero of *No Place to Be Somebody,* Gordone is a light-skinned African American. The son of William and Camille (Morgan) Gordone, he grew up in Elkhart, Indiana, where his family lived in a white neighborhood. He says that after graduating from high school he was run out of town, "not by white people, but my own people, black people, because I tried to date a black girl."

After a semester at the University of California, Los Angeles, Gordone did his military service in the United States Air Force. He then returned to college, studying music at Los Angeles City College and drama at Los Angeles State College. On earning his B.A. from Los Angeles State College in 1952, he headed for New York City in search of work as an actor—despite the advice of his drama professor, who said there was no future there for black actors. As if to prove his professor wrong, Gordone landed a part almost immediately and launched his career in fine style by playing on Broadway. He played the role of the half-breed Logan in Moss Hart's *Climate of Eden.* However, he was soon looking for work again, because the play closed after only twenty performances.

During the next few years, Gordone slowly but surely made his way in the theater. He appeared in several plays, including the all-black production of John Steinbeck's *Of Mice and Men* (1953), for which he won an Obie Award as best actor. Another of his parts was in Greer Johnson's *Mrs. Patterson* (1957), which starred Eartha Kitt.

By the mid-1950s Gordone was working as a director as well as an actor, having formed his own theater, named Vantage. There he put on such plays as *Tobacco Road* and *Three Men on a Horse.* As his reputation spread, other companies offered him work, and in the

Charles Gordone

early 1960s he directed *Moon of the Caribbees* and several other plays for the Equity Library Theater. In 1964 he made a brief foray into films as associate producer for the movie *Nothing But a Man,* and in the late 1960s he produced and directed a theater version of Goethe's *Faust* at Judson Memorial Church in Greenwich Village.

Gordone's acting roles in the 1960s included a second performance as Logan in a television production of *Climate of Eden.* He had a long run from 1961 to 1965 playing the part of the valet in Jean Genet's *The Blacks,* and in 1967 he performed in *The Trials of Brother Jero.*

Prizewinning playwright

During much of the 1960s Gordone was working on his play *No Place to Be Somebody,* which took him seven years to complete. He rewrote it five or six times and even staged a tryout performance in Greenwich Village—

which proved to be a disaster—before he came up with a version that was acceptable. When the play opened in 1969, it was staged with money from a Rockefeller Foundation grant in the experimental Other Stage Theater in Joseph Papp's Shakespeare Festival Public Theater in New York City. Despite its difficult birth, it was an instant success. The *Wall Street Journal* reviewer wrote, "It would be difficult to find a better reason for the existence not only of foundations and Mr. Papp's theater but of theater itself." Walter Kerr, writing in the *New York Times,* was equally rapturous, saying that "Charles Gordone is the most astonishing new American playwright to come along since Edward Albee."

The idea for *No Place to Be Somebody* grew out of Gordone's experience in the 1950s when, between acting jobs, he worked as a waiter in a bar in Greenwich Village. Like himself, many of the customers were semi-employed people who had "no place to be somebody." The play is set in a similar New York bar, which is owned by the white-hating Johnny Williams, who "learned early to hate white society and not to trust anybody." The racial theme is strong throughout the play. Like Gordone himself, the hero, Gabe Gabriel, is an unemployed, light-skinned black actor who is too white for black roles and who struggles to find his racial identity. Gabe introduces each of the three acts with a monologue, commenting in an often-humorous tone on both the absurdity and tragedy of racism.

In 1969 and 1970 *No Place to Be Somebody* had a total of 903 performances off Broadway before going on tour with three national companies, and in 1971 it was brought back to New York in a production directed by Gordone at the Morosco Theater on Broadway. In addition to winning the Pulitzer Prize in 1970, it won the New York Drama Critics Circle Award and the Vernon Rice Award.

Gordone quickly followed up this success with *Gordone Is a Mullah,* a combination of poems and monologues he produced at the Carnegie Recital Hall in 1970. His other dramatic works include *Baba-Chops* (1975) and *The Last Chord* (1977).

In keeping with the theme of his Pulitzer-winning play, Gordone has made it his mission to help those who have "no place to be somebody." As far back as 1962 he was co-founder of the Committee for the Employment of Negro Performers. In 1977-78 he turned his attention to prisoners, as an instructor at the Cell Block Theater in Yardville and Bordontown Detention Centers in New Jersey, and in 1978-79 he was an instructor at the New School for Social Research in New York.

After Gordone won the Pulitzer in 1970, he asked himself "Can I do it better?" He may not have written a better play since then, but those whom he has coached may feel that he has indeed done better—or at least as well—in his role as sympathetic helper to those who have "no place to be somebody."

Berry Gordy, Jr.

Recording industry executive
Born November 28, 1929, Detroit, Michigan

"Songs are more than rhymes. Songs need a beginning, middle, and an end. Like a story."

Berry Gordy, Jr.'s famous Motown record label has produced hit records from many of its artists, including Stevie Wonder, the Supremes, the Jackson Five, and Marvin Gaye. Several popular movies, including *Lady Sings the Blues* and *The Last Dragon,* and a host of videos, books, and television specials, have also been produced by its sister company, Motown Industries. The company Gordy formed in 1959 as Motown Record Corporation grew from the small Detroit-based record label specializing in rhythm and blues to a multi-level entertainment corporation in Los Angeles. In 1973 *Black Enterprise* magazine named Motown the number one black-owned or -managed business. On January 20, 1988, Gordy was inducted into the Rock 'n' Roll Hall of Fame.

Gordy's songs hit the charts

Gordy was born on November 28, 1929, in Detroit, Michigan, to Berry and Bertha Gordy. Considered well-to-do, his father owned a plastering and carpentry service, a general store, and a printing business. In 1951 Gordy was drafted into the army, where he received his high school equivalency diploma. Two years later and out of the service, he married Thelma Coleman. They had three children, Hazel Joy, Berry IV, and Terry, before divorcing in 1959. Employment on an automobile assembly line and as a prizefighter occupied Gordy during the early 1950s. Around 1955 he also opened a jazz-oriented record store, the 3-D Record Mart. Largely financed by his family, the record store folded a short time after it started.

Meanwhile Gordy was writing many songs and submitting them to magazines and contests. In 1957 Gordy, his sister Gwen, and Tyran Carlo wrote "Reet Petite," which was recorded by Jackie Wilson. This would be the first of many hits for Wilson. Gordy's team wrote four more hits for Wilson over the next two years: "To Be Loved" and "Lonely Teardrops" in 1958 and "That's Why" and "I'll Be Satisfied" in 1959.

By the late 1950s Gordy became interested in producing, forming the basis for what would become Motown Records. He recorded and released recordings of the Miracles, Marv Johnson, and Eddie Holland to the nationally distributed labels Chess, United Artists, and End. To publish his songs, he established Jobete, named for Gordy's children Hazel Joy, Berry IV, and Terry.

Motown label appeals to all races

Gordy received small royalty checks from the national labels, and as a songwriter he had to split his royalties with the music publisher, so he needed his own corporation to take control of his work. He created Motown Record Corporation in 1958 with six employees in an apartment on Gladstone in Detroit. The songwriting-production team consisted of Gordy, Smokey Robinson, Raynoma Liles, Janie Bradford, Robert Bateman, and Brian Holland. Gordy's family provided him with a loan of $800 to get started.

Because many of the performers were in their teens or early twenties and Gordy himself was barely thirty, he tried to foster a family feeling at Motown in the early days. As performers signed with the company, they became members of the "Motown family." The company released its first single in 1959 on the newly formed Tamla label (Tamla was a variation on "Tammy," a popular song of the period sung by Debbie Reynolds). The Motown label was established in 1960, and the third major label, Gordy, debuted in April 1962. Although the Motown sound had its roots in urban rhythm and blues, Gordy intended to appeal to young people of all races with a kind of music that would retain some of its origins while adding other sounds, an idea he conveyed in his advertising slogan, "The Sound of Young America." Motown had its first number-one pop hit in 1961 with the Marvelettes' "Please, Mr. Postman."

Although Motown's early releases were popular with black audiences, Gordy wanted his albums to be successful with the record-buying white audience. In 1962 four singles made the Top Ten on the pop charts. The next year Motown placed six more singles on the pop Top Ten, with Stevie Wonder's "Finger-

Berry Gordy, Jr.

tips, Part 2" reaching number one on the pop charts.

Motown turned the corner in 1964 when four of the company's five Top Ten pop hits went to number one, including "My Guy," "Where Did Our Love Go," "Baby Love," and "Come See About Me." Another song, "Dancing in the Street," went to number two. The company also wrote songs that the Supremes were making famous. The next year five Motown releases reached number one.

Although Gordy was a talented songwriter and hands-on producer, he didn't build the company by himself. He surrounded himself with talented songwriters that were complemented by a group of gifted writers and producers. Almost like a music factory, it churned out hit after hit.

As the hits rolled along, Motown was placed under closer scrutiny. Rumors circulated that the company was under the control of the mob. Gordy vigorously denied these rumors, saying that they were made up by rival companies to discredit Motown.

Relocates Motown to Los Angeles

With Motown on solid footing, Gordy expanded the business into other entertainment opportunities. In 1966 he established a West Coast office to secure film roles for Motown stars and to encourage the use of Motown songs in film sound tracks. By 1968 Gordy moved to Los Angeles and began establishing additional offices. In 1972 Los Angeles became Motown's official home.

The Jackson Five was a Motown discovery of the late 1960s. The group, and especially the youngest member, Michael, enjoyed close ties to Gordy. He used to let the entire family stay at his California home. Gordy headed a songwriting and production team within Motown, called the Corporation, that wrote and produced several chart-topping lists for the Jackson Five.

In 1973 Gordy resigned as president of Motown Records to direct Motown Industries' record, motion picture, television, and publishing divisions full time. Diana Ross was his major talent, and she starred in her first solo television special, "Diana," in 1971. Her first film, *Lady Sings the Blues,* which Gordy produced and edited, premiered in 1972 to critical acclaim, and Ross received an Academy Award nomination for her performance. Ross's second movie, *Mahogany,* was produced in 1975 and marked Gordy's debut as film director. It was followed by *The Wiz*, a 1978 Universal/Motown musical version of *The Wizard of Oz*. However, *The Wiz* was panned and did poorly at the box office. Motown did not make another movie until 1985 when Gordy produced *The Last Dragon,* a kung-fu musical that did well at the box office.

Motown produced a 1983 special for NBC television, "Motown 25—Yesterday, Today, and Forever." The two-hour special was taken from a four-hour tribute to Gordy. The show featured a reunion of the Jackson Five, the Miracles, and the Supremes, as well as solo performances by Michael Jackson and Marvin Gaye. It received nine Emmy nominations for Motown and was the most-watched variety special in the history of television. Two years later Motown produced "Motown Returns to the Apollo," which coincided with the reopening of the newly restored Apollo Theater in

Harlem. The special won an Emmy for best variety, music, or comedy program. Trying to reach as wide an audience as possible, Motown has made several of its productions available for home video use.

Despite Gordy's success as Motown chairman, there are a lot of artists who intensely dislike him, although he made them successful. A common complaint was that Gordy was no longer readily available to address their needs. Many of the executives entrusted by Gordy mistreated the artists, botching their lives and affairs.

Gordy sold Motown Records to MCA Inc. in 1988 for $61 million. The sale did not include Motown's publishing division (Jobete Music Co. and Stone Mountain Music), nor its film and television divisions. Gordy continues to run these operations as the Gordy Company.

Dick Gregory

Comedian, social activist, nutrition advocate
Born October 12, 1932, St. Louis, Missouri

"Laughter is the best way to release tensions and fear. If I fall down three flights of stairs, you just stand there and hold your breath. But if I get up and laugh about it, you laugh too. Then we can get together and fix any bones that got broken."

As well known for his nutritional advocacy as for his comedy, Dick Gregory is a man of several careers. He has been an athlete, comedian, civil rights activist, author, nutritionist, and a spokesman for progressive social and political causes. He has fasted to emphasize the plight of Native Americans, run marathons to ease world famine, and once ran for president to promote social justice.

Comedy spared him from court martial

Gregory was born on October 12, 1932, in St. Louis, Missouri, to Presley and Lucille Gregory. He was raised by his mother, who often worked late into the evening to support the family. To help out, Gregory started shining shoes and did other odd jobs. He was a bright student, but his living conditions at home (there was often no electricity or food) made it difficult for him to concentrate on his studies.

Gregory tried out for the high school track club since he knew team members could have hot showers every day after practice. At first the coach would not let him try out, so while the team ran around the field, Gregory ran around a city block. Eventually the coach let him shower with the team, and by the next year he was on the team. He was soon winning championships and setting records. By his senior year, Gregory was captain of the track and cross-country teams, and he successfully ran for class president.

He received a scholarship to Southern Illinois University, where he continued to set records and win championships. He began to notice, however, that the predominately white university treated its black athletes with less respect. He did satirical comedy work at some of the school's variety shows and found the work rewarding. Satirical phrases began slip-

Dick Gregory

ping into his everyday coversation as he developed a wisecracking nature. He took this nature with him when he was drafted by the army in 1954.

His wisecracks eventually led to an argument with a colonel who challenged him to win the comedy competition at that night's talent show—or face a court martial. Gregory won and was transferred to the army's Special Services entertainment division.

Tried to earn his living as a stand-up comedian

After being discharged, Gregory eventually headed to Chicago, Illinois, to find a job as a stand-up comedian. He got some low-paying, short-term jobs as a host at various black nightclubs. He supplemented his income by working as everything from a postal clerk to a car washer. In 1958 he borrowed money and opened his own nightclub, the Apex, on the city's outskirts. Things looked promising at

first, but as bad weather kept many clients away, the Apex closed before the year ended.

In late 1959 he rented the Roberts Show Club in Chicago and organized a party for the Pan-American Games, with himself as master of ceremonies. The party was so successful that the owner hired Gregory as regular MC. Since the best black acts in the country played at the club, Gregory learned from such professional entertainers as comedian Nipsey Russell and actor Sammy Davis, Jr. The job only lasted for a year, and Gregory was soon forced back into one night stands at small clubs.

Achieved big break at Playboy Club

Gregory got his big break in early 1961 when his agent called, saying a replacement was needed for a comic scheduled to work at Chicago's Playboy Club. When Gregory reached the club, the club's booking agent tried to turn him away, saying the room had been booked to a convention of delegates from the South who would probably be critical of a black comedian. Gregory refused to be turned away, and he convinced the management to let him perform. The audience was hostile and insulting. But Gregory returned their comments with humor and soon had the audience laughing. The fifty-minute show lasted an hour and forty minutes.

After that the Playboy Club offered him a two-month contract. His career suddenly took off—he was featured in *Time* magazine, and Jack Paar invited him to appear on his television show. He was now one of the hottest acts on the nightclub circuit and became the first black comedian to break the color barrier by performing for white audiences. His key to success was his satirical approach to race relations and his non-derogatory jokes about race. After starting with a few self-deprecating jokes, he would switch to a topical joke: "They asked me to buy a lifetime membership in the NAACP, but I told them I'd pay a week at a time. Hell of a thing to buy a lifetime membership, wake up one morning and find out the country's been integrated."

As his fame spread, Gregory spent less time hunting for work and more time on social issues, such as black voting rights. He appeared at civil rights marches and rallies throughout the United States and performed benefits for the Student Nonviolent Coordinating Committee (SNCC) and the Congress on Racial Equality (CORE). At one time he traveled daily from San Francisco to Chicago to play a gig in a nightclub and still attended a series of demonstrations. He was arrested and jailed several times and was beaten severely by police in a Chicago jail.

Launched career in health and well-being

In 1966 Gregory ran in Chicago's mayoral race, and two years later he ran for president as a member of the Freedom and Peace Party. His platform called for civil rights, racial and social justice, and peace in Vietnam. Neither of his campaigns were successful, but Gregory said they drew attention to issues that were often overlooked. He earned about 200,000 votes for president, and some of his supporters decided to name him "President in Exile."

In the late 1960s Gregory made several changes in his personal life. Due to his belief in nonviolence, he became a vegetarian and

discovered that the switch put an end to his ulcer and sinus problems. He began to research diet and health and became a spokesperson on the benefits of vegetarianism and the ill effects of the average American diet. He quit the nightclub circuit to speak at churches, schools, and universities.

Gregory began to explore other areas of health care and nutrition in the 1970s. He became interested in fasting and marathon running. He has fasted many times to publicize world hunger, to draw attention to the nation's drug epidemic, and to emphasize the plight of Native Americans. He has also run marathons for similar causes.

Angelina Weld Grimké

Poet
Born February 27, 1880, Boston, Massachusetts
Died June 10, 1958, New York, New York

"Whatever I have done it sems to me is a reflection of some mood which gives the spiritual atmosphere and significance."

A ngelina Weld Grimké wrote plays and short stories as well as poetry, but she is especially known for her beautifully crafted verse. Her poetry is lyrical and delicate, often using leaves, flowers, trees, and other natural objects as symbols. Her best-known poems are "The Black Finger," "A Mona Lisa," and "El Beso."

Some of Grimké's poems were so personal that she did not attempt to get them published. Others appeared in magazines and newspapers, or in anthologies such as *The New Negro* (1925). Grimké never brought out a book of her verse in her lifetime, nor has one been published since her death. However, in 1920 she published her play *Rachel*, which was first performed in 1916 under the sponsorship of the National Association for the Advancement of Colored People (NAACP).

Rachel is about racism and persecution, a subject Grimké explored in a number of poems, though she more often wrote love poems. Her work was much admired in the 1920s by the poets of the Harlem Renaissance, who included her poetry in their anthologies. But in recent years Grimké has received little attention in literary circles.

Raised in privileged circumstances

Angelina Weld Grimké was born into a prominent biracial family. Her mother, Sarah (Stanley) Grimké, was a white Methodist who wrote a number of tracts. Her father, Archibald Grimké, had both black and white ancestors and was a practicing lawyer, diplomat, and publisher. A champion of black rights, he served for many years as vice-president of the NAACP.

When Angelina Grimké was three, her mother left her father and took her to live with her parents. Grimké stayed with them until she was seven, when she was returned to her father. She never saw her mother again. Nevertheless, she did not lack affection, for she developed a close relationship with her father, whom she adored.

Raised in a cultured and comfortable home, Grimké had a privileged upbringing compared with that of most African Americans in the late nineteenth century. Nor was she very conscious of racism or discrimination, for she was so pale skinned that she could pass for white. She attended white upper-class schools, including Carleton Academy in Northfield, Minnesota, and Cushing Academy in Ashburnham, Massachusetts. She then studied at the Boston Normal School of Gymnastics, from which she graduated in 1902. Between 1906 and 1910 she took courses at Harvard University during the summer vacations from her teaching job.

Grimké taught high school English in Washington, D.C., from 1902 until 1926, when she retired because of ill health. In Washington she made friends with other poets and scholars, and she wrote some of her best poetry. This was by far her most productive period as a writer. Although she had composed some poetry during her early years, she wrote nothing after 1930, when her father died and she left Washington for New York City.

Suffered from despondency

At some point before Grimké arrived in Washington she had an unpleasant experience that focused her attention on racism and caused her to write about it with great despondency. Unlike the intellectuals of a later era, Grimké did not fight against the injustices of racism. Her attitude was defeatist—racism was a fearful thing, but it was something black people could not avoid. Only occasionally did she take a more aggressive tone, as in the poem "Beware Lest He Awakes!" (1902), which warns of the revenge black men may take one day.

The other major theme of Grimké's poetry was unhappiness in love. As a teenager she had a lesbian relationship with a girl called Mamie Burrill, and she may well have had other relationships in her early twenties. As Grimké grew older she suppressed her desires and thus suffered all the frustrations of an unfulfilled love life. These frustrations are expressed in many of Grimké's poems—which is why she did not seek to get them published. In the 1920s and 1930s lesbianism was simply not acceptable. Nevertheless, some of Grimké's love poems were veiled enough to be published without problems. One of the strongest was "El Beso." Written in 1909, this poem reflects on various aspects of love and expresses the loneliness and pain of being rejected by a loved one.

Sadness also permeates Grimké's poems about race. One of her few positive poems is "The Black Finger," which she wrote for the fiftieth anniversary celebrations of Washington's Dunbar High School, where she taught for several years. In this poem Grimké describes a cypress tree that resembles a black finger pointing upward; she presents the tree as a symbol of hope that a promising future is in store for African Americans.

Wrote *Rachel*, a play with a somber message

Grimké took a far more gloomy view in her play *Rachel,* which is about persecution. The main characters are Rachel and her brother, Tom, who live in a New York tenement. In the first act of the play their mother tells them of their father's lynching many years earlier. While Tom reacts angrily, Rachel accepts the

Angelina Weld Grimké

situation, thinking of the grim future in store for black children and of the burden this places on their mothers. "Everywhere, everywhere, throughout the South, there are hundreds of dark mothers who live in fear, terrible, suffocating fear," mourns Rachel.

The second act takes place four years later, when Rachel learns of the abuse suffered by a neighboring little girl and by Jimmy, a small boy Rachel adopted after his parents die of smallpox. Jimmy has terrible nightmares, reliving the time he was stoned by white boys. In the third act, one week later, Rachel turns down a proposal of marriage so that she can care for Jimmy and other black children. She does not want to marry and bear children of her own because they will only add to the number of those who suffer. The play ends with Jimmy weeping in the next room, and Rachel running to comfort him.

Rachel has not been performed often, for it is too sentimental and far too negative to be popular. When it was staged by the NAACP at the Myrtilla Miner Normal School in Washington in 1916, the program announced: "This is the first attempt to use the stage for race propaganda in order to enlighten the American people relating to the lamentable condition of ten millions of Colored citizens in this free republic." Some critics have taken up this point, categorizing *Rachel* as propaganda rather than drama. Nevertheless, it is a powerful work and is important historically as one of the first plays written by and for African Americans.

Similarly, although Grimké produced a relatively small body of work, she has an important place in African American literature. She was a sophisticated writer, wonderfully lyrical, with great poetic art, and she made her own unique contribution to that flowering of black literature known as the Harlem Renaissance.

Bryant Gumbel

Television morning-show host
Born September 29, 1948,
New Orleans, Louisiana

"I'm good at communicating ideas. I deal it straight, and I have the confidence to win people through the lens of the camera no matter what the subject matter."

For nine years Bryant Gumbel announced professional sporting events. For "NBC Sports" Gumbel hosted the World Series, the Superbowl, major golf tourna-

ments, and numerous other athletic events. In 1982 NBC officials applied his quick-wittedness and charisma to their sagging "Today" morning show. With Gumbel's on-screen grace and knack for commentary, the "Today" show slowly began crawling from the bottom of the ratings to the top. His colleague, the late Jessica Savitch, called Gumbel "the greatest natural-born TV commentator I've ever seen."

Talent helped more than affirmative action

Gumbel was born on September 29, 1948, in New Orleans, Louisiana, to Richard and Rhea Gumbel. His father was a probate court judge and a major influence in his life. His parents insisted he attend Roman Catholic schools and stressed speaking, writing, and listening well at home. Gumbel spent most of his childhood in Hyde Park, a racially and ethnically integrated area near Chicago's south side.

From 1966 to 1970 Gumbel attended Bates College in Lewiston, Maine. He was one of only three blacks in a student body of 900. Gumbel wore his hair long and maintained a casual attitude about his studies (he majored in Russian history). He also played baseball and football. After suffering a sports-related injury, he was ruled ineligible for the Vietnam draft, so he headed to New York City to become a salesman with Westavaco Corporation, a packaging manufacturer. He soon discovered that this was not the life he wanted to lead, and he also rejected his family's advice to enter law school.

Gumbel began a new career in 1971 when he submitted an article to *Black Sports* about Harvard University's first black athletic direc-

Bryant Gumbel

ing with a band playing behind him, making it impossible for him to hear the cues the producers were giving him. As usual, Gumbel remained calm, completing his piece smoothly and with perfect timing. Another incident involved his eloquent, off-the-cuff, ninety- second commentary about UCLA legend John Wooden after coaching his final basketball game in 1975. Gumbel was soon asked to co-host "Grandstand," an NFL pregame show from New York that combined live events, features, and sports news. Though the show folded after a few years Gumbel's future was assured.

Prize-winning sportscaster

While sports director of KNBC from 1976 to 1980, Gumbel traveled to New York City on weekends to anchor major league baseball, NFL football, and NCAA basketball games. He won an Emmy Award in 1976 for producing an Olympic sports special. His job responsibilities soon increased to include anchoring a World Series, three Super Bowls, five Thanksgiving Day parades, and several golf tournaments. He won another Emmy the next year and Los Angeles Press Club Golden Mike Awards in 1978 and 1979. He was chosen to co-anchor NBC's coverage of the 1980 Summer Olympics in the Soviet Union, but the U.S.-led boycott scuttled the position.

In June 1980 Gumbel signed a three-year contract with NBC that included co-hosting a short-lived show called "Games People Play" with Cyndy Garvey. He also anchored three sports segments a week on the "Today" show and anchored "NFL '81" for the network. In 1981, "Today" show executive producer Steve

tor. Nine months later Gumbel was the magazine's editor. Then a friend at KNBC-TV in Los Angeles asked him to audition for the weekend sports anchor job. Gumbel was so impressive that a newswriter said it was the best audition by someone without experience he had ever seen. Eight months later Gumbel became the weeknight sportscaster on the 6 P.M. news, and in 1976 he was named the station's sports director.

Although he attributes some of his early success to affirmative action hiring practices, he remarked to *People* magazine: "The kinds of jobs I've gotten are not the kind people give out as token measures. If anything, race becomes an issue primarily when other blacks ... find [me] 'not black enough.'"

Gumbel is well known for his ability to handle any situation. Scheduled to give courtside commentary at a National Collegiate Athletic Association (NCAA) title basketball game, Gumbel found himself compet-

Friedman asked him to sit in for co-host Jane Pauley during her temporary absence and, soon after, to test for the opening created by Tom Brokaw's departure to the "NBC Nightly News." The auditioning Gumbel appeared at ease while discussing such topics as heroin, crime, cellulite, computers, seal hunting, desegregation, and Auschwitz and interviewing celebrities William F. Buckley, Treat Williams, and Peggy Class. Friedman called Gumbel "unbelievably warm" and chose Gumbel over the other candidates, including the late Jessica Savitch, Garrick Utley, John Palmer, and Phil Donahue. NBC officials hoped Gumbel would help close the gap between the "Today" show and "Good Morning America." The Cincinnati-San Diego American Football Conference title game in January 1982 was the last event Gumbel covered during his nine-year sportscasting career.

Gumbel debuted on the "Today" show January 4, 1982, with other "Today" members Chris Wallace, Jane Pauley, Gene Shalit, and Willard Scott. Gumbel told *People* that it would be "nothing as glitzy as ('Good Morning America'), but ... will appeal to a younger, upscale crowd." Comparing his personal delivery style with his predecessor's, Gumbel remarked, "I am more prone to lighten things up than (Tom) Brokaw was, and the changes we have been trying reflect my personality more." Gumbel delivers his commentary, news scripts, and pieces on popular culture without set scripts or retakes. "I'm good at communicating ideas," he told *Newsweek*. "I deal it straight, and I have the confidence to win people through the lens of the camera no matter what the subject matter."

Rocketed "Today" show to number one

By 1985 the show was rated the most popular morning show. Gumbel sharpened his interviewing skills until he could speak with anyone—even politicians, diplomats, or economists. In 1984 he earned the Edward R. Murrow Award from the Overseas Press Club for his interviews with high-ranking officials in Moscow. He teamed with Jane Pauley the next year for stories involving the Vatican and America's heartland. The *Washington Review Journal* in 1986 named him the best morning interviewer. In 1988 Gumbel was chosen to host TV's most expensive undertaking ever—the NBC coverage of the Olympics in Seoul, South Korea.

Despite Gumbel's success, his reputation has been dogged with accusations of arrogance and self-righteousness. He has allegedly stated that he only wants to associate with people who meet his high standards, and this is given as the reason he cut ties with colleagues Connie Chung, David Letterman, and Linda Ellerbee. Friends and family say there is a big difference between the private and public Gumbel. The private Gumbel is prone to fits of anger and coldness and reportedly carries a list of prospective pallbearers. Gumbel told *Sports Illustrated* that he keeps this list because he doesn't "want to wait until something happens to see who my friends are. It's not that I dislike many people. It's just that I don't like many people."

When Gumbel is not working, he spends time with his wife, June, and his children, Bradley and Jillian. He currently lives in New York City.

Lucille C. Gunning

Pediatrician, medical services administrator
Born February 21, 1922, New York City, New
 York

*"If the child is retarded we should review the
whole issue of 'retardation' as well as the issue
of retardation of the black child; rather than
dealing with the intellectual impairment, deal
with their asset profile and see what they are
good at."*

Lucille C. Gunning

Best known for her methods of caring
for children with mental retardation and
other handicaps, Lucille C. Gunning tested
her theories at a developmental center for children with Downs Syndrome that she opened
at Harlem Hospital in New York City. There
parents worked with their children to make
them more self-sufficient. Later she developed a program at the Children's Medical
Center in Dayton, Ohio, where children with
disabilities could be with other children. Her
visionary ideas have greatly benefited disabled children across the country.

Driven to a medical career

Gunning was born on February 21, 1922, in
New York City to Roland and Susan Gunning.
Her father was an assistant druggist who later
became a doctor and her mother taught school.
When Gunning was thirteen months she experienced poor health and was taken to live
with her paternal grandmother in Jamaica. Her
paternal aunt looked after her when she was
five years old. Her aunt was a well-known
midwife, and Gunning accompanied her on a
late-night delivery. Soon there was plenty of
commotion, and she later learned that the baby
had died. Through all the crying and scream-
ing, she remembered a doctor arriving in a
horse-drawn carriage, carrying a black bag.
She sensed what everyone was thinking—if
the doctor had arrived earlier, the baby would
have lived. This episode remained fixed in her
mind and helped drive her towards a medical
career.

After Gunning completed high school in
Jamaica, she wanted to attend college in England, but the Second World War forced her to
return to her parents in New York. When she
told her family that she wanted to be a doctor,
her grandmother and father tried to talk her
out of it. They advised Gunning to become a
nurse or a teacher, since these were the traditional work roles for women. Her mother was
very supportive of her choice, and her father
eventually gave his support as well.

She attended New York University and earned a B.A. in 1945. She graduated from Women's Medical College of Pennsylvania with an M.D. degree in 1949, interned at Harlem Hospital Center in New York City, and started a residency in infectious diseases at Hermann Kiefer Hospital in Detroit, Michigan, in 1950. She served as chief resident in the department of pediatrics at Harlem Hospital from 1951 to 1952, was pediatric chief resident at Women's Medical College of Philadelphia Hospital, then became a fellow in pediatric cardiology at Grace New Haven Hospital at Yale University from 1953 to 1954.

Recognized needs of disabled children

In 1954 Gunning opened a private practice in pediatrics in the Bronx (this office closed ten years later) and in New Rochelle, New York; she was also a child health physician for the Department of Health in New York City and was visiting attending physician in the pediatric departments of several major hospitals. In 1965 she was a fellow in medicine at the Albert Einstein College of Medicine at Montefiore Hospital Medical Center, then became assistant attending physician at Morrisania (a city hospital) in the department of rehabilitation medicine.

As a firm believer that disabled children should be with other children rather than disabled adults, Gunning established and directed the division of pediatric rehabilitation at Montefiore Hospital and the Medical Center in the Bronx from 1966 to 1971 and served as chief of pediatric rehabilitation at the Harlem Hospital Center in New York City in 1971.

While at Harlem Hospital she worked with children with Downs Syndrome and concluded that parents must play a vital role in treating the child. Gunning established a developmental center where the parents were trained in techniques to make their children as self-sufficient as possible.

From 1976 to 1979 Gunning was a field-work supervisor for the Sophie Davis School of Biomedical Education of City College of the City University of New York. This program provided admission for minority students into any New York State medical school upon successful completion of the premedical college courses. Gunning also helped found the Susan Smith McKinney-Steward Medical Society of New York City, an organization of black American women physicians who provide counseling to minority female medical students.

Gunning published numerous articles on childhood disabilities, pediatric rehabilitation, physical medicine and rehabilitation, child abuse, mental retardation, and other topics. She has suggested that the adult caregiver for the chronically ill or disabled child should work closely with the psychologist or psychiatrist and take an active role in the child's rehabilitation.

Mainstreamed disabled children in the hospital setting

While she was at Harlem Hospital, Gunning wanted to establish an extended-care facility for children with chronic illnesses in the Harlem community, similar to Blythedale in Westchester. She believed that when chronically ill children are sent away from the community and the family is unable to visit the child, they become alienated from each other and from the community. She proposed creating facilities akin to nursing homes, but for children.

Gunning was given an opportunity to test her theories as director of physical medicine and rehabilitation in the Children's Medical Center in Dayton, Ohio. She was also appointed associate clinical professor of rehabilitative medicine at Wright State University Medical School. She developed a program incorporating her idea of children with disabilities being with other hospital children, and by the time her contract ended two years later, she had proof that her idea worked.

Currently the deputy director of medical services for the New York State Office of Mental Retardation and Developmental Disabilities in Tarrytown, New York, Gunning is responsible to insure the best care of developmentally disabled people in state residences. She is committed "to the art of medicine; you must go that extra step to provide quality care for the patient."

Clara Hale

Humanitarian
Born April 1, 1905, Philadelphia,
    Pennsylvania
Died December 18, 1992, New York, New
    York

"The children here know that someone loves them and they're happy.... I tell them to be proud of their Blackness, to be proud of one another, and to pull together."

For more than fifty years Clara Hale was the guardian, friend, and protector of young children who had had been abandoned or had been born with drug addictions because of the lifestyle of their parents. She nursed more than a thousand babies through the pains of withdrawal from drug addiction, and toward the end of her life she also cared for babies born with AIDS.

"Mother Hale," as she was called, originally cared for the children in her own small apartment in Harlem, New York City, but in the 1970s she was provided with Hale House, a five-story brownstone building. Her work was strictly nonprofit, and at first she and her family paid most of the expenses themselves. Only after her efforts became widely known did she receive large grants of money and private donations, which enabled her to employ a trained staff as well as the many volunteers who offered their services.

Enjoyed mothering her foster children

Clara Hale was born Clara McBride, the youngest in a family of four. Her mother was the main influence during her childhood, for her father died when she was a baby. Her mother was a strong character who supported the family by taking in lodgers. She taught her children to be proud of themselves and face the world with confidence. "Always look people in the eyes," she said.

Soon after leaving high school Clara married Thomas Hale and moved with him to New York City, where he opened a floor-waxing business. As this did not bring in much money, Clara helped out by cleaning theaters at night.

Clara Hale

The couple had three children—Lorraine, Nathan, and an adopted son, Kenneth—and a happy family life. But their life changed greatly when Thomas Hale died of cancer in 1932.

Clara Hale was twenty-seven at the time, and with three children to support she worked doubly hard, cleaning homes in the daytime as well as theaters at night. But this was not a satisfactory arrangement, for she hardly saw her children. Worse still, she often had to leave them alone.

Since Hale particularly enjoyed looking after children, she had the idea of taking in other people's kids and caring for them along with her own while their parents were at work. This was more than day care, because most of the mothers were live-in maids who came home only at weekends, and not always then. It also meant a drop in income for Hale—the parents earned so little money that she could not charge them much—but she made enough to cover the basics.

Hale's unofficial fostering developed into the role of licensed foster mother when in 1941 she began to take in children who were wards of the city. She was paid two dollars a week for each foster child, and in her five-room apartment she could house seven or eight foster children at a time. Over the next twenty-seven years Hale brought up a total of forty foster children. Some were black, some white, and all called her Mommy. "My daughter says she was almost sixteen before she realized all these other kids weren't her real sisters and brothers," Hale told a reporter years later. She went on to extol the achievements of her foster children, all of whom had gone to college: "They're doctors, lawyers, everything. Almost all of them stay in touch. I have about sixty grandchildren."

Mother Hale of Hale House

In 1968, at age sixty-three, Hale decided to retire—but her retirement lasted barely a year. In 1969 her daughter Lorraine came across a young woman heroin addict sitting in a Harlem park holding a two-month-old baby. Like her mother, Lorraine could not ignore someone who obviously needed help, so she gave the young woman her mother's address—and, of course, Hale took in the baby.

Word of this charitable deed spread quickly. "Before I knew it," Hale recalled, "every pregnant addict in Harlem knew about the crazy lady who would give her baby a home." Within two months she had twenty-two babies in her apartment. Her three children rallied round to help support the infants, working at two jobs to bring in the needed funds. Meanwhile, Hale had her hands full, for all the babies were born suffering from drug addiction.

For a year and a half Hale and her family supported the babies through their own efforts, but when the City of New York learned of her work, it gave money for the project through its Department of Social Services for Children. In 1975 the city provided Hale with a five-story building—named Hale House—at 154 West 122nd Street. Private donors also came forward to help, including rock star John Lennon, who contributed $20,000 in 1978. After his assassination in 1979, his widow, Yoko Ono, set up a foundation to donate $20,000 to Hale House each year.

The children at Hale House ranged in age from ten days to four years. The babies suffering from withdrawal slept in Hale's bedroom so that she could comfort them when they cried in the night and clean them when they vomited—which they all did as part of their withdrawal. After several weeks or months, when the babies were able to sleep peacefully, they were moved to the nursery on the second floor, where they were looked after for by child-care workers. The older children shared bedrooms on the fourth floor. Very few of the children were ever put up for adoption. Hale's aim was to return them to their parents, many of whom were undergoing treatment to break free of drugs. The parents were encouraged to visit their children regularly to keep in touch.

Meanwhile, Hale built up the self-confidence of the youngsters in her care as well as looking after their health."The children here knows that someone loves them and they're happy," she said. "I make sure that they're always clean and well fed and comfortable. I tell them how pretty they are and what they can accomplish if they get an education. And I tell them to be proud of their Blackness, to be proud of one another, and to pull together." In fact, Hale took in every child who was brought to her by the clergy, hospital, social workers, police, or anyone else. Whether the kids were black or white, male or female, babies or toddlers, they were always made welcome by Mother Hale.

In 1985 Hale was formally honored for her work by President Ronald Reagan, who invited her to Congress for his State of the Union Address, in which he praised her as a "true American hero." Hale also received tribute from John Jay College of Criminal Justice, which awarded her an honorary doctorate of humane letters, and she was given the Salvation Army's highest award, the Booth Community Service Award. Yet Hale never considered herself at all heroic. "I love children and I love caring for them," she said. "That is what the Lord meant me to do."

Alex Haley

Writer
Born August 11, 1921, Ithaca, New York
Died February 10, 1992, Seattle, Washington

"Roots is the simple story of all black people. Every one of us goes back ancestrally to someone who lived in one of those African villages, was caught, brought across the ocean and worked on a plantation, went through the Civil War. That's the saga of the whole race."

When Alex Haley wrote *Roots: The Saga of An American Family*, people for the first time began to realize and appreciate the ordeal slavery had been to black Americans.

The book, which was turned into one of the most popular television series ever, renewed black interest in history and genealogy and is credited with improving race relations in the United States.

Heard stories about Kin-tay during summers at grandparents' home

Haley was born on August 11, 1921, in Ithaca, New York, to Simon and Bertha Haley. His father was a college professor who taught at several institutions throughout the Southern states. During the school year, Haley and his brothers lived with their parents, and they spent summers with their maternal grandparents at Henning, Tennessee. Haley listened to his grandmother and great aunts on their front porch discuss their African ancestor named Kin-tay, captured and sold into slavery in America during the late 1700s.

Haley graduated from high school at age fifteen and briefly attended college before joining the U.S. Coast Guard in 1939. To banish boredom during weeks at sea, he wrote love letters for his less literary crewmates. He also wrote several adventure stories involving life on the seas, which he tried to sell—without much success—to various magazines. Those he did sell encouraged him that he could become a successful writer. The Coast Guard also created the public relations position of chief journalist, just for him. Haley retired from the service in 1959 to become a full-time freelance writer.

Interview with Malcom X led to a best-seller

Wanting to give all his energies to writing, Haley lived in a basement apartment in Greenwich Village and did not seek a job. Only after magazines like *Reader's Digest* began buying his stories on a regular basis was Haley able to live on anything more than a strict budget. His first big break occurred when *Playboy* asked him to interview jazz trumpeter Miles Davis for a piece that launched the magazine's well-known interview feature. He was soon given another assignment—to interview black American Muslim leader Malcolm X. During the interview, Malcolm X asked Haley to write his autobiography. The book was completed just a few weeks before his assassination in 1965 and was published later that year. *The Autobiography of Malcolm X* received excellent reviews and sold over 6 million copies. The book was translated into eight languages.

As his reputation grew, Haley was able to earn a living lecturing and taking writing assignments that he found interesting. Haley received advances from Doubleday and the *Reader's Digest* to research his family history. He consulted libraries, archives, and other research centers. He also worked with a linguist who helped him to link the many "k" sounds his ancestor Kin-tay used with that of the Mandingo people of Gambia in West Africa.

Researched his ancestry in Africa

In 1967 Haley traveled to Gambia to meet with a griot, or oral historian, of the Kinte clan in the Mandingo village of Juffure. Working with an interpreter, Haley learned the story of the Kinte clan, including marriages, births,

Alex Haley

deaths, and other events. Eventually he heard the story of a young man named Kunta Kinte, who left his village to chop wood and was never seen again. The story of Kunta Kinte paralleled the tale he had heard from his grandmother and great aunts. Kunta Kinte and his ancestor Kin-tay were probably the same person.

Haley conducted more research and discovered records that supported the story that Kunta Kinte was kidnapped and sent to America on a British slave ship. After a decade of research, Haley wanted to write his family's story, but it seemed almost impossible. He wanted the book to be a "buoy for black self-esteem—and a reminder of the universal truth that we are all children of the same creator."

He overcame his writer's block on board a ship for America from Liberia. Haley was making the trip to help him understand what the voyage across the Atlantic would have

been like for Kunta Kinte. He spent the nights, stripped to his underwear and lying on boards as his ancestor would have done, but he still couldn't get a proper understanding of what Kunta Kinte went through. Haley became deeply depressed, not only because of his inability to write the story, but he was also facing financial troubles, and the deadline for his manuscript was fast approaching. One night he stood at the ship's railing and considered jumping overboard. As he looked into the water, he heard the voices of his ancestors telling him to continue working on the book. He was later quoted in *Ebony* magazine that he "felt for the first time that I was Kunta Kinte. From that moment on, I had no problem with writing."

Achieved phenomenal success with *Roots*

In 1976 Haley's book *Roots: The Saga of an American Family* was published, and it soared to the top of the bestseller list. In January 1977 it was broadcast as a television miniseries that attracted 130 million viewers, a record two-thirds of the possible audience (it still ranks as the thirteenth highest rated show of all time). The U.S. Senate passed a resolution paying tribute to Haley and comparing *Roots* to *Uncle Tom's Cabin* by Harriet Beecher Stowe in the 1850s. *Roots* also received a special Pulitzer Prize, a National Book Award, and nearly 300 other honors. The television show received an Emmy Award. Haley received more honorary doctorates from colleges and universities as well as the National Association for the Advancement of Colored People (NAACP) Springarn

Medal. Four thousand deans and department heads of colleges and universities throughout the country in a survey conducted by *Scholastic Magazine* selected Haley as the country's foremost achiever in the literature category.

Roots created an unprecedented interest in black history and genealogy. It also renewed discussions about race relations in the United States. Some analysts said most whites knew about slavery, but the story made them feel it through a black perspective. It also made blacks realize what they have had to overcome to get to their status today. Although some criticized Haley's story for weaving fact with fiction, most acknowledged that the story enabled whites to become sensitive to the black-American situation. Paul D. Zimmerman, a *Newsweek* critic, wrote, "Instead of writing a scholarly monograph of little social impact, Haley has written a blockbuster in the best sense—a book that is bold in concept and ardent in execution, one that will reach millions of people and alter the way we see ourselves."

In the aftermath of the book's success, Haley kept busy by lecturing, making personal appearances on radio and television, and writing. He signed at least 500 books daily, spoke to an average of 6,000 people a day, and traveled round trip coast-to-coast at least once a week. His new writing projects included his father's family history, a detailed account of his twelve years researching *Roots*, and a profile of Henning, Tennessee, as it was when he spent his summers there.

In February 1992 Haley was in Seattle for a lecture when he suffered a heart attack and died. His body was returned to Henning and was buried on the grounds surrounding his grandparents' home, a few steps away from the porch where he once listened to his grandmother's stories. The home is now a state museum.

Arsenio Hall

Actor, talk show host
Born February 12, 1955, Cleveland, Ohio

"I'm not after Johnny's crowd. I'm going after Johnny's crowd's kids."

A s a child, late-night talk show host Arsenio Hall used to pretend he was Johnny Carson. He started in the entertainment business as Arsenio the Magician and performed his tricks at local parties. After college he worked at comedy clubs for ten dollars a night. Now the host and producer of "The Arsenio Hall Show," Hall is the most successful black late-night talk show personality in history. With Johnny Carson now retired, people are beginning to wonder if Hall will be the Carson of his generation.

Preferred watching Carson to children's TV shows

Hall was born on February 12, 1955, to Fred (a minister) and Annie Hall in Cleveland, Ohio. His parents were twenty years apart in age and did not share a lot in common. They divorced when he was six years old, and he went to live his grandmother. As an only child, Hall spent a lot of time watching television, but he wasn't watching typical children's shows. Hall watched talk shows such as Dinah Shore, Merv Griffin, and Johnny Carson. After being sent to bed, Hall would sneak out to the living room and watch Carson on "The Tonight Show."

Carson soon became the hero for the young Hall. As a twelve-year-old he would arrange chairs in the house to make a pretend "Tonight Show" set and make believe he was Carson. He took music lessons, studied puppetry, and learned magic tricks and performed as Arsenio the Magician at parties, bar mitzvahs, and weddings. Hall began appearing on local television programs and knew entertainment would be his field.

Hired as Nancy Wilson's regular warm-up act

After graduating Hall enrolled in Ohio University at Athens, then transferred to Kent State University, where he received a degree in speech. Hall once told the *New York Times* that at Kent, "I stood up in front of a speech class and said, `I plan on making a living with my oratory skills, and I'd like to be a talk-show host.' There was a pause, then the most incredible laughter you've ever heard in your life. I guess they thought I was crazy. No one stands up in speech class at Kent State and says he wants to be the next Johnny Carson."

Although this was exactly what he wanted, his next job was for Noxell, manufacturer of Noxzema skin cream. While watching "The Tonight Show," he decided to quit his job and chase his dream. He moved to Chicago, Illinois, and started working in stand-up comedy clubs for ten dollars a night. He slowly built a name for himself, and received book-

ings to warm up for touring rock bands. In 1979 singer Nancy Wilson hired Hall to host her show in Chicago. She arrived late, so Hall had to improvise for twenty minutes. He was such a hit that Wilson hired him as her regular warm-up act.

Hall moved to Los Angeles in the early 1980s. He appeared several times on the ABC television program "Half Hour Comedy Hour," and in 1983 appeared as Alan Thicke's sidekick in the short-lived "Thicke of the Night" talk show. Hall then landed a spot as host of Paramount's syndicated rock-and-roll show "Solid Gold."

Filled in for Joan Rivers

Hall got his big break in 1987 when he got a call to fill-in as guest host for the "Joan Rivers Show." He did so well that he was asked back twice the next week. He was given a thirteen-week contract, but the show was already

Arsenio Hall

scheduled to be cancelled. Determined the make the most of the situation, Hall began taking chances. He played with the band, took cameras on the street, did improv, sang, wrote sketches, and asked tough questions. He hoped somebody would give him a job and sure enough, one night two executives from Paramount Studios asked him if he wanted to be in a movie.

Hall signed a three-movie deal with Paramount. The first one was entitled *Coming to America*, in which he co-starred with Eddie Murphy. Paramount twice asked Hall to try his own talk show, but he turned down the offer both times because he was already committed to other projects. Shortly after rejecting the second offer, he made a guest appearance on "The Tonight Show" to promote his new movie. After meeting his hero, Hall changed his mind and accepted the offer to do his own show.

Hall produces his own talk show

"The Arsenio Hall Show" debuted in 1989. Not a duplication of the Carson set, Hall has done away with the desk and couch—which he felt sets the host apart from the guests—for plush living room chairs. His show has a party atmosphere; Hall might sing with the band or joke with the audience. Some critics have complained that he doesn't ask his guests tough enough questions, but he says he is an entertainer and not a journalist. Just the same, he has been learning interviewing skills from a New York media consultant. Despite this criticism, there is no doubting his popularity. The show is seen on 175 television stations and reaches 95 percent of the television audience. He is the first successful black late night talk show host.

Besides writing the show's theme music, Hall is also its executive producer. He approves guests and hires staff. On a typical day he arrives at the studio around 11 A.M. to review the mail, look at the newspapers, and begin getting ready for the show. By 5 P.M. he is ready to take the stage. After the show, he reviews it with his staff and will take a videotape home to study before finally going to sleep.

One of the secrets to his success is that instead of competing for Carson's audience, Hall is appealing to their kids. "The Tonight Show" began in 1958 and much of Carson's audience has aged with the show. Hall is trying to become the Carson for the next generation. "He's like the Johnny Carson for the younger viewers," David Klein, executive editor of *Electronic Media*, a trade newspaper, told the *New York Times*. "It's hard to remember now, but back in the '60s Carson was kind of daring and hip. Arsenio is the first late-night host since Carson who clearly has his own personality—warm, friendly, daring, sexy—the perfect TV personality."

When "The Arsenio Hall Show" premiered in January 1989, he finished fourth after Carson, Pat Sajak, and David Letterman. By the summer he had moved into second place behind Carson. Now that Carson has retired, only time will tell if he becomes the most popular talk show host on television.

Fannie Lou Hamer

Civil rights activist, sharecropper
Born October 6, 1917, Montgomery county,
  Mississippi
Died March 15, 1977

"The landowner said I would have to go back to withdraw or I would have to leave and so I told him I didn't go down there to register for him. I was down there to register for myself."

It's easy to understand how Fannie Lou Hamer became involved in the civil rights movement. By the time she was six, Hamer sweated in the cotton fields for the promise of candy. There was no time for school, housing conditions were deplorable, and food was hard to come by. Hamer worked hard to change these conditions by working with the Student Nonviolent Coordinating Committee (SNCC), and later with the Mississippi Freedom Democratic Party (MFDP) and many other organizations. For her actions she was beaten, lost her job, was arrested, and faced many other brutalities perpetuated by whites against blacks. Her determination inspired self-reliance and self-determination among many blacks and other poor people of the world.

The twentieth child of the family

Hamer was born the twentieth child in the family to sharecropper parents. They lived in terrible poverty. When it looked like their luck was finally about to turn for the better, an envious white neighbor poisoned their mules and cows. When Hamer was six years old, the plantation owner enticed her to work in the cotton fields by promising her candies. Each week she was expected to pick more cotton. By the time she was thirteen years old, Hamer was picking three to four hundred pounds.

Since she spent so much time in the fields, Hamer had little time for school. She had only six years of schooling, most of that from December to March, when she wasn't needed in the fields. Even then, she could only attend for about a month since she lacked warm clothing during the winter.

In 1942 she married Perry "Pap" Hamer, a tractor driver from another plantation. Since they were unable to have children, they adopted two girls, one of whom died in 1967. They continued working as sharecroppers, but because Hamer was a hard worker, she was eventually promoted from cotton-picking to plantation time keeper.

Life on the plantation was extremely hard, but Hamer's life took a turn for the better after meeting members of the Southern Christian Leadership Conference (SCLC) and SNCC. In 1962 these groups were mobilizing people to fight for civil rights in Mississippi. Hamer was interested in their activities, and she became involved in politics in Mississippi, especially in Ruleville. When civil rights leaders asked for volunteers to challenge the unjust voting laws, Hamer was among them. On August 31, 1962, she and eighteen others boarded an old school bus owned and driven by a black man from another county to go to Indianola to register to vote. They were given literacy tests, but they all failed. They reboarded the bus and headed back to Ruleville. Along the way they

Fannie Lou Hamer

were stopped by a highway patrolman, and the driver was arrested for driving a bus that was "too yellow." The patrolman said the bus looked too much like a school bus and could create potential confusion. When the group refused to be separated, the one-hundred-dollar fine was reduced to thirty dollars, which they were able to collect among themselves.

Forced to leave the plantation

After she returned to the plantation, the owner insisted Hamer withdraw her application to vote or be forced to leave. Hamer decided to leave, but her new home was soon riddled with gun shots, and the family left the plantation.

Hamer tried two more times to pass the literacy test before she was finally able to become a registered voter. She became SNCC supervisor in Sunflower County and taught blacks to pass the literacy test. After attending a civil rights workshop in Charleston, South Carolina in 1963, Hamer and a group of nine-teen activists stopped at a bus terminal in Winona, Mississippi, to get something to eat. They decided to challenge the whites-only policy at the restaurant, but were attacked by state troopers, arrested, and thrown in jail. Hamer was taken to a cell with two black male prisoners who were given a black leather clutch loaded with metal and told to beat her or face worse consequences. She was so badly beaten that she was permanently injured. Later Hamer was returned to her jail cell, where she and the other civil rights workers were released upon the intervention of James Bevel and Andrew Young.

This experience made Hamer even more determined. In spring 1964, she helped organize the MFDP. Hamer was given the position of vice-chairman, which she used to campaign for Congress from the Second Congressional District of Mississippi. She gained national recognition as the MFDP challenged the white Mississippi delegation to the 1964 National Democratic Convention in Atlantic City. Hamer was given the opportunity to tell her story before the credentials committee. Many were shocked to hear her talk about her beatings and the other brutalities she suffered. Despite her best efforts, the MFDP did not get what it wanted. They only received two seats on the sixty-eight member delegation. Hamer was quoted as saying, "we didn't come all this way for no two seats when all of us is tired."

Besides being on the political stage, Hamer also spent a great deal of time building her own community. She helped to bring the Head Start Program, the most successful part of the War on Poverty program, to Ruleville. In 1969 she founded Freedom Farm in Sunflower County, Mississippi, and fed fifteen hundred people with the food that was grown. Hamer became involved with the Young World Developers, an organization that built homes for the poor. When a needy white man moved to the farm and sought food, clothing, and shelter for his family of five children, the organization ensured his needs were met. Hamer also helped to start a low-income day care center and she was involved in bringing a garment factory to the town.

Teaches at Shaw University

Hamer had an interest in education and she agreed to teach a course in contemporary black history at Shaw University in the late 1960s. When her class met, "sometimes parents would be there. Sometimes teachers would be there. It was a great experience for me," she said.

Hamer was often quoted on what she believed to be the rights and responsibilities of black women. She had learned a great deal about the plight of black women through her grandmother, a former slave who was 136 years old when she died in 1960.

Since Hamer spent much of her life fighting for the civil rights movement, many colleges and universities awarded her honorary doctoral degrees, including Shaw University, Tougaloo College, Columbia College in Chicago, Howard University, and Morehouse College.

Throughout her life she was endangered and threatened many times. She finally succumbed to diabetes, heart trouble, and breast cancer on March 15, 1977. L.C. Dorsey paid tribute to Hamer in an Action Memorial: "A proper memorial would be one where all of us who loved her would dedicate and rededicate our lives to serving others and helping all of us achieve a greater measure of freedom, justice and love."

Virginia Hamilton

Writer
Born March 12, 1936, Yellow Springs, Ohio

"Few writers of fiction for young people are as daring, inventive, and challenging to read—or to review—as Virginia Hamilton."—Ethel L. Heins

With her many novels about black children, Virginia Hamilton has established herself as a brilliant writer of stories for young people. All her books have gripping plots, though their subjects vary enormously, ranging from present-day to historical novels and science fiction to ghost stories.

Many of Hamilton's books are set in rural Ohio where she grew up, and most include elements of African American history and folklore. As she explained in an essay on her writing, "What I am compelled to write can best be described as some essence of the dreams, lies, myths, and disasters befallen a clan of my blood relatives whose troubled footfall is first discernible on this North American continent some one hundred fifty years ago."

Writer in training

The youngest of five children, Virginia Hamilton was born and raised in Yellow Springs,

Ohio, on land that had been in her mother's family since the nineteenth century. The land had been bought by her grandfather after his escape from slavery.

Hamilton's parents, Kenneth and Etta (Perry) Hamilton, farmed part of the land, as did other relatives. Although they had very little money, they gave their children a secure and happy home. "My childhood was particularly fine if we allow for the fact that I had no concept of dollar poverty," wrote Hamilton many years later. "We had land and plenty to eat."

One of the delights of Hamilton's childhood was listening to the stories her father told—intriguing accounts of local folklore and history, and stirring tales about the achievements of famous African Americans. Because of the knowlege imparted by her father and other relatives, Hamilton received a fairly broad education, even though the local schools offered a limited curriculum. After graduating from high school, she won a scholarship to Antioch College in Yellow Springs (1952–55), after which she studied for two years at Ohio State University.

Longing to get away from small-town life, Hamilton spent her summer vacations working in New York, and after leaving college she moved there permanently. Her plan was "to find a cheap apartment, a part-time job, write, and have a good time"—and she did just that. Among New York's artistic community Hamilton met the Jewish teacher and poet Arnold Adoff, whom she married in 1960. Meanwhile, she wrote in every spare moment and took a creative writing course at the New School for Social Research. Although her first manuscripts were rejected by publishers, she was encouraged to continue writing, and in 1967 her first novel was published.

Hamilton remained in New York for fifteen years before returning to Yellow Springs in the early 1970s. There she and her husband brought up their children, Leigh and Jaime, and there they have made their home ever since.

Prolific author

Hamilton is an extremely prolific author. Since the publication of her first novel, *Zeely* (1967), she has brought out a new book almost every year. *Zeely* attracted considerable attention because, instead of offering the usual stereotype of black children, it portrayed a sensitive and imaginative child who was bursting with character— and was not living in extreme poverty. The heroine is a girl named Geeder, who pays a summer visit to her uncle's farm and fantasizes that Zeely, the tall young woman looking after the pigs, is an enslaved Watusi queen. The story is set in farmland typical of the Yellow Springs area.

Hamilton's second book, *The House of Dies Drear* (1968), also is based in Yellow Springs, though it is a historical novel about the Underground Railroad. A gripping tale involving a strange house with secret passages and a mysterious character called Mr. Pluto, it won the Edgar Allen Poe Award for best juvenile mystery.

In 1969 Hamilton brought out *The Time-Ago Tales of Jahdu,* the first of her books about the character Jahdu. The Jahdu stories include a wealth of African and African American folklore and mythology, elements that are strong in many of Hamilton's novels. Works such as *The Magical Adventures of Pretty Pearl* (1983) have drawn particular praise for their skillful blending of history, mythology, and folklore. Hamilton's fascination with folklore led her to publish a collection of folktales in 1985. Titled *The People Could Fly: American Black Folktales,* it includes animal fables, slave stories, and various tales involving the supernatural.

Of all Hamilton's books dealing with the supernatural, one of the strongest is *Sweet Whispers, Brother Rush* (1982). Written in dialect, the book tells of two children who meet their uncle's ghost, who shows them the past. By understanding the past, the children are better able to cope with the difficulties they have to face in their daily lives. *Sweet Whispers* won the John Newbery Honor Book Award, the Coretta Scott King Award, and the Boston Globe–Horn Book Award, as well as receiving a Certificate of Honor from the International Board on Books for Young People for its "outstanding example of literature with international importance."

Another novel that won many awards, including the National Book Award and the John Newbery Medal, was *M. C. Higgins, the Great* (1974). The setting is Hamilton's familiar region of southern Ohio, only in this case it is in the hills bordering the Ohio river. Here, high on Sarah's Mountain, the fictional Higgins family lives below a huge spoil heap, created by strip mining, which threatens to destroy their home. The story centers on thirteen-year-old Mayo Cornelius Higgins, who is torn between worries for his family's safety and his love for his home. Among the many

who heaped praise on this book was the poet Nikki Giovanni, who commented, "It is warm, humane and hopeful and does what every book should do—creates characters with whom we can identify and for whom we care."

As well as writing of the present and the past, Hamilton sometimes takes her readers into the future, as in her science fiction trilogy: *Justice and Her Brothers* (1978), *Dustland* (1980), and *The Gathering* (1981). These books are about four children—Justice, Levi, Thomas, and Dorian— who are able to go forward into the future, where they find a dust-covered land inhabited by strange creatures. The theme of the trilogy is survival. Like all Hamilton's books, these three give the reader plenty to think about as well as telling a good story.

In contrast to the Justice trilogy, *Willie Bea and the Time the Martians Landed* (1983) is not science fiction. Set in 1938, it is a

Virginia Hamilton

delightful story of a young girl who hears the broadcast of Orson Welles's radio drama *War of the Worlds* and believes that the Martians have invaded Earth. Going out into the fields to investigate, she thinks the harvesting machines are aliens.

In addition to her novels, Hamilton has written two biographies: *W. E. B. Du Bois: A Biography* (1972), about the well-known black civil rights leader and author, and *Paul Robeson: The Life and Times of a Free Black Man* (1974), about the famous actor and singer. She has also brought out an edition of the works of Du Bois for teenage readers in *The Writings of W. E. B. Du Bois* (1975).

While Hamilton's books are all steeped in African American culture, they are marvelously diverse in subject and approach so that one never knows just what to expect from her next. The only sure thing is that her next book will be totally absorbing, just as her last one was. As the reviewer Katherine Paterson wrote of *Sweet Whispers*, "To the more timid reader, young or old … I say: Just read the first page, just the first paragraph, of 'Sweet Whispers, Brother Rush.' Then stop— if you can.'"

Hammer

Rap singer
Born 1962, Oakland, California

"I was a sharp businessman and could have joined up with a top (drug) dealer…. I thought about that just like any other entrepreneur would."

If Hammer had managed to reach his first dream, we would be watching him on television playing professional baseball. When that dream fell through he turned to his second love—music. For the millions who enjoy rap music, the choice was the right one. He has won Grammy Awards for best rap solo and for best rhythm and blues song for his phenomenal hit "U Can't Touch This." His albums have sold in the millions, and he has one of the most energetic stage shows in the history of music. Instead of being a ballplayer, Hammer has had to settle for being one of the world's most successful rap artists.

A baseball and music fan

Hammer was born in Oakland, California, with the given name Stanley Burrell. He was the youngest of his parents' seven children, and they lived mainly on government assistance in a tough area of the city. Hammer managed to stay out of trouble by playing baseball and music. He was a big fan of the Oakland Athletics, and if he couldn't see a game, he would hang around the parking lot hoping to meet one of the team's stars. When he wasn't watching baseball, Hammer would fill the time copying the dance moves of James Brown, the O'Jays, and other musicians. He also used to write commercial rhymes for his favorite products.

One day while Hammer was dancing in the Oakland Coliseum's parking lot, Charlie Finley, the Athletic's owner, walked by. Finley noticed Hammer and the two struck up a conversation. Eventually Finley offered Hammer a job working in the team's clubhouse and acting as batboy for road games. Finley even gave him the honorary title of executive vice-president. The ball players used to call him Hammer because of his resemblance to the batting champion, Hammerin' Hank Aaron.

After graduating from high school Hammer tried his hand at playing professional baseball, but he was not good enough. He took classes in communications, but decided he was not interested in pursuing a career in that area. Worried about the future, Hammer began to consider joining the lucrative drug trade that was underway in his old neighborhood. In a *Rolling Stone* interview Hammer said, "I was a sharp businessman and could have joined up with a top dealer. I had friends making $5,000 to $6,000 a week, easy....I thought about that just like any other entrepreneur would." Although the easy money was enticing, Hammer decided to follow his conscience. He joined the navy and was sent on a three-year stay in Japan and California.

When his time in the navy was over, Hammer decided to take the discipline he learned and apply it to the music field. He formed a religious rap duo named the Holy Ghost Boys. Although religious rap may seem to have limited marketability, Hammer managed to convince two record companies into taking a chance on producing an album. But before the project could be completed, he and his partner parted ways.

Forms Bust It Records

Dwayne Murphy and Mike Davis, two of Hammer's friends from the Oakland Athletics, each invested $20,000 to form Bust It Records, Hammer's own company. He made a debut single, "Ring 'Em" and sold it on the

Hammer

streets. At the same time he was auditioning and working with musicians, dancers, and his female backup trio known as Oakland's 3-5-7. Hammer wanted to stage a sophisticated show, so he held rehearsals seven days a week, sometimes for fourteen hours a day.

Hammer released a second single, "Let's Get Started" before he met Felton Pilate, a producer and musician from the group Con Funk Shun. The two worked in Pilate's basement studio and compiled a full-length album for Hammer entitled *Feel My Power*. The album was produced on a shoestring budget and didn't have a major record company to market it. Still, it sold sixty thousand copies.

In 1988 Hammer happened to be at the same Oakland music club that Joy Bailey, an executive at Capitol Records, was attending. She didn't know who he was, but his presence and attitude impressed her. Bailey introduced herself and later arranged for him to meet with some of the company's top executives in Los

Angeles. At the meeting, Hammer impressed the company with his music, dancing, and keen business sense. With rap music starting to boom, Capitol wanted in on the action, and Hammer convinced them that he was the one to take them to the top. He walked away from the meeting with a $750,000 advance and a multi-album contract. Capitol reworked Hammer's *Feel My Power* album and retitled it *Let's Get It Started*. The album was an immediate sensation, climbing to sales of more than 1.5 million copies.

Hammer hit the road and was soon making appearances across the country with well-established rap stars like Tone-Loc, N.W.A., and Heavy D and the Boyz. He had recording equipment placed in the back of his bus and turned out a hit single "U Can't Touch This" for about $10,000 (nearly the same cost of *Feel My Power*). Capitol embarked on a unique marketing campaign to sell "U Can't Touch This." It included sending cassettes to a hundred thousand children, along with personalized letters urging them to request the song on MTV. "U Can't Touch This" had already sold more than five million copies in late 1990, easily surpassing the previous record held by the Beastie Boys' *Licensed to Ill*. It also became the theme song for the Detroit Pistons basketball team during and after their second NBA championship campaign in 1990.

"U Can't Touch This" was released with the album, *Please Hammer Don't Hurt 'Em*, in 1990. Shortly after the release, Rick James took legal action against Hammer for allegedly stealing from his early 1980s hit song "Super Freak." *Jet* magazine reported that the entertainers reconciled, with James telling Hammer to "keep doing it."

Hammer puts on one of the most enthusiastic shows in the business. Before each performance, he leads his fifteen dancers, twelve backup singers, seven musicians, and two deejays in prayer. He united his Bust It Records company with Capitol in a $10 million joint-venture agreement in 1991. Hammer also makes commercial endorsements for Pepsi and British Knights athletic wear. He plans to make an action-comedy film tentatively titled *Pressure*. He told *Rolling Stone*, "I'm not a singer-want-to-turn movie star. I've always been an actor."

For the future, Hammer intends to maintain his image as a wheeler-dealer and sleek entertainer. He is looking forward to putting out more albums. "I'm on a mission," he said in *Rolling Stone*. "The music is in me, and I have to get it out."

Lionel Hampton

Bandleader, percussionist
Born April 20, 1908, Louisville, Kentucky

"Sometimes, when I play jazz, it's like a spiritual impulse comes over me."

O ne of the most spirited performers in the history of jazz, Lionel Hampton has captivated audiences throughout the world with his spectacular showmanship and his terrific sense of rhythm. Whether leading his own big band or playing with his small jazz combo, he has made each performance an exciting happening—so much so that his fans have often joined in, stomping enthusiastically in time with the music. At a 1954 performance at the Apollo Theater in Harlem, the audience stomped so vigorously that they cracked the mezzanine balcony.

Hampton is also known as the musician who popularized the vibraphone as a jazz instrument. His band was at the top of the hit charts during the 1940s and 1950s, and he continued to draw audiences as he grew older. Describing Hampton's performance as a sixty-nine-year-old, the music writer Arnold Jay Smith commented, "He is always smiling, enjoying his playing and that of others, expressing that pleasure by 'yeah-ing' whenever the spirit moves him."

The young musician

Lionel Leo Hampton inherited his musical talents from his father, Charles Hampton, who was a professional pianist and singer—though only briefly. He had barely begun his career when he was sent overseas to fight in World War I and almost immediately was reported missing. Since "missing" was assumed to mean "dead," Lionel and his brother grew up without a father. They did not discover until years later, when they were adults, that their father was in fact alive—a blind, elderly man living in a veteran's home.

Unable to cope on her own, the boys' mother, Gertrude (Whitfield) Hampton, took them to live with her parents in Chicago. There Hampton was raised as a Roman Catholic and sent to St. Monica Elementary School and St. Elizabeth High School. By the time he was at high school he had become such a keen drum-

mer that he had worn out all the toy drums he had ever been given. In order to afford real drums, he took a job as a newsboy with the *Chicago Defender*. This served a double purpose because the paper sponsored a jazz band for its newsboys. Within a week of starting the job, Hampton was playing in the band on his own set of drums.

On graduating from high school, Hampton headed for Los Angeles, where he was taken into the band of Les Hite, a long-time friend of his grandmother. Hampton stayed with the Hite band for the next four years, and for two years he attended classes in music theory at the University of Southern California. Very soon he gained a reputation as a talented drummer—and also as a vibraphone player.

Popular performer

Hampton's switch to the vibraphone came about almost by accident. When Louis Armstrong was in Los Angeles in 1930, he asked Hampton to stand in as his drummer for recording dates. During one of these sessions Hampton found a vibraphone in the studio and tried it out. He was fascinated by the instrument, and about an hour later he played it on Armstrong's recording of "Memories of You" (which has since become famous for containing the first jazz vibraphone solo ever recorded).

The more Hampton played the vibraphone, the more he marveled at its versatility. It was like the xylophone, only better, in that it had metal rather than wooden bars and motor-driven resonators that could produce a "wah-wah-wah" vibrato. Before Hampton took up the vibraphone, it had been used mainly to produce chimes, but he made it work as a wonderfully rhythmic jazz percussion instrument.

Clarinetist Benny Goodman, "the King of Swing," was so taken with Hampton's performance on the "vibes" that in 1936 he persuaded Hampton to join him in a quartet with drummer Gene Krupa and pianist Teddy Wilson. During the next four years, the quartet was tremendously successful, with such hits as "Dinah," "Exactly Like You," "My Last Affair," and "Moonglow."

As a member of the Benny Goodman Quartet, Hampton was one of the first black musicians to play with a predominantly white group. Hampton also performed and recorded with Goodman's full band. He made recordings with other jazz groups, too, for companies such as RCA Victor and also for his own record company, Glad-Hamp Records, which he founded with his wife Gladys, whom he had married in 1936.

By 1940, when the Benny Goodman Quartet broke up, Hampton was a leading figure of the Swing Era, and he had no difficulty forming his own big band. Such talents as saxophonist Charlie Parker and singer Dinah Washington were eager to join the Lionel Hampton Orchestra, which became a showpiece of brilliant jazz musicians. All the players were given full opportunity to display their talents, for Hampton was one of the first bandleaders to let a number continue until every player had done a solo.

Hampton himself was the inspirational spirit of the band, spreading excitement and euphoria among players and audience alike. As well as conducting, he sang, played the vibes and drums, and sometimes even played

Lionel Hampton

the piano—rippling along at great speed, using his two forefingers only, as if they were vibraphone mallets. With such superb showmanship, Hampton's band was the most popular in the field for some twenty years, from its first big hit, "Flyin' Home," in 1941 right through to the 1960s.

By the 1960s big bands were losing their popularity, so Hampton reduced his orchestra to an eight-man combo called The Inner Circle. Since then he has toured widely, visiting Europe, Japan, the Philippines, Australia, North Africa, Israel, and many other places. His visit to Israel, a country he fell in love with, inspired him to compose his only major work, the jazz symphony *King David*.

Hampton has made numerous albums, ranging from the uproarious *Apollo Hall Concert, 1954* to the more recent *At Newport '78*. In 1981 he was appointed a professor of music at Howard University, and in 1985 he was made United Nations Ambassador of Music.

Like many people who love their work, Hampton has never really retired from it. He was still touring when he was in his eighties—and still spreading happiness among his audiences. As he once told a reporter, "We just act the way the music and the spirit moves us. That's all. Remember what the Bible says. It says 'Blow the trumpet, beat the cymbals.' That's what we're doing."

Lorraine Hansberry

Playwright
Born May 19, 1930, Chicago, Illinois
Died January 12, 1965

"I told them this wasn't a 'negro play.' It was a play about honest-to-God, believable, many-sided people who happen to be black."

T he famous dramatist who wrote *A Raisin in the Sun*, Lorraine Hansberry came from a family long engaged in the struggle for black civil rights. During her brief lifetime she wrote insightful dramas about the most controversial subjects of her time. She also wrote articles and essays on a wide range of topics, including homophobia, world peace, the House un-American Activities Committee, and the Cuban missle crisis. Many considered her to be one of the sharpest observers and most talented playwrights of her time.

Quit college to work with Paul Robeson

Hansberry, the youngest of four children, was born on May 19, 1930, in Chicago, Illinois, to Carl and Nanny Hansberry. The Hansberrys were well known in the struggle for black liberation. Her grandfather was a slave who had tried to run away. Her mother was a schoolteacher who dedicated herself to the struggle for political and social reform by serving on a ward committee. Her father was a strong believer in black civil rights and moved the family into an all-white neighborhood in 1938.

As Hansberry went to school in the morning she was confronted by angry whites throwing bricks at her. One concrete slab narrowly missed her head. Her family barely lived there a year when a lower court ordered them to leave. Her father fought the case all the way to the U.S. Supreme Court, and eventually won in 1940.

In 1948 Hansberry decided to attend the University of Wisconsin, instead of Howard University, her parents' choice. She became interested in writing after watching Sean O'Casey's play, *Juno and the Paycock*. As her interest in writing grew, her studies bored her and left her feeling unfulfilled. In 1950 she left the university to work as a reporter for Paul Robeson's radical black newspaper, *Freedom*, in New York. She started by writing political articles and book and drama reviews, and by 1952 she was an associate editor.

That year she went to the International Peace Congress in Uruguay as Robeson's representative (the State Department had refused him a passport). The congress broadened her awareness of such issues as poverty, dictatorships, the arms race, and American interference in Latin American countries. She enjoyed the chance to meet women of color

Lorraine Hansberry

from other countries, and she used material from this experience to write the essay: *Simone de Beauvoir and the Second Sex: An American Commentary, 1957.*

Married Robert Nemiroff

In 1953 she married Robert Nemiroff, a white Jewish intellectual, member of the Communist party, and unknown to her at the time, a homosexual. For this reason they separated four years later, but they remained close. In fact, Nemiroff maintains control over her papers and holds the rights to her published work. Shortly before her death she entrusted him with revisions of *Les Blancs* (her last play that was left unfinished) and named him as her literary executor.

Hansberry realized that her struggle against the white power elite would have to be through her writing. In 1953 she resigned as editor of *Freedom* to concentrate on her own work. She held several odd jobs until Nemiroff

wrote a hit song with Burt D'Lugoff in 1956. The money from this venture allowed her to quit working and write full time.

In 1957 Hansberry wrote the play *A Raisin in the Sun*, about the bleak social conditions that force a black family to defer their dreams until their own strength and pride help them struggle toward opportunity. Philip Rose, a friend of Nemiroff, wanted to produce the play on Broadway, but no producers who would take a chance on it. Rose began raising the money through small investors. After he was refused bookings on Broadway, he opened it for test runs in New Haven, Philadelphia, and Chicago where it enjoyed a brief but successful run. The play then opened at New York's Barrymore Theater on March 11, 1959.

A Raisin in the Sun had great impact

A Raisin in the Sun was the first play on Broadway by a black female playwright. It received very good reviews and ran for 538 shows. The play appealed to both black and white people, and theaters had to cope with racially mixed audiences. This led to demonstrations and boycotts in some cities. The play created many opportunities for black theater artists across the country and was the first serious black drama to have real impact upon mainstream society. Twenty-five years after it opened, *A Raisin in the Sun* was revived across the country and given important productions at the Kennedy Center and on PBS.

In May 1959 Hansberry became the first black playwright and one of the few women ever to win the coveted New York Drama Critics Circle Award for Best Play of the Year.

Because the play dealt with the oppression of blacks, she became a spokesperson for and symbol of American blacks.

However, since the play appealed to whites, militant black groups criticized it, saying it caused blacks to be blended into white culture. Influential black playwright Amiri Baraka did not at first consider it to be true black art, but he reversed that decision in 1987 in an article that appeared in the *Washington Post*.

Walked out on Robert Kennedy

In 1964 Hansberry created her second drama, *The Sign in Sidney Brustein's Window*, about a white Jewish male intellectual. Not a commercial success, its intellectual content went right over the heads of its audience. It frustrated critics and disappointed viewers, who wanted to see a sequel to her first play. Another reason the play failed was because Hansberry was ill when it was first released and did not have the strength to perform a final edit.

Hansberry also contributed to civil rights causes. In 1961 she donated money for the station wagon used by Freedom Riders James Chaney, Andrew Goodman, and Michael Schwerner, who were murdered in Mississippi. The next year she gathered support for the Student Nonviolent Coordinating Committee (SNCC) and was a strong critic of the House un-American Activities Committee and the Cuban missle crisis.

Perhaps her biggest moment in the civil rights movement occurred on May 24, 1953, when she and several prominent blacks met with Attorney General Robert Kennedy.

Rather than endorsing America as a land of freedom and opportunity, Hansberry led a walk-out, saying she was worried about the state of oppression most blacks faced.

Cancer ended career

At the age of thirty-four, Hansberry's activities were severely curtailed because of cancer. She suffered a paralyzing stroke, losing her speech and eyesight. She fought back and regained both. Hansberry left her sickbed to raise money for SNCC, to meet with Robert Kennedy, and to attend reheasals for *The Sign in Sidney Brustein's Window*. She went through two unsuccessful operations and received heavy doses of chemotherapy.

During her last year she published a radical volume, *The Movement: Documentary of a Struggle for Equality*. The book features a collection of photographs of racist brutality, including hangings, and an equally disturbing text. She began working on a new play, *Les Blancs*, and when she realized she was too ill to complete it, she had many long conversations with Nemiroff so he could finish it after her death. *Les Blancs* was produced in 1970 at the Longacre Theater in New York. The story concerns a man who must choose between his white wife and a comfortable family life in England or leading his people in the fight against colonial oppression. It received mixed reviews and ran for only forty-eight shows.

Hansberry's play *The Sign In Sidney Brustein's Window* continued running for 101 performances, mainly through the efforts of Nemiroff and his influential friends. The show closed when Hansberry died on January 12, 1965.

The Harlem Globetrotters

Basketball team
Born 1927

"I think what it is with the Globetrotters is that the kids have to believe in something, and they don't believe in Santa Claus anymore. The Globetrotters give them the myth with the reality." —Marie Linehan, former assistant to original owner Abe Saperstein

Adorned in their red, white, and blue uniforms, the Harlem Globetrotters are part show business, part sporting event, and part slapstick. For over sixty years this band of basketball players has been entertaining millions around the world with their antics and skills. Once billed as the Ambassadors of Goodwill, they now refer to themselves as family entertainment. "I think what it is with the Globetrotters is that the kids have to believe in something, and they don't believe in Santa Claus anymore," Marie Linehan, a former assistant to original owner Abe Saperstein, told *Sports Illustrated*. "The Globetrotters give them the myth with reality. They win every game, so they are miracle men, which means the kids don't have to make a decision about them. And the kids know what's going to happen in every game, they know the whole scenario. But you see, this doesn't disturb them. On the contrary, it makes the kids more a part of it."

The Globetrotters have had a lengthy list of popular players since their inception in 1927. They have had comedians like Sweet Lou, Goose Tatum, Meadowlark Lemon, and Geese Ausbie; dribbling sensations such as Jimmy Blacklock, Clyde Austin, Marques Haynes, and Curley Neal; dunkers like Derrick Refigee; and three-point shooting stars such as Billy Ray Hobley.

Globetrotters owner kept NBA from integrating

The team was formed by millionaire Abe Saperstein, who signed players from club, college, and a few professional squads. Since the National Basketball League did not accept black players, and there was no organized black league to compete for talent, the Globetrotters attracted the most gifted college and club players in the country. "We were just happy to be playing ball," former member Sweetwater Cliffton told *Sports Illustrated*. "I guess they'd call that Tomming today."

The players were poorly paid, and it was a buyer's market. Saperstein kept it that way by threatening to boycott National Basketball Association arenas if the league broke the color barrier. Saperstein did not want his black players jumping to the higher-paying NBA. His pressure helped hold off integration until 1950, when the Boston Celtics drafted Chuck Cooper.

In the 1940s the Globetrotters were considered one of the best entertainment acts in the world because of their clowning. Inman Jackson was one of the first to act as a funnyman on the court, but it was Goose Tatum who was the premier showman when the team rose to national prominence after World War II.

Even after the color barrier was broken, Saperstein held total authority over the players. No player would even dare to shoot a jump shot when Saperstein was at a game. He believed the jump shot was a defilement of the sport, and he threatened to fire anyone who tried one. Saperstein would also pay informants on the team who would disclose player secrets to him.

Another tactic Saperstein used to control his team was to force some veterans to try out for the team each fall. Some of the shrewder Globetrotters managed to beat the boss at his own game: One would call him up nearly every off-season, and moan into the phone, "Skip, you got to help me out with $500. The white mens down heah gwanna sho nuff put me in jail lessen you send me $500 right prompt." Saperstein would chuckle at the player's request, wire the money, and then notify the coach to make sure the fellow made the team again—so he could get the $500 back out of his salary.

Although Saperstein was frugal when it came to paying his players, he frequently did not know how to handle his money. It is rumored that he left a paper bag with $40,000 in gate receipts in a restaurant. He ran the company so badly that few people had a true idea of its value when he died. Despite these faults, Saperstein was tremendously loyal to his friends. In many cities he stuck with bad promoters who were old buddies.

Owner used Globetrotters to gain support for NBA franchise

Saperstein hoped the NBA would one day grant him a franchise in Los Angeles. To round up support for his bid, he would have the Globetrotters perform on the same bill as struggling NBA teams to help the gate. When the Minneapolis Lakers were transferred to Los Angeles, Saperstein felt he was double crossed. In retaliation he formed the American Basketball League and had the Globetrotters play on the same bills with teams in the ABL.

Saperstein died in 1966, and his estate sold the Globetrotters the following year for $3.7 million—a startling price at the time, but a bargain in hindsight. The buyers were three Chicago businessmen, Potter Palmer, George Gillett, and John O'Neil. They went public with the company, calling it Globetrotter Communications Inc. They also diversified by adding radio stations and sporting goods. In 1972 the corporation made a profit of $1.8 million, of which $875,000 came from the Globetrotters.

Despite the money the Globetrotters were making, very little ended up in the players' hands. Larry Lindberg, a film director who traveled with the team for a month in 1971, felt so sorry for some of the players that he bought meals for them since they did not have enough money to buy food. "It was hard to expect people to be funny for a camera when they were hungry," he told *Sports Illustrated*. In 1972 the players decided to go out on strike. The strike lasted about three weeks, but the players finally settled, mainly because the owners were recruiting a replacement team.

The Globetrotters have played in more than 89 countries, traveled more than six million miles, played before 75 million people, and once in Berlin they played before the largest basketball crowd in history, 75,000. The team has also played before 5 papal audiences and met the late Soviet Union leader Nikita Khrushchev and the Duke of Edinburgh. They have played in bull rings, fish markets, airplane hangars, and in the bottom of a drained swimming pool.

The Globetrotters have a "International Unit" that travels abroad in the winter, and every spring a combined team plays Europe for a few months. The full contingent for traveling in Europe is about thirty-five. This includes Globetrotters, the opposition, other acts, wives, children, and support personnel. Their opposition has been called the Washington Generals, New York Nationals, Jersey Reds, Boston Shamrocks, Atlantic City Gulls, or Chicago Demons. Much of the opposition were run-of-the-mill, small college heroes recruited by word of mouth. They are usually single, recent graduates, who like the idea of travel and meeting people.

Every game is almost a duplicate of the previous one. The early minutes of each quarter are reserved by tradition to mostly straight basketball. The clowning does not begin until there are about six minutes left in a period. If there is no scoreboard clock, as is often the case in Europe, someone at the scorer's table lets the Globetrotters know how much time is remaining with code words.

Woman joined team and increased audience size

In 1986 the Globetrotters tried to spruce up their act by hiring Earl Duryea, former marketing director for Ringling Brothers and Barnum & Bailey Circus, as president. One of his first moves was to add a woman to the

The Harlem Globetrotters

team. Lynette Woodard made the team after beating out eighteen of the best black women basketball players in a tryout camp. With Woodard in the act, attendance was up over 20 percent from the previous year. Ninety percent of the games are sell outs. Most of the players now make $70,000 a year, and a few of the bigger-name veterans make more. The Globetrotters are involved in marketing a variety of items, and they pick up extra money by handling sales of their theme song, Brother Bones's version of "Sweet Georgia Brown."

Despite the success of the Globetrotters, their parent company, International Broadcasting Corporation, went into bankruptcy in 1993. Mannie Jackson, a former Globetrotter, announced in March 1993 that he was leading an investment firm that had reached an agreement to acquire the assets of the team. He hoped to take control of the team after it emerged from bankruptcy proceedings later that year.

Barbara Harris

Bishop
Born June 12, 1930, Philadelphia,
  Pennsylvania

*"A fresh wind is indeed blowing.... To some
the changes are refreshing breezes. For others,
they are as fearsome as a hurricane."*

When Barbara Harris was ordained a suffragan (assistant) bishop of the U.S. Episcopal Church in 1989, she broke a 2000-year-old tradition stretching back to the time of Christ. She was the first woman to be made a bishop by any of the three major branches of Christianity—Anglicanism, Roman Catholicism, and Eastern Orthodoxy.

The U.S. Episcopal Church is part of the worldwide Anglican communion that grew out of the Church of England, and it has many traditionalists among its members. While some of them welcomed Harris's appointment, others were outraged. They protested that it was "sacrilegious" and "theologically unsound" for any woman to be a bishop, because bishops were successors of the twelve apostles, all of whom had been men. Others attacked Harris personally as a left-wing radical and as a divorced black woman who lacked the necessary qualifications. They complained that she had no college degree or seminary training, and had not been a full-time priest with her own parish.

Harris agreed that her background was unusual, for she had been a businesswoman for much of her life, but she did not feel that made her unsuitable. "I've had an active ministry all my life," she said, "a lay ministry." This was indeed true, for she had been an active member of the church even as a child.

Social worker and activist

Barbara Clementine Harris was taught from an early age "to love the Lord your God with all your heart" and "to love your neighbor as yourself." Along with her sister and brother, she was regularly taken to church by her parents, Walter and Beatrice (Price) Harris. Her mother was choir director and organist of St. Barnabas Church in the Germantown district of Philadelphia where the Harrises lived, and young Barbara played the piano for the church school in her teenage years. As a teenager, Barbara also started a Young Adults Group, which was so popular that it attracted some seventy members and became the largest youth group in the city.

On graduating from Philadelphia High School for Girls in 1948, Harris went to work for Joseph V. Baker & Associates, a black-owned public relations firm in Philadelphia. The work involved representing white companies in black communities, mainly in the South, a role Harris performed so effectively that after ten years she was made president of the firm. She served in this position from 1958 until 1968, when she was hired away by Sun Oil, where she became head of the community relations department. It was during her term as president of Baker & Associates that she had her brief marriage, which ended in divorce. She had no children.

Alongside her busy career, Harris was equally busy doing volunteer work connected with her church. She was a member of the St. Dismas Society, which visited the local jails to hold services and befriend the prisoners. She was also a board member of the Pennsylvania Prison Society. Despite such community work, Harris felt that her church was not sufficiently involved in the vital issues of the times. Although most of the congregation supported the civil rights movement, their support was quiet and undemonstrative, since they were rather conservative and did not want to get involved in political action. In the 1960s, with her rector's blessing, Harris therefore moved to the more activist Church of the Advocate in north Philadelphia.

Under its energetic rector the Reverend Paul Washington, the Church of the Advocate had become the center of the black protest movement in Philadelphia. It provided buses to take people to civil rights protests in the South, and many of its congregation—includ-

Barbara Harris

ing Barbara Harris—joined Martin Luther King, Jr., on his Selma march in 1965. Three years later, the church hosted a Black Panther convention which attracted ten thousand Panthers.

Harris was deeply involved in all the church's activities. She served in the vestry, helped the poor in the surrounding community, volunteered in the soup kitchen, and helped get a Philadelphia orphanage desegregated. The Reverend Washington greatly admired what he called her "strong sense of justice and compassion for the poor," and when she told him of her wish to become a minister, he gave her full support.

Deacon and priest

In the early 1970s, although a woman could be ordained a deacon in the Episcopal Church, she was not allowed to be ordained a priest. In other words, she could be an assistant but not a full member of the clergy. Harris thought this an outdated rule that made no sense in the twentieth century. Others were of the same view, and in 1974 three retired bishops took matters into their own hands and ordained eleven women deacons as priests—thereby causing a great furor in the Episcopal church. But their action had the desired effect: two years later, the church policy was changed to admit women priests.

Harris had shown her support for the "Philadelphia 11" by leading a procession of parish women into the ordination service, and within the next two years she became convinced that she, too, should train for the priesthood. Since she had a full-time job, she could not enroll at a theological college, but she worked out a schedule that allowed her to acquire the necessary number of credits by studying in the evenings and on weekends. In 1976, she enrolled at Metropolitan Collegiate Center in Philadelphia, and between 1977 and 1979, she took several course at Villanova University. After a final three months at the Episcopal Divinity School in Cambridge, she had completed all the necessary qualifications and was duly ordained deacon in September 1979. One year later, in October 1980, she was ordained priest.

Harris then gave up her job with Sun Oil, though she continued to do some consulting work. Meanwhile, she served for four years as priest at St. Augustine of Hippo Church in Philadelphia and as chaplain at Philadelphia County Prison. Then, in 1984, she was appointed executive director of the Episcopal Church Publishing Company. It was in this role that she came to national attention, as editor of the *Witness,* a left-wing church journal. Harris had already written a number of articles for the *Witness,* protesting such matters as racism in the church and raging against President Ronald Reagan's policies. Like her sermons, her articles were powerful and hard-hitting, and they evoked a strong reaction among her readers.

Bishop Harris

When, in 1988, Harris was elected bishop after a heated campaign, many people objected on the grounds that she was too liberal. However, by far the greatest opposition came from those who were vehemently against the idea of women bishops, even though the Anglican church had recently opened the door to women by ruling that national bodies could choose their own bishops. There were also a few people who based their objections on Harris's color, but this was not a major issue, for there were already twenty-eight black bishops within the church.

During the time between Harris's election and her ordination, it looked as if the church might split over the issue. But Harris stood firm, and in February 1989 she was duly consecated suffragan bishop of the Episcopal Diocese of Massachusetts. Preaching the following week in her home parish, she told the congregation: "A fresh wind is indeed blowing. We have seen in this year alone some things thought to be impossible just a short time ago. To some the changes are refreshing breezes. For others, they are as fearsome as a hurricane." Bishop Harris has since won over many of her opponents. Meanwhile, as church consultant Myrtle Gordon has pointed out, Harris remains what she has always been—"a strong black woman, small in stature, fiercely strong in her beliefs, loyalties, and concerns for people's welfare in relation to the witness of the church."

Marcelite J. Harris

Military officer
Born January 16, 1943, Houston, Texas

fter years of distinguished military service, Marcelite J. Harris was rewarded in 1990 by being named the first black woman general in the Air Force. She was the Air Force's first woman aircraft maintenance officer and one of the first two women to be "air officers commanding" at the Air Force Academy in Colorado. Harris was not only the first woman appointed maintenance squadron commander in Strategic Air Command, but she was also Air Training Command's first woman wing commander. She is currently the vice-commander of the Oklahoma City Air Logistics Center at Tinker Air Force Base.

Great-great grandfather was a politician

Harris was born on January 16, 1943, in Houston, Texas, to Cecil O'Neal Jordan, Sr., a postal supervisor, and Marcelite Jordan, a high school librarian. She has a sister, Elizabeth, and a brother, Cecil O'Neal, Jr. Her great-great grandfather, Pierre Landry, the son of a slave woman and her master, was born on the Provost plantation in Ascension Parish in Louisiana. He lived the first thirteen years of his life in virtual freedom. After being sold, he opened a plantation store, which sold approved items to other slaves, and he became the plantation's head carpenter. After the Civil War ended and he received his freedom, Landry moved to Donaldsonville, the parish seat, where he became mayor in 1868. From 1870 to 1884 he served in the state house of representatives and in the state senate. He eventually left politics to practice law. On her maternal side, Harris's great grandfather, I.M. Terrell, was an educator who founded a school for blacks in Fort Worth, Texas.

In 1960 Harris graduated from Kashmere Gardens Junior-Senior High School, and four years later she received a bachelor of arts degree in speech and drama at Spelman College in Atlanta, Georgia. She later received a bachelor of arts degree in business management from the University of Maryland. She took the Air Force's Squadron Officer School by correspondence and Air War College by seminar. Harris also completed Harvard University's Senior Officers National Security and the Defense Department's CAPSTONE course for general officers in residence.

Harris entered the United States Air Force in September 1965 through the Officer Training School at Lackland Air Force Base in Texas. After graduating in December, she was named assistant director for administration at the 60th Military Airlift Wing at Travis Air Force Base in California. In January 1967 Harris became the administrative officer for the 388th Tactical Missile Squadron at Bitburg Air Base in West Germany. She was reassigned as the maintenance analysis officer with the 36th Tactical Fighter Wing at the same base in May 1970.

After completing her tour in Germany, Harris returned to the United States, where she graduated in May 1971 from the Aircraft Maintenance Officer Course at Chanute Air Force Base in Illinois. She was the first woman in the Air Force to become an aircraft maintenance officer. Three months after graduating, she became the maintenance supervisor for the 469th Tactical Fighter Squadron at Korat Air Base in Thailand. Upon her return to the United States, she was named the job control officer for the 916th Air Refuelling Squadron at Travis Air Force Base in California. In September 1973 she became the squadron's field maintenance supervisor.

Two years later Harris became a personal staff officer at Headquarters, United States Air Force, in Washington, D.C. One of her assignments was to act as White House social aide to President Jimmy Carter. In May 1978 she became commander of Cadet Squadron Thirty-nine at the United States Air Force Academy in Colorado. She was one of the first two women to be an "air officer commanding."

Harris became maintenance control officer for the 384th Air Refuelling Wing at McConnell Air Force Base in Kansas in July 1980. The next year she became the first woman maintenance squadron commander in Strategic Air Command, assuming command of the 384th Avionics Maintenance Squadron at McConnell Air Force Base. Eight months later she became commander of McConnell's 384th Field Maintenance Squadron.

Air Force's first woman deputy commander for maintenance

In November 1982 Harris moved to the Kadena Air Force Base in Japan, where she was assigned to the Pacific Forces Logistic Support Center. She became the Air Force's first woman deputy commander for maintenance in March 1986, when she assumed the position at Keesler Air Force Base in Mississippi. On December 3, 1988, she became the commander of the 3300th Technical Training Wing at Keesler Training Center at Keesler Air Force Base in Mississippi. At that time she was the first woman wing commander in Air Training Command.

Harris became a brigadier general on September 8, 1990, and is currently vice-com-

Marcelite J. Harris

mander of the Oklahoma City Air Logistics Centre at Tinker Air Force Base. *Jet* magazine stated she "helps oversee 26,000 workers in the maintenance of all types of military aircraft and missiles."

Throughout her distinguished career, Harris has received many military honors, including the Bronze Star, Meritorious Service Medal with three oak leaf clusters, Air Force Commendation Medal with one oak leaf cluster, Presidential Unit Citation, Air Force Outstanding Unit Award with eight oak leaf clusters—one with valor, Air Force Organizational Excellence Award with one oak leaf cluster, National Defense Service Medal, Vietnam Service Medal, Air Force Overseas Ribbon—Short Tour, Air Force Overseas Ribbon—Long Tour with one oak leaf cluster, Air Force Longevity Service Award Ribbon with four oak leaf clusters, Republic of Vietnam Gallantry Cross with Palm, and the Republic of Vietnam Campaign Medal.

Harris married Maurice Anthony Harris, a native of Portsmouth, Virginia, a retired Air Force lieutenant colonel who studied law at Louisiana State University. They have a son, Steven, and a daughter, Tenecia.

Patricia Harris

Lawyer, government official
Born May 31, 1924, Mattoon, Illinois
Died March 23, 1985

"I didn't start out as a member of a prestigious law firm, but as a woman who needed a scholarship to go to school. If you think I have forgotten that, you are wrong."

Patricia Harris

Patricia Harris was the first black woman to serve in a U.S. president's cabinet. Serving as the secretary of Housing and Urban Development and as secretary of Health, Education, and Welfare, Harris was interested in good government and racial harmony. Other firsts for Harris included being the first black woman to serve her nation as an ambassador and to head an American law school.

Importance of education stressed early

Harris was born on May 31, 1924, in Mattoon, Illinois, to Bert and Chiquita Roberts. Her father was a dining car waiter for the Illinois Central Railroad, who abandoned the family while Harris was still a child. Her mother did not have a lot of money, but she stressed upon Harris the importance of an education. As one of the few black families in town, Harris was often subjected to racist comments from her classmates.

After finishing her secondary education in Chicago, Illinois, Harris entered the School of Liberal Arts at Howard University in 1941. She graduated summa cum laude in 1945 with a bachelor's degree and was later elected into Phi Beta Kappa. While at Howard Harris took an interest in civil rights, and she joined other students in one of the first student sit-ins at the Little Palace Cafeteria, which refused to serve blacks.

After finishing graduate school and working several years at the Chicago YWCA, Harris became executive director of Delta Sigma Theta in 1953. She also married William Beasley Harris, a lawyer who encouraged her to attend law school. In 1957 she enrolled in George Washington University School of Law and quickly became a stellar student. She was a member of the law review; was elected to the Order of the Coif, a national legal honor society; and graduated at the top of her class in 1960.

Harris joined the appeals and research staff of the criminal division of the U.S. Department of Justice, where she stayed until she rejoined Howard as a part-time lecturer on law in 1961. Harris spent the rest of her time as associate dean of students at the university. Her appointment to the law faculty made her the fifth woman to teach at Howard's law school.

Harris was appointed a full-time position around 1963, becoming one of two women on the law faculty. In June 1965 she took a leave to accept an appointment by President Lyndon Johnson to serve as ambassador to Luxembourg. She stayed until 1967, and later that year received the Order of Oaken Crown for her distinguished service in Luxembourg.

After retiring as ambassador, Harris returned full time to Howard. She also served as an alternate U.S. delegate to the Twenty-first and Twenty-second General Assembly of the United Nations, and as the country's alternate to the Twentieth Plenary Meeting of the Economic Community of Europe.

First woman dean of Howard University School of Law

In 1969 Harris was appointed dean of Howard University School of Law, but she held it for only a month. Although her term was short because of a host of issues, ranging from a student uprising and faculty disagreements to a disagreement with the president of Howard University, she was the first black woman to head a law school. Afterwards she joined the Washington, D.C.-based firm of Fried, Frank,

Harris, Shriver & Kampelman. She practiced corporate law until President Jimmy Carter named her secretary of Housing and Urban Development in 1977. During her Senate confirmation hearings she was questioned by Senator William Proxmire, who wondered if she was "sympathetic to the problems of the poor." Harris's response appeared in every major newspaper in the country: "You do not understand who I am.... I am a black woman, the daughter of a Pullman car waiter. I am a black woman who even eight years ago could not buy a house in parts of the District of Columbia. I didn't start out as a member of a prestigious law firm, but as a young woman who needed a scholarship to go to school. If you think I have forgotten that, you are wrong."

As a public official Harris was concerned with good government, racial harmony, and the elimination of racial and sexual discrimination. She often spoke on the need for jobs for minorities and minority youth, racial discrimination in housing, and the role of women in the future. Harris once said: "I want to hear the Speaker of the House addressed as Madam Speaker and I want to listen as she introduces Madam President to the Congress assembled for the State of the Union. I want Madam President to look down the podium at the women of the Supreme Court who will be indicative of the significant number of women judges throughout the Federal and State judicial systems."

After serving for three years as Housing and Urban Development Secretary, President Carter named her secretary of the Department of Health, Education, and Welfare. She served until President Carter was defeated in 1980.

Lost bid for D.C. mayor to Marion Barry

Two years later Harris unsuccessfully ran for the mayor of the District of Columbia. The campaign was tough and bitter. She lost the Democratic primary to Marion S. Barry, Jr., but still received 36 percent of the vote. In 1983 she was appointed a full professor of law at George Washington University. She held this position until she died of cancer on March 23, 1985—shortly after the death of her husband.

Harris lived by a philosophy to do "what I think I ought to be able to do." As a promoter of racial harmony, Harris felt segregation limited the number of experiences people could have. Although a lawyer, she was "suspicious of those who believe that the protector of minorities is in the courts," and she realized that it took "a combination of action—the enactment of legislation and the courts—to protect the rights of minorities" in the United States. Believing that social change could be accomplished through corporations, Harris consequently joined the board of directors of several major corporations including Chase Manhattan Bank, Scott Paper Company, and IBM, and she served as a trustee of the Twentieth Century Fund.

Robert Hayden

Poet
Born August 4, 1913, Detroit, Michigan
Died February 25, 1980, Ann Arbor, Michigan

"I can't imagine any poet worth his salt today not being aware of social evils.... But I feel I have the right to deal with these matters in my own way."

Robert Hayden was the first African American to be appointed consultant in poetry to the Library of Congress, a post equivalent to poet laureate (not until six years after Hayden's death did the United States formally introduce the title "poet laureate").

Hayden wrote beautifully crafted poems in the modernist style, often choosing subjects from black history as his theme. After attracting little notice for many years, he came to prominence in the 1960s, and by the 1970s his work was widely known. However, it was not universally praised. Black nationalists regarded Hayden as a traitor because he declared himself an American poet, rather than a black poet, and because he chose to write in a "white" style. Hayden would not change his approach to please his critics. Although deeply concerned about social issues, he did not believe that black literature should be written solely for an African American audience or that its main purpose should be propaganda.

Faced difficult family circumstances

Robert Hayden had an unhappy and disturbed childhood, largely because of the conflict between his mother and his foster parents. Hayden was the son of Asa and Ruth Sheffey, who named him Asa Bundy Sheffey, but his parents divorced when he was a baby, and he was taken in by William and Sue Hayden, who renamed him Robert Earl Hayden.

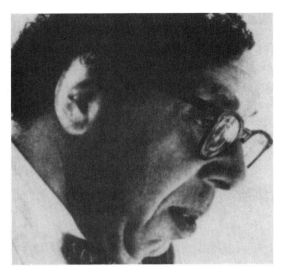

Robert Hayden

The Haydens lived in a grim, low-income district of Detroit nicknamed Paradise Valley. There, Hayden grew up in an atmosphere of constant strife, for his foster parents quarreled frequently, sometimes taking out their frustrations on him. The situation was made more difficult when Hayden's mother came to live next door. Since she and Hayden's foster mother disliked each other and since both were competing for Hayden's affections, life was very complicated for the growing boy, who was constantly challenged by divided loyalties.

Another problem was Hayden's eyesight, which often prevented him joining in games with other children. Feeling isolated, he turned to books for companionship, though he had to hold them close to his face in order to read them. Hayden's sight improved slightly as he grew older so it did not inhibit his schoolwork. On graduating from Detroit Northern High School in 1932, he won a scholarship to Detroit City College (now Wayne State University), where he studied Spanish and English.

Like most poets, Hayden started writing young, and at college he had the chance to show some of his poetry to the celebrated author Langston Hughes. Hughes was not impressed. Nevertheless, Hayden continued to write, and after earning his B.A. in 1936 he joined the Federal Writers' Project in Detroit, where he researched local black folklore and history. He also took a part-time job as theater and music critic for the *Michigan Chronicle,* a black weekly newspaper, and in 1940 the paper's editor published Hayden's first book of poems, *Heart-Shape in the Dust.* The book was very much a first effort, and the poems were not remarkable, but they exhibited great pride in the African American heritage.

The year 1940 saw Hayden's marriage to musician Erma Morris, who supported them both by teaching school while Hayden studied for his M.A. at the University of Michigan. Hayden studied under the poet W. H. Auden, who was a visiting professor at Michigan and had a lasting influence on Hayden's style. "He stimulated us to learn more about poetry and even to search ourselves," wrote Hayden, "and he made us aware of poetry in a way that we never would have been had it not been for him."

While at Michigan, Hayden twice won the university's Hopwood Award for poetry, and after completing his master's degree in 1944 he stayed on for two years as a teaching fellow. Hayden was the first African American to be a member of the university's English Department. However, he was not sure the position would be permanent, so in 1946 he moved south with his wife and young daughter, having accepted a teaching position at Fisk University, the black university in Nashville, Tennessee. Hayden remained at Fisk for the next twenty-three years.

First black poet to be consultant at Library of Congress

Hayden's teaching took up much of his time and energy, and in the late 1940s and 1950s he produced only two slim volumes of poetry, *The Lion and the Archer* (1948) and *Figure of Time* (1955). Yet this period represented an important phase in Hayden's development. Not only did he perfect his style, but these were the years when he wrote most of his black history poems, which were published in periodicals and in the classic anthology *The Poetry of the Negro* (1949).

Hayden's three major history poems are "Middle Passage," "Runagate Runagate," and "Frederick Douglass." By far the best known is "Middle Passage," a long narrative poem about the slave ships sailing between Africa and America. "Runagate, Runagate" is a dramatic poem about Harriet Tubman, heroine of the Underground Railroad, while "Frederick Douglass" is an unrhymed sonnet.

Although Hayden's work was admired by a small coterie of fellow poets, it attracted little attention until the publication of *A Ballad of Remembrance* (1962), which won the Grand Prize for Poetry at the first World Festival of Negro Arts in Senegal in 1966. Suddenly a great many people were interested in Hayden's poetry, and a revised version of the *Ballad*, with thirteen additional poems, was published in 1966 as *Selected Poems*. The book was arranged by subject matter, beginning with poems on black history (including "Middle Passage") and then moving on to other themes, some of which had a religious slant. Hayden had been a member of the Bahá'i faith since 1943.

With the civil rights movement at its peak, white as well as black Americans were eager to read the work of black poets, and Hayden quickly gained many admirers. But his broad appeal was the very thing that brought him criticism from the more nationalist black intellectuals, who believed that black poets should use poetry to arouse a black audience to action. To such critics Hayden replied: "There's a tendency today—more than a tendency, it's almost a conspiracy—to delimit poets, to restrict them to the political.… I can't imagine any poet worth his salt today not being aware of social evils.… But I feel I have the right to deal with these matters in my own way."

In 1969 Hayden accepted the position of professor of English at the University of Michigan, where he remained until his death in 1980. During these years he published four more volumes of very fine poetry, including *Words in the Mourning Time* (1970) and *American Journal* (1978), both of which were nominated for the National Book Award. Honors were heaped upon Hayden in his latter years, and from 1976 to 1978 he made history as the first African American to serve as consultant in poetry to the Library of Congress.

By the end of his life, Hayden had clearly proved that a person could be both a black poet and an American poet. Although he chose to write in a modernist style, his verses celebrated the Afro-American heritage and represented a moving record of black suffering and survival. As an article in *Nation* pointed out, Hayden was "an American poet, deeply engaged by the topography of American myth in his efforts to illuminate the American black experience."

Dorothy Height

President of National Council of Negro
  Women
Born March 24, 1912, Richmond, Virginia

"White power in the system in which we live is a reality.... We have to see that we have been treating the symptoms instead of the causes. I think this does call for the more direct approach to the societal conditions."

As the president of the National Council of Negro Women since 1957, Dorothy Height has helped the council address global issues that affect women. She also served as president of Delta Sigma Theta sorority for nine years, was a member of numerous national committees involving women's issues, won countless service awards, and traveled extensively to promote women's issues.

Attended university on $1,000 scholarship

Height was born on March 24, 1919, in Richmond, Virginia, to James and Fannie Height. Four years later the family moved to Rankin, a small mining town in Pennsylvania. Height attended Rankin High School, and after graduating applied to Barnard College in New York City. The college told her they already had two black students and she would have to wait to be admitted. She decided to attend New York University instead, using $1,000 scholarship she won from an Elks Fraternal Society's national oratorical contest. While in New York she lived with her sister and supported herself by working at odd jobs. After three years she completed her undergraduate work and the next year started working on her master's degree in educational psychology. She finished her course in 1933.

Height took a practice teaching position at Brownsville Community Center in Brooklyn. After the United Christian Youth Movement was founded in 1935, Height became an active member and quickly become one of its leaders. She traveled across the United States and Europe as a member. In 1937 she represented the organization at the International Church Youth Conference in Oxford, England, and served as a youth delegate at the World Conference of Christian Youth in Amsterdam, Holland. In 1938 Height became a representative for Harlem Youth Council and became one of ten American youths to help Eleanor Roosevelt plan the World Youth Congress that year at Vassar College in Poughkeepsie, New York. Later that year Height took a position with the YWCA. She realized she could put her skills to better use in an organization that included all races and was international in its approach. She moved to Harlem for her new job as assistant director of the Emma Ranson House, a shelter for black women.

Height soon became an advocate for the large number of black women working under deplorable conditions in domestic service jobs. In 1938 she testified before the New York City Council about the practice of young black girls bargaining with passing motorists for a day's housework at poor wages. She still maintains the fight for better wages for domestic workers and urges them to organize into unions.

While working for the YWCA, Height met Mary McLeod Bethune, president and founder of the National Council of Negro Women. She was so impressed with Bethune that she quickly joined the organization and attended all key functions.

Became more militant during civil rights era

In 1939 Height became executive secretary of the YWCA Phillis Wheatley Home in Washington, D.C. She also became a member of the Delta Sigma Theta sorority. At an executive committee meeting in June 1940, Height suggested that the sorority adopt a national job analysis program that would look at the reasons why black women were excluded from jobs that were open to other women. The program would also increase the number of positions for black women on jobs already accessible to other women and improved conditions under which many unskilled laborers were forced to work.

Height was elected vice-president of Delta Sigma Theta in 1944 and three years later became its national president. Paula Giddings, who wrote a history of the organization, said, "Neither the direction nor the substance of the initiatives changed under [her] leadership, but the breadth and interest in them did." One of her priorities was to focus the sorority on the relationship between black women in America and in Third World countries. In 1952 Height was invited by the World YWCA to teach for four months at the Delhi School of Social Work in India. When she returned, she relayed the dreadful conditions of women in India and convinced her sorority to establish a scholarship for two Hindu women.

After participating in Haiti's bicentennial celebration in 1950, Height organized the sororities first international chapter. She also established a Haitian relief fund, which was instrumental in helping those left homeless by Hurricane Hazel in 1954. Height introduced the sorority board to members of the United Nation's Department of Information and the Political and Economic Committee on the Rights of Women.

Dorothy Height

When her term as sorority head ended, Height became president of the National Council of Negro Women in 1957. The NCNW is an umbrella group for local and national women's organizations. The following year New York governor Nelson Rockefeller appointed her to the state Social Welfare Board. In 1960 the Committee on Correspondence sent Height to study women's organizations in five African countries. With this experience, Height became a consultant to the secretary of state.

During the early years of the civil rights movement, Height was known as a moderate. She did not support the call for black power as a means to attain civil rights. But by 1972 she altered her stance: "White power in the system in which we live is a reality.... We have to see that we have been treating the symptoms instead of causes. I think this does call for the more direct approach to societal conditions."

This change in attitude was evident in her activities in the council and the YWCA. Height was able to build financial and administrative capabilities that positioned the NCNW to become eligible for large foundation grants, a first in the history of black women's organizations.

Height managed to convince the Ford Foundation to grant the council $300,000 to begin Operation Woman Power, a project to help women start their own businesses and provide funds for vocational training. As well, the U.S. Department of Health, Education, and Welfare supplied the means for a job training program for teenagers. The council spent time in areas where community needs were not being addressed: it went to rural areas and bought seed and feed for poverty-stricken farmers and started food cooperatives.

Leads National Council of Negro Women

For the past thirty years the council has been a catalyst for bringing about social change. Their focus is currently on the revival of black family life, with annual celebrations they call Black Family Reunions. These events encourage and renew the concept of the extended black family. Height hopes these reunions will overcome juvenile delinquency, drug use, and unwanted teen pregnancy.

Under Height's leadership the council publishes *Black Woman's Voice* and operates a Women's Center for Education and Career Advancement for minority women in nontraditional careers. It also runs an Information Center for and about black women and the Bethune Museum and Archives for black women's history. It has offices in West and South Africa, working to improve women's conditions in Third World countries. Height has also spoken at length on the responsibilities of the United States, United Nations, and local organizations in pursuit of these improvements.

The council is now a competent umbrella for 240 local groups and 31 national organizations. In different ways each organization has been striving toward the unified goal of equal rights for black women around the world. Through hard work, determination, strong managerial skills, and networking, Height has left an undeniable mark on the organizations she has led.

Jimi Hendrix

Singer, songwriter, guitarist
Born November 27, 1942, Seattle,
 Washington
Died September 18, 1970

T o Jimi Hendrix, the guitar was much more than a musical instrument. It was almost a living being that needed the proper coaxing to perform. Hendrix is arguably the most innovative electric guitarist of all time. Although his career was short-lived and controversial, Hendrix created music that still sounds as fresh and breathtaking today as it did when he took the pop world by storm in the 1960s. He manipulated the guitar to create shrieks and a bullet-spitting rattle, while he used his huge hands to perform reaches and funky chordings. Hendrix had the unique ability to play clean leads and distorted rhythm simultaneously. Many have tried to duplicate his style, but none have ever reached the success of Hendrix.

Quits school
to become a paratrooper

James Marshall Hendrix was born on November 27, 1942, in Seattle, Washington, to James and Lucille Hendrix. He started playing the guitar when he was eleven and within a short time was playing in local clubs. With his father's permission, he quit school when he was sixteen and joined the army a year later as a paratrooper. While in the service, Hendrix met bassist Billy Cox, and the two often jammed together. Hendrix became a big fan of music by blues artists Muddy Waters, Howlin' Wolf, Albert and B.B. King, and Lightnin' Hopkins. He even started sleeping with his guitar because he heard his idols did the same thing.

Hendrix was discharged from the service after he was injured on his twenty-sixth jump. He began concentrating on music and worked as a guitarist for several popular rock and rhythm-and-blues artists including Little Richard, Jackie Wilson, the Isley Brothers, Curtis Knight, Wilson Pickett, King Curtis, and James Brown. By 1962 Hendrix was beginning to incorporate new crowd-pleasing antics into his performance. He sometimes played the guitar with his teeth, behind his back, and between his legs.

In 1964 Hendrix arrived in New York and performed under the name Jimmy James. He fronted his own band called the Blue Flames.

Jimi Hendrix

John Hammond, Jr., a guitarist, heard the group playing in a small club in Greenwich Village called the Cafe Wa and asked Hendrix to join his group. A few weeks later their partnership ended. With his amazing ability, Hendrix constantly upstaged the band. Many other bands, including the Beatles and the Animals, heard this up-and-comer and realized he had enormous potential.

Former Animals bassist, Chas Chandler, convinced Hendrix to head to London, England, with him. The music industry was catching fire at the time, and Chandler told Hendrix he would introduce him to Eric Clapton. While in London, Hendrix formed a new band entitled the Jimi Hendrix Experience, which featured Mitch Mitchell on drums and Noel Redding on guitar. They were managed by Chandler and Michael Jeffrey who convinced the trio to frizz their hair and dress as outlandishly as possible to create a sensation. Their first single, "Hey, Joe," went all the way to number six on the British charts in 1967. They followed that with "Purple Haze," a song that was a tribute to Hendrix's distorted guitar-playing ability.

Burns his guitar on stage

In 1966 Beatle Paul McCartney used his influence to persuade the Monterey Pop Festival to book Hendrix even though his first album had not been released. His performance made him a superstar. Although he was shy offstage, his showmanship floored the audience, and he ended his performance by burning his guitar. The Jimi Hendrix Experience was then booked as the opening act for the Monkees in 1967, but since the styles of the two acts were totally opposite, the partnership was short-lived. But by then it didn't matter. Hendrix's debut album, *Are You Experienced?* was climbing to the top of the record charts. It featured a barrage of hit songs including: "The Wind Cries Mary," "Third Stone From the Sun," "Fire," and "Foxy Lady." *Guitar Player* called it the "most revolutionary debut album in rock guitar history."

Hendrix was a true innovator. He manipulated the guitar's tone and volume controls to make unique effects and became the first to fully realize the vibrato arm's usefulness by creating dive-bombing shrieks and bending full cords. He custom shaped the bar to obtain a three-step variation instead of the stock bar's one step. His rapid-fire flicking of the toggle switch produced a machine-gun effect, while his hands allowed for funky recordings.

Unlike most guitarists, Hendrix limited his use of special electronic effects. His setup included a Univibe (to stimulate a rotating speaker), a wah-wah, and a fuzz-box. The key, however, was to channel this through a stack of amplifiers with the volume wide open. Hendrix harnessed the feedback, whereas most could barely control it. How he managed to play clean leads at the same time as distorted rhythm is a mystery.

Jeffrey became sole manager of the Experience in 1968 after Chandler quit. Hendrix was not happy with the arrangement (even twenty years after his death, Hendrix's estate is still a financial nightmare). He also released his second album in 1968, *Axis: Bold as Love*, which contained several memorable tunes like "Little Wing," "If 6 Was 9," and "Castles Made of Sand." Nine months later he produced the double set, *Electric Ladyland*, which featured guest performances by Steve Winwood and Jack Cassidy.

Band breaks up

All three albums went gold and Hendrix's popularity soared. At the same time, he began drinking, smoking dope, popping pills, and sleeping with groupies. The constant pressures on the band caused their breakup in 1969; they played their last show at the Denver Pop Festival on June 29. That same month, they released *Smash Hits*, which featured their first and only Top 20 single, "All Along the Watchtower."

Hendrix resurfaced with the all-black band, Band of Gypsys. He played with his former army buddy, Bill Cox, on bass and Buddy Miles on drums. The group only lasted a few months, but a live performance was captured on the *Band of Gypsys* album. The band headed for the Isle of Wight Festival in England, and Hendrix made his final performance at the Isle of Fehmarn in West Germany on September 6, 1970. Twelve days later Hendrix died after choking on his own vomit caused by barbiturate intoxication.

Although gone, Hendrix's legacy lives on. Guitarists like Robin Trower and Stevie Ray Vaughan have introduced his music to a new generation of listeners. Others, like Randy Hansen's Machine Gun, even try to recreate Hendrix's image and sound. For the most part, however, these acts still fall far short of the original.

Matthew Henson

Co-discoverer of North Pole
Born August 6, 1866, Charles County, Maryland
Died March 9, 1955, New York, New York

"The Commander gave the word, 'We will plant the stars and stripes—at the North Pole!' and it was done.... As in the past, from the beginning of history, wherever the world's work was done by a white man, he had been accompanied by a colored man."

For centuries, explorers braved the Arctic wastes in their eagerness to "stand on top of the world." In 1909, when Commander Robert E. Peary achieved his long-sought goal of becoming the first Arctic explorer to reach the North Pole, he was accompanied by Matthew Henson and four Eskimos. Which of these six men was actually the first to stand at the exact site of the Pole we will never know, though it was very likely Henson. However, Peary claimed that he himself was the first, and when they returned to the United States, he made no attempt to share the glory with Henson or even to acknowledge his contribution. While Peary was showered with honors, Henson struggled to find work.

As a key member of the expedition, Henson endured the same hardships as Peary and faced the same dangers. Yet until quite recently, few people knew anything about him. On the rare occasions when he was mentioned in the accounts, it was usually as "Commander

Peary's negro servant"—as if a black person could not possibly be an explorer. This insult was finally rectified in 1988, some thirty-three years after Henson's death, when his body was moved to Arlington National Cemetery and buried with due honor next to the grave of Robert Peary. The black granite tombstone bears a gold-leaf likeness of Henson and is inscribed with the words "co-discoverer of the North Pole."

The young adventurer

Matthew Alexander Henson was the son of Maryland sharecroppers, Lemuel and Caroline Henson. The accounts of his childhood vary, but it seems that he was orphaned when he was about eight years old and lived for a while with an uncle in Washington. There he went to school and worked as a kitchen helper in a restaurant, where he met a sailor called Baltimore Jack, who thrilled the small boy with tales of the sea.

When Henson was thirteen, he decided that he too would to go to sea, so he walked to the waterfront district of Baltimore and persuaded the captain of a merchant ship to take him on as a cabin boy. For the next six years, Henson sailed the seas, visiting Europe, North Africa, China, and other distant places. The captain taught him to read and write, instructed him in mathematics and the classics, and instilled in him a love of books. It was a sad day for Henson when the captain died, for he lost a father figure as well as an employer.

By the time Henson was nineteen, he was an experienced sailor and could speak several languages. On returning to the United States, he had no difficulty finding work, and over the next two years he took a variety of jobs, ranging from stevedore to coachman. He was working in a hat store in Washington, D.C., when in 1887 he met Robert Peary.

Peary, who was then a lieutenant in the U.S. Navy, had come into the store to buy a helmet to wear on an engineering survey in Nicaragua. While choosing the hat, he happened to mention that he was looking for a personal servant to accompany him on the expedition. By the time Peary left the store, he had engaged one—Matthew Henson. An expedition to Central America was just the type of adventure that appealed to Henson.

The years as explorer

For the next twenty-two years, Henson accompanied Peary on his expeditions, first to Nicaragua and then on seven journeys to the Arctic. On the Nicaraguan trip, he soon proved his worth. Because of the navigation skills he had learned at sea, he was able to chart a course through thick jungle, and he was quick to learn new skills, such as surveying. This type of versatility could make all the difference between life and death to a group of explorers alone in the wild.

Henson again proved invaluable when he accompanied Peary to Greeenland in 1891. He was the only member of the expedition who bothered to learn Eskimo, and he became a skilled hunter and one of the best dog-drivers in the group. From then on, Henson and Peary returned to the Arctic every few years. At first they continued to explore in Greenland, but in 1898 they set out on the first of their three attempts to get to the North Pole. On their second attempt, in 1905–06, they came within about 175 miles of the Pole. Next time they hoped to make it.

Like Peary, Henson was by now a seasoned explorer with a wealth of experience on how to survive even the worst Arctic blizzards. But while Peary was fast becoming a national hero, Henson was so little known that the only work he could get between expeditions was as a janitor or railway porter. Yet Peary relied heavily on Henson. "He must go with me. I cannot make it without him," Peary said before setting out on his final—and successful—attempt to reach the Pole in 1908.

Henson was a newlywed when he left for the Arctic in 1908, having recently married Lucy Ross, a New York bank clerk. As usual, he was one of the most experienced members of the expedition, though this group included four other Americans, a Newfoundland sea captain, and eighteen Eskimos. (The Eskimos had agreed to take part largely because of

Matthew Henson

their affection for Henson. They called him *Maye-Paluq,* "the kind one.") Peary divided his men into seven teams, six of which were support teams whose role was to drop supplies at certain points along the way and then turn back. The remaining team, which was to make the last dash to the Pole, consisted of Peary, Henson, and four Eskimos: Ootah, Egingwah, Seegloo, and Ooqueah.

On April 6, 1909, Henson was out in front, breaking the trail, when he reached the spot he thought was the Pole. "I think I am the first man to sit on top of the world," he said when Peary caught up with him. Peary, annoyed at not being first, took some readings and decided that the Pole was three miles farther north. He then went the three extra miles, taking two of the Eskimos with him. But he would not shake hands when Henson tried to congratulate him, and he barely spoke to Henson on the return trip. Back home, he dropped Henson altogether. Why he so abruptly ended their long-standing friendship is not clear. It may have been because Henson had in fact reached the Pole first, or possibly Peary was worried that his readings were inaccurate and they had all failed to reach the Pole, as a rival explorer tried to claim when the party returned home.

Despite these problems, Peary was hailed as a hero and promoted to rear admiral. And Henson? He found a job as a parking attendant. He could not even give lectures about his experiences, because Peary had made him promise not to do so. Henson kept this promise until he was so desperate for money that he had to break it. Meanwhile, members of the black community were aware of the neglect

Henson was suffering, and in 1913 they pressured President William Taft to find him a position with the U.S. Customs House in New York City. Henson worked there as a messenger and clerk until his retirement in 1936.

Toward the end of his life, Henson did at last receive some recognition. In 1937 he was admitted to the Explorers Club, and in 1950 and 1954 he was honored at White House ceremonies. This was partly the result of the book *Dark Companion* (1947), which he wrote with Bradley Robinson and which attracted more public notice than his earlier book, *A Negro Explorer at the North Pole* (1912).

Nevertheless, it was not until the 1980s that there was full public acknowledgement of Henson's role, largely as a result of petitioning by Dr. S. Allen Counter, a promoter of black historical figures. On April 6, 1988, exactly seventy-nine years after Henson had reached the North Pole, his body was moved to Arlington National Cemetery, where it was given a hero's burial. At the ceremony, Dr. Counter stated, "Matthew Henson, we give you the long overdue recognition you deserve. We lay you to rest to right a tragic wrong, to correct a shameful record."

Aileen Hernandez

Feminist, labor relations specialist
Born May 23, 1926, Brooklyn, New York

"As a black woman, I particularly think that it is important to be involved in women's liberation, largely because black women are desperately needed in the total civil rights movement."

Recognized for her influence in the areas of labor relations, women's rights, and equal-opportunity employment, Aileen Hernandez has represented the U.S. State Department as a specialist in labor education; served as the only woman on the Equal Employment Opportunity Commission; and was president of the National Organization of Women. Hernandez has also organized her own public relations and management firm assisting government, private businesses, labor, and other organizations that use minority groups and women.

Training in equality began early

Hernandez was born in Brooklyn, New York, on May 23, 1926, to Charles and Ethel Clark. Charles worked for an art supply house, and Ethel worked in the garment industry during the Depression. Hernandez was the middle of three children and the only daughter. The Clarks believed that each child should be treated equally, so they all learned to cook, sew, and care for their personal belongings. Hernandez graduated from Bay Ridge High School in 1943 as class salutatorian. She received a scholarship at Howard University in Washington, D.C., majoring in political science and sociology, and also volunteered for the National Association for the Advancement of Colored People, wrote a column for the *Washington Tribune* dealing with university activities, and during her junior and senior years edited the *Hilltop*, the student newspaper.

After graduating, Hernandez worked as a research assistant in the political science department at Howard University. From 1947 to

1959 she attended several universities, including the University of Oslo, where she studied comparative government and participated in the International Student Exchange Program; New York University, where she took public administration classes; the University of California at Los Angeles, where she studied adult and nursery education; and the University of Southern California. Hernandez received a master's degree in government from Los Angeles State College in 1959. That same year she married an African American garment cutter from Los Angeles, though she divorced him two years later.

During the 1950s Hernandez worked for the International Ladies Garment Workers Union (ILGWU). This group wanted to expand educational programs for its members by providing qualified staff to conduct classes on a variety of subjects including languages, fine arts, and government. Hernandez was director of public relations and education at the West Coast office in Los Angeles from 1951 to 1961.

Appointed to civil rights commission

Representing the State Department in 1960 as a specialist in labor education, Hernandez toured several South American countries—including Venezuela, Colombia, Chile, Peru, Argentina, and Uruguay to discuss American trade unions, minority groups, the status of women, and the American political system.

The next year she left ILGWU to serve as campaign coordinator for Democrat Alan Cranston, who was running for state comptroller. After he was elected, Hernandez was appointed assistant chief of the California Fair Employment Practice Commission (FEPC). She supervised a staff of fifty, covering activities in the San Francisco, Los Angeles, Fresno, and San Diego field offices. She also developed a technical advisory committee that studied the effects of industrial testing in hiring minority group members. Due to her work with ILGWU, she was named "Woman of the Year" by the Community Relations Conference of Southern California.

As her reputation grew, President Lyndon B. Johnson appointed her to the Equal Employment Opportunity Commission (EEOC). The commission was charged under the 1964 Civil Rights Act with enforcing federal laws that prohibit employment discrimination because of race, color, religion, national origin, and sex. Hernandez was the only woman on this five-member commission. She was instrumental in ending the airlines' policy to terminate women flight attendants if they married, but after eighteen months Hernandez resigned her position, believing that the EEOC lacked true enforcement powers to implement its policies.

In 1966 she started Hernandez and Associates, a public relations and management firm. She advised private business, government, labor, and other organizations on programs that use minority groups and women.

Succeeded Betty Friedan as NOW president

A year later Hernandez was appointed western vice-president with the National Organization of Women (NOW). In 1971 she became president, succeeding Betty Friedan,

NOW's founder and first president, at a time when NOW and the women's liberation movement were viewed by black women as unwanted competition. Many considered NOW to be an elitist white women's organization. However, Hernandez perceived NOW as a natural extension of the civil rights movement and stated: "As a black woman I particularly think that it is important to be involved in women's liberation, largely because black women are desperately needed in the total civil rights movement. Until women, black as well as others, gain a sense of their own identity and feel they have a real choice in the society, nothing is going to happen in civil rights. It's not going to happen for blacks, it's not going to happen for women."

Other local and national organizations have involved Hernandez. She is or has been a member of the board of directors of the National Committee Against Discrimination in Housing, the executive committee of Common Cause, the steering committee of the National Urban Coalition, the task force on employment of women of the Twentieth Century Fund, American Civil Liberties Union, National Association for the Advancement of Colored People, Industrial Relations Research Association, American Academy of Political and Social Sciences, board of trustees for Working Assets Money Fund, board of overseers for Civil Justice, RAND Corporation, adviser for the National Institute for Women of Color, treasurer of Eleanor R. Spikes Memorial Fund, cofounder and member of Black Women Organized for Action, and the National Hook-up of Black Women.

Aileen Hernandez

Hernandez has received many awards and honors, including the Bay Area Alumni Club's Distinguished Post Graduate Achievement Award, Charter Day Alumni Post Graduate Achievement in Labor and Public Services Award, and the Ten Most Outstanding Women in the Bay Area Award. She also received a Doctorate of Humane Letters from Southern Vermont College; Equal Rights Advocate Award; Friends of the Commission on the Status of Women Award; and the San Francisco League of Women Voters Award.

Hernandez still lectures on civil rights, equal employment opportunities, trade unionism, and similar issues. Her public relations firm, located in San Francisco, has several major clients, including United Airlines, Standard Oil, United Parcel Service, National Alliance of Businessmen, University of California, and the California cities of Richmond, Berkeley, and Los Angeles.

Anita Hill

Lawyer and social activist
Born July 30, 1956, Morris, Oklahoma

"I am hopeful that others who have suffered sexual harassment will not be discouraged, but instead will find the strength to speak out about this serious problem."

In October 1991, Anita Hill's life was changed forever. The quiet, reserved law professor suddenly found herself the focus of national attention, required to appear before the Senate Judiciary Committee during its televised hearings. The committee had the task of deciding whether to recommend that Judge Clarence Thomas be appointed a justice of the U.S. Supreme Court. According to Hill, he had sexually harassed her some years earlier.

Anita Hill

If true, this could make him unsuitable for such an important position.

The hearings were watched by millions of viewers across the world, for this was the stuff of high drama. It was a terrible ordeal for Hill as she sat in the glare of the spotlight, submitting to the committee's grilling. Yet she felt it was her duty to speak out, partly to help other women. An important result of the hearings was to raise the level of public awareness of sexual harassment and of the problems it involved. For Hill, the main result was that she had become a public figure. Her life would never be quite the same.

The young lawyer

Anita Hill's childhood on her parent's farm near the small town of Morris, Oklahoma, set the standards that would guide her as an adult. She was the thirteenth and youngest child of Albert and Irma Hill and was brought up to be dutiful and diligent. On Sundays, the family went to the Lone Pine Baptist Church, and on weekdays the children helped with the farm chores and attended school.

Hill was an exceptionally good student, and she graduated as valedictorian and National Honor Society student from her integrated public school. After high school, she gained a degree in psychology at Oklahoma State University and then a degree in law from Yale University. Her first position after qualifying as a lawyer was with the Washington law firm of Ward, Harkrader, and Ross. But after about a year, she left to become personal assistant to Clarence Thomas, who had just been made assistant secretary of civil rights at the Department of Education.

In her testimony to the Senate committee, Hill said that Thomas started harassing her soon after she began working for him in 1981. He pestered her for dates, she said, and when she refused to go out with him he made dirty remarks to her and described pornographic movies he had seen. Apparently, all this stopped when Thomas began to date someone else, so Hill felt safe following him to a better job, when he was made chairman of the Equal Employment Opportunity Commission (EEOC) in 1982. But soon he started harassing her again, and this so upset Hill that she was hospitalized with stress-related stomach problems.

Unable to stand it any longer, Hill resigned from the EEOC, and in 1983 became a civil rights professor at Oral Roberts University in Tulsa, Oklahoma. This conservative, religious school suited Hill well, and she likely would have remained there had not its law school been moved to Virginia in 1986. Since Hill wanted to stay near her family, she moved to the University of Oklahoma, where she became a professor specializing in contract law. After only four years, she was given tenured status, and it looked as if she had a quiet academic career ahead of her. But then came President George Bush's nomination of Judge Clarence Thomas to be the new Supreme Court justice.

The Senate committee hearings

When the Senate Judiciary Committee began its deliberations to decide whether the Senate should confirm or reject Thomas's nomination, Anita Hill kept silent. She had not filed a complaint against Thomas ten years before, and she did not want to do so now. But she had told her friends about the harassment, and the Senate committee heard rumors about this. As a result, she was asked if she would appear before the committee to answer questions on the matter.

At first Hill said no, but then she agreed provided she could remain anonymous. This was impossible, she was told, because Thomas would have to be informed of any accusations made against him. After much soul searching, Hill agreed to appear, and she wrote a personal statement for the committee to study. Meanwhile, Thomas issued a sworn statement forcefully denying Hill's allegations. He said that all he had done was ask her for a few dates.

As the drama unfolded, Thomas made a series of emotional statements, complaining that he was under attack simply because he was black and that the hearings were a "high-tech lynching." Meanwhile, Hill was attacked by his supporters. She was accused of making up the whole thing and of acting out of jealousy because Thomas was not attentive enough. She was even accused of being part of a Democratic plot to discredit Thomas.

Many African Americans were not concerned so much about whether Thomas had or had not harassed Hill. What offended them was that Hill had violated the code that blacks should not criticize each other in front of whites. Nevertheless, Hill had many supporters, both black and white, who believed she was telling the truth and felt that she had been the victim of sexism—and that in fact she still was being victimized because of the aggressive grilling by the committee and the assault on her character.

In the end, the all-white, all-male Senate committee decided in favor of Thomas, and he was duly sworn in as a Supreme Court justice. But the attacks against Hill did not end. Some people called for action against her; some branded her a liar. In 1993 journalist David Brock published a book called *The Real Anita Hill,* which claimed to produce evidence that she had lied to the Senate committee.

Meanwhile, Hill had quietly gone back to teaching. She did not capitalize on her celebrity by writing a book or by selling her story as a television movie. Nor did she take the opportunity to make a fortune on the lecture circuit. On the rare occasions when she has agreed to speak, it has generally been for no fee, and she has spoken not about herself but about the larger issue of sexual harassment .

It is in this area that the most important results of the Hill-Thomas controversy can be seen, for recently many more women have followed Anita Hill's example and dared to go public with charges of abuse. In addition, the sight of a male Senate committee judging a woman's complaints of sexual harassment caused more women to run for all levels of public office in the 1992 elections. Although Anita Hill and her supporters may have lost the battle in the Senate hearings, they undoubtedly made a major advance in the war against sexism.

Chester Himes

Writer
Born July 29, 1909, Jefferson City, Missouri
Died November 12, 1984, Moraira, Spain

"Himes has produced … the most complete and perfect statement of the nature of native American racism to be found in American literature." —Stephen F. Milliken

T he author of more than twenty books, Chester Himes wrote a wide range of works, including novels, crime thrillers, satire, autobiographies, and short stories. All his books deal with racism in one way or another, and all are angry, powerful statements about injustice and oppression. Even Himes's detective novels smoulder with rage and violence.

Himes's detective stories were his only works that sold well during his lifetime. His first five books—all strong protest novels—attracted little notice and brought in very little income. Today, the protest novels are considered Himes's best works. They have been compared to such classics of African American literature as Richard Wright's *Native Son.*

"Grew into manhood" in the penitentiary

Chester Himes had a difficult childhood, partly because of the constant friction between his light-skinned mother and dark-skinned father. His mother, Estelle (Bomar) Himes, felt she was superior because of her lighter color. Himes's father, Joseph Himes, seemed also to consider whites superior, and this angered Himes, for he greatly admired his father.

Himes had two older brothers, one of whom was blinded in an accident during his teenage years. In the hope of finding good medical attention for the boy, the family frequently moved to a new city. Himes lived in six different cities during his childhood, the last being Cleveland, Ohio, where his parents bought a house when he was fifteen.

Two years later, in 1926, Himes graduated from Glenville High School in Cleveland and took a vacation job as a busboy at a local hotel. After only two days he fell down an elevator shaft and hurt his back. He was still wearing a brace when, that autumn, he enrolled at Ohio State University.

Although Himes's back was to trouble him for the rest of his life, he was soon fit enough to enter wholeheartedly into university life—which he did with a vengeance. His unsettled childhood, the constant bickering at home, and the racism he encountered at Ohio State all combined to make him an exceptionally wild student, and he was expelled in 1927, after leading a romp through Cleveland's red-light district.

Himes then drifted into a life of crime in Cleveland, where he broke into a house, held up the owners at gunpoint, and robbed them of goods worth $53,000. Arrested soon afterwards, he was sentenced to twenty years hard labor. He served seven years of this sentence before being let out on parole. "I grew to manhood in the Ohio State Pentitentiary," Hines later wrote. "I was nineteen years when I went in and twenty-six years old when I came out.... I learned all of the behavior patterns necessary for survival, or I wouldn't have survived."

Ohio State Pentitentiary was a violent and desperate place. During Himes's years there he witnessed beatings, killings, and prison riots. In 1930 there was a terrifying fire in which more than 300 prisoners were burned to death in their cells. All these events were later described in Hines's fiction.

Wrote novels now regarded as classics

Himes began his writing career while he was in prison. His first works were short stories, which were published in black weekly newspapers, and in 1934 he had two stories accepted by *Esquire* magazine. Both of these stories were based on Himes's prison experiences—one of them was about the fire—and both appeared signed with his name and prison identification number.

After Himes was paroled in 1936 he took part-time jobs as a waiter and bellhop, which left him time to continue with his writing. In 1937 he married his long-standing girlfriend, Jean Johnson, and soon afterwards began work with the Federal Writers' Project. A few years later they moved to California, where Himes

Chester Himes

wrote his first novel while working in ship-yards and for aircraft companies in Los Ange-les and San Francisco.

Himes had hoped that by moving to the West Coast he would leave racism behind, but he found it as strong there as anywhere else. His anger at West Coast attitudes surged through his first novel, *If He Hollers, Let Him Go* (1945). The story covers five tense days in the life of Bob Jones, a black foreman in a Los Angeles shipyard. Jones is demoted when he trades insult for insult with a white woman employee, and when the woman later tries to seduce him he almost gets killed by the white shipyard workers.

Himes's second novel, *The Lonely Cru-sade* (1947), had a similar plot and theme, whereas his next three novels were largely autobiographical. *Cast the First Stone* (1952) was based on Himes's prison experiences; *The Third Generation* (1954) was based on his early years as a member of a family whose light-skinned mother despised blacks; and *The Primitive* (1955) was based on an interracial love affair Himes had after separating from his wife.

Today, these five novels are considered classics of black American protest literature, especially *Cast the First Stone,* which is viewed as one of the world's major prison novels. But the books attracted little attention at the time, and very few copies were sold. To support himself, Himes had to rely on laboring jobs—his prison record made it difficult to find other work. In 1953 he decided he could stand America no longer, and he moved to Europe, where he lived at first in France and then in Spain. During these years he had sev-eral long-term relationships with white women, and in the 1960s he married an Engish woman, Lesley Packard.

Wrote popular—and prize-winning—detective novels

Himes was very short of money during his first years in France, but at least he was recog-nized as a writer; his first two novels had been translated into French and received good re-views. Among those who admired Himes's work was publisher Marcel Duhamel, and in 1956 Duhamel asked Himes to write a detec-tive novel for the popular crime series, La Série Noire. Himes did not particularly want to do so—he was a serious novelist, not a thriller writer—but he agreed because he so desperately needed the money.

Himes took only three weeks to write the story, which was then translated into French and published in 1957 as *La Reine des Pommes.* (The book has since been published in English as *A Rage in Harlem.*) It is a fast-paced action story about two black detectives, Coffin Ed Johnson and Grave Digger Jones, who track down criminals in Harlem and kill some of them while doing so. Like all Himes's detective novels, this one contains a great deal of violence, but it proved extremely popular and won the Grand Prix Policier—France's top prize for crime fiction.

During the next ten years Himes wrote eight more thrillers about Johnson and Jones, including *The Heat's On* (1960) and *Cotton Comes to Harlem* (1964), which were made into movies. As before, Himes wrote the thrill-ers very quickly, completing each book in about three weeks. By contrast, his serious novels could take him a year or more, and then he might have to wait several more years before he could get them accepted by a publisher. In 1961 Himes at last found a publisher for his satiric novel *Pinktoes,* which he had completed four years earlier.

Himes's major works during his final years were his two volumes of autobiography, *The Quality of Hurt* (1972) and *My Life of Absurdity* (1977). He also brought out a book of short stories, *Black on Black* (1973). Whatever his subject and whatever type of book he was writing, Himes never strayed far from his main theme—the perniciousness of racism and the misery it causes. As literary critic Stephen F. Milliken so aptly said, "Himes has produced ... the most complete and perfect statement of the nature of native American racism to be found in American literature, and one of the most profound statements about the nature of social oppression, and the rage and fear it generates in individuals, in all of modern literature."

Gregory Hines

Dancer, actor
Born February 14, 1946,
    New York, New York

I n an age in which tap dancing is almost obsolete, Tony Award-winning Gregory Hines is determined to bring this art form back from the brink of extinction. Trained in tap before he was three years old, Hines has used his unique dance steps to become of the country's most popular black entertainers. He

has starred in comedies, dramas, plays, and has even produced his own album.

Cried his way into tap-dancing class

Hines was born on February 14, 1946, in New York City and raised in middle-class, integrated Washington Heights. For many years his family had been involved with show business. His grandmother, Ora Hines, was a dancer at the Cotton Club in Harlem. His father, Maurice, Sr., played drums for several rock and roll bands, including the Flamingoes.

When his parents learned that free tap lessons were available for children, they enrolled their older son, Maurice, Jr. Gregory Hines, at two-and-half-years old, was too young for the classes, but he cried so much when Maurice was being dropped off at class that the teacher decided to let him attend.

In 1952 the boys met Henry LeTang, a well-known tap dancing teacher and choreographer, who taught them some new dance routines. They began performing at several nightclubs under the name of the Hines Kids. While performing, Hines met tap greats like Sandman Sims and Teddy Hale, who further developed him as a dancer.

Danced on Broadway

Maurice, Sr., joined his sons' act as a drummer in 1963, and they became known as Hines, Hines, and Dad. They appeared on television shows including "The Tonight Show" and "The Ed Sullivan Show." The group also toured internationally, playing in the Palladium and Olympia theaters in London, England. Despite their success, tap dancing was

Gregory Hines

falling out of style, and by the late 1960s the trio became a musical-comedic lounge act, with Maurice as straight man and Hines as comedian.

In 1968 Hines married Patricia Panella, but they separated five years later. His family act also ended in 1968. Hines moved to Venice, California, where he began experimenting with sex, drugs, and rock and roll. He quit dancing and started a jazz band called Severance. He played the guitar and began wearing a left earring, which would later become his signature. He also joined a single fathers' group and a men's sensitivity group. The support from these groups, as well as from his daughter Daria, helped him to get his life in perspective.

While in California, Hines met Pamela Koslow, a divorced guidance counselor, and they soon became lovers. In 1977, his band broke up, and his brother told him there was work for tap dancers in New York. He re-turned to the city with Koslow and divorced his first wife. In 1978 the Hines brothers reunited in the Broadway show "Eubie." Hines did so well in the show that he was nominated for a Tony Award for best featured actor. He was nominated for another Tony in 1980 after appearing in the broadway show "Comin' Uptown." He appeared on Broadway in 1981 in "Sophisticated Ladies." Frank Rich in the *New York Times* wrote, "This man is human lighting and he just can't be contained." Hines received his third Tony nomination for the play.

Fell in love with movie acting

He married Koslow in 1981 and made his first movie appearance. He portrayed a medical examiner in *Wolfen* and a Roman slave in Mel Brooks's *History of the World, Part I.* Hines fell in love with acting and began seeking more roles. He received parts in *Deal of the Century* in 1983 and a year later appeared in *The Muppets Take Manhattan.*

When he heard producer Robert Evans was casting a major film about the Cotton Club, Hines aggressively called Evans every day and went to his house to tell him how good he was for the starring role. Eventually he landed the role of Sandman Williams, an upwardly mobile Cotton Club dancer. When director Francis Ford Coppola heard about the history of fights between Hines and his brother Maurice, he cast Maurice as Hines's film brother. The two played tap dancing brothers who split up, but get back together again. The Hines brothers have never overcome their differences and only occasionally speak to each other. When the movie was released in 1984 it received poor reviews, but most critics said Hines did an excellent job.

His role in *The Cotton Club* and a now-classic performance on the television show "Saturday Night Live" boosted his popularity. Audiences were thrilled with his fast-paced and jazz-tap routines, many of which featured improvisation that went beyond traditional tap dancing. His dance skills were put to the test against Soviet ballet star Mikhail Baryshnikov in the movie *White Nights*. Hines excelled, matching the classically trained Baryshnikov step for step in a film that had good box office numbers, despite a somewhat uninspired plot.

Danced with other black all-stars of tap

In 1986 Hines co-starred with Billy Crystal in the action-comedy film *Running Scared*. The film was a hit and solidified Hines's position as a emerging star. In 1987 he teamed up with Luther Vandross to release a record. A duet with Vandross, the single hit number one on the black music charts. He followed it with an album titled *Gregory Hines* a year later. He also co-starred with Willem Dafoe in *Off Limits* in 1988. Previously Hines had only played likable, good guy roles, but in this movie he played a tough detective.

In 1988 Hines became the leading man in *Tap*, playing opposite his idol, Sammy Davis, Jr., and other black all-stars of tap including Jimmy Slyde, Harold Nicholas, Bunny Briggs, and Sandman Sims. The film documented the influence black Americans have had on tap dancing.

In 1991 Hines appeared in *Eve of Destruction*, playing a counterterrorism expert

assigned to track a female android gone berserk. He also starred in the critically well received big-budget drama *A Rage in Harlem*.

Earned his first Tony Award

Hines landed the lead role in the 1992 Broadway musical "Jelly's Last Jam." He plays Jelly Roll Morton, a light-skinned Creole musician who rejects his black heritage. Although he found the role taxing, critics have called his performance moving and powerful. He received his first Tony Award for this play.

Since tap dancing is a taxing profession, many have wondered when Hines's performances will begin to deteriorate. He has kept in peak form by exercising regularly and working on new steps. Many of the tap dancers of old see him as the one who will introduce tap to a new generation.

Billie Holiday

Singer
Born April 7, 1915, Baltimore, Maryland
Died July 17, 1959, New York, New York

"I don't think I'm singing. I feel like I'm playing a horn.... What comes out is what I feel. I hate straight singing. I have to change a tune to my own way of doing it."

B illie Holiday was one of the earliest and probably the greatest of all jazz singers, yet her life was dogged by tragedy and her career cut drastically short. A superb artist, she seemed to be at one with the music, phrasing without effort and using her warm, sensual voice like a finely played instrument. "She could swing like a trumpet player," said one of her colleagues.

Holiday made music come alive with personal meaning, especially when singing of heartbreak and loneliness. She once said, "If you find a tune that's got something to do with you, you just feel it; and when you sing it, other people feel it too."

Earned her living in a brothel

At her birth Holiday was named Eleanora Fagan, given her mother's surname because her parents were not married. Although they did marry three years later, the child saw little of her father, Clarence Holiday, for the marriage soon broke up.

Holiday's mother worked as a domestic, and Holiday earned what she could by running errands and scrubbing floors in a local brothel. It was there she first heard the music

Billie Holiday

of the popular blues singer Bessie Smith, and before long young Billie decided that she, too, would be a famous singer one day.

When she was ten, Holiday was raped by a neighbor, blamed for the incident, and sent to a reformatory—sentenced to stay there until twenty-one. However, two years later, as punishment for some small offense, she was locked in a room with the body of a child who had been killed in an accident. When her mother heard of this, she created such a fuss that she managed to get her daughter released.

Holiday joined her mother in Harlem, but their rented rooms were in a brothel, so within a year Holiday became a prostitute. When she refused to obey the demands of a customer, the customer had her arrested for prostitution. In an effort to prevent her from being sent back to the reformatory, her mother told the judge that Holiday was eighteen. So the judge sent the thirteen-year-old girl to an adult prison for the next four months.

Nicknamed Lady Day

By 1928 Billie Holiday was living with her mother on 139th Street in the heart of Harlem. As usual, they were desperately in need of money, so the fifteen-year-old girl visited various night spots, trying to get hired as a singer or dancer. She had no formal training in either, and her attempts at dancing were laughed at, but the owner of a basement bar let her try out as a singer. The customers liked her so much that she was hired on the spot.

Holiday soon became a regular in the Harlem clubs, and in 1932 she was discovered by the jazz record producer John Hammond. Her first recording was made a year later with

Benny Goodman's orchestra, and after that she began to record for Columbia Records, usually with Teddy Wilson's ensemble. A member of Wilson's group gave her the nickname she became known by—Lady Day.

Lady Day soon became one of the most sought-after singers. Her light, buoyant style set a new fashion, transforming well-known love songs into exciting jazz originals. As well as performing in the New York clubs, she toured with Count Basie's orchestra in 1937, and the following year she was hired as the female soloist in Artie Shaw's white band. Shaw was considered brave for taking on a black singer, for the music world was almost totally segregated; but in fact it was Holiday who had to be brave, especially when they went on tour.

As one of the first black singers to perform with a white band, Holiday faced countless insults. In some places the audiences booed her. In others she was not allowed to perform and had to sit outside in the bus while a stand-in sang the songs that had been written for her. Usually, she had to eat apart from her fellow perfomers and lodge in a different hotel. The whole business was thoroughly humiliating, and Holiday gave it up in fury when she was barred from entering a hotel through the front door.

Back in New York she continued her career as a solo artist. Holiday now had a large and admiring audience among both whites and blacks. With gardenias in her hair and eyes half closed, she looked dramatic and seemed to sing with her whole body. She was at her most dramatic when singing "Strange Fruit," a disturbing and outspoken ballad about lynching—the "strange fruit" being the black men hanged on the trees. As an early protest song, "Strange Fruit" caused shock and anger and was banned in some places, but it touched the hearts of thousands of people and became a major hit. In the late 1930s the public couldn't get enough of the wonderful Lady Day.

Plagued by drug addiction

Although Holiday was now at the peak of her career, her private world had begun to fall apart. The men in her life—her boyfriends and both the men she married—all mistreated her in one way or another. She had long been a heavy drinker, and in the early 1940s her first husband introduced her to opium and heroin. For the rest of her life, she struggled against drug addiction.

Holiday's songs in the 1940s matched her mood: they were heart-breaking ballads of rejection and despair, but they were even more popular than her earlier work and they brought her award after award. But her addiction was becoming too well known, and in 1947 she was arrested on drug charges and sentenced to nine months in prison.

When released from prison, Holiday was banned from singing anywhere that had a liquor license. This was a bitter blow, for it meant that she could not perform in the clubs, though she could still make recordings and appear in theaters. She continued to do so through the 1950s, and she also went on tour in Europe. But the drugs gained an increasing hold. In the last years of her life, Holiday was in and out of prison and in very poor health. She died of a heart attack at the age of forty-four.

On Holiday's death, the papers made much of her addiction, but her friends in the music business mourned the loss of a brave spirit and a superb musician. Despite so many early disadvantages, Holiday rose to the top of her profession. The body of music she left behind is still being enjoyed by millions of jazz lovers throughout the world.

Benjamin L. Hooks

NAACP executive director, attorney, clergyman
Born January 31, 1925, Memphis, Tennessee

"The civil rights movement is not dead. If anyone thinks that we are going to stop agitating, they had better think again. If anyone thinks that we are going to stop litigating, they had better not close the courts. If anyone thinks that we are not going to demonstrate and protest ... they had better roll up the sidewalks."

For fifteen years Benjamin L. Hooks led the NAACP, the country's largest and most influential organization for blacks. At a time when it was in decline, Hooks was named executive director and helped the organization get back on its feet.

Hooks kept the NAACP vital by addressing national issues from a minority perspective. He has visited the White House, hosted his own television programs, confronted racism as a public defender, and preached sermons as a Baptist minister.

Encouraged to study

Hooks was born in Memphis, Tennessee, in 1925 to Robert and Bessie Hooks. His father operated a photography studio, and the family was considered comfortable by black standards. He used to wear second-hand clothes and watched his mother stretch the food bill so they would have enough to eat. His grandmother was the second black woman in the United States to graduate from college, so Hooks was encouraged to pursue secondary education.

Hooks was a shy youngster and took an interest in the ministry, but his father discouraged this pursuit. Hooks enrolled in a pre-law class at LeMoyne College in Memphis. At the same time he became interested in the black civil rights movement and hoped for the end of segregated bathrooms, lunch counters, water fountains, and other public facilities. "I wish I could tell you every time I was on the highway and couldn't use a restroom," he said in an interview with U.S. News and World Report. "My bladder is messed up because of that. Stomach is messed up from eating cold sandwiches."

Couldn't eat in the same restaurant as the prisoners he guarded

When the Second World War broke out, Hooks joined the armed forces and ran into racism. He was assigned to guard Italian prisoners of war who were allowed to eat in restaurants that were off-limits to him, because of his race. He retired from the army with the rank of staff sergeant. When no law school in Tennessee would accept him, Hooks went to Chicago, Illinois, to study law at DePaul University.

In 1948 he earned his J.D. degree and returned to Memphis with every intention of ending racial segregation. He passed the Tennessee bar and opened his own practice, confronting racism at every turn. In an interview later with Jet magazine, Hooks recalled: "At that time you were insulted by law clerks, excluded from white bar associations and when I was in court, I was lucky to be called 'Ben.' Usually it was just 'boy.' [But] the judges were always fair. The discrimination of those days has changed and, today, the South is ahead of the North in many respects in civil rights progress."

In 1949 Hooks met Frances Dancy, a twenty-two-year-old teacher, at the Shelby County fair and married her three years later. Frances Hooks recalled in Ebony magazine that her husband was "good looking, very quiet, very intelligent." She added, "he loved to go around to churches and that sort of thing, so I started going with him. He was really a good catch."

Worked as lawyer, judge, and minister

Despite his growing popularity as an assistant public defender, Hooks still felt a pull towards the ministry, and contact with civil rights leader Martin Luther King, Jr., and the Southern Christian Leadership Conference proved decisive for him. Hooks was ordained a Baptist minister and began to preach regularly at the Middle Baptist Church in Memphis in 1956. He also took part in many events sponsored by the National Association for the Advancement of Colored People (NAACP), such as restaurant sit-ins and economic boycotts.

In 1954 Hooks entered politics, making an unsuccessful bid for the state legislature that year and for juvenile court judge in 1959 and 1963. Despite these defeats Hooks attracted both black and liberal white votes. By 1965 he was so well known that Tennessee governor Frank G. Clement appointed him as the first black criminal court judge in state history. The next year he won election to a full term as a judge in Division IV Criminal Court of Shelby County.

By the late 1960s Hooks was a judge, a businessman, a lawyer, and a minister. He flew to Detroit twice a month to preach at the Greater New Mount Moriah Baptist Church. He also participated in many NAACP civil rights protests and was a producer and host of several local television shows, including "Conversations in Black and White," "Forty Percent Speaks," and "What Is Your Faith."

Hooks's wife worked with him constantly as his assistant, secretary, adviser, and traveling companion, even though it meant sacrificing her career as a teacher and guidance counselor. "He said he needed me to help him," she told Ebony magazine. "Few husbands tell their wives that they need them after 30 years of marriage, so I gave it up and here I am. Right by his side."

Appointed to Federal Communications Commission

In 1972 Hooks became the first black appointee to the Federal Communications Commission (FCC). He addressed the lack of minority ownership of television and radio stations, the minority employment statistics for the broadcasting industry, and the image of blacks in the mass media. While he was a FCC member, minority employment in broadcasting rose from 3 percent to 15 percent.

Hooks was elected NAACP executive director on November 6, 1976. At its peak, the civil rights organization enjoyed nationwide acclaim for its nonviolent protests and its membership numbered almost a half million. By the time Hook took over, the NAACP had declined to nearly 200,000 members. Hook was determined to add money and new members without compromising the organization's ideals. During his early years, he ran into trouble with Margaret Bush Wilson, chairperson of NAACP's board of directors. Wilson suspended Hooks in 1983 after they argued about organizational policy, with Wilson accusing Hooks of mismanagement. With the charges never proven, the majority of the board's sixty-four members backed Hooks, and he never officially left his post.

Rebuilt the NAACP as its executive director

Secure in his position, Hooks has since overseen the organization's positions on affirmative action, federal aid to cities, foreign relations with repressive governments (such as South Africa), and domestic policy decisions. Membership has grown by several hundred thousand.

Hooks and several black civil rights leaders met with President George Bush on November 17, 1989, to discuss the increasing tensions between the races. They told Bush that racism was rising in some areas of the country and urged him to upgrade black education, housing, and employment. They

Benjamin Hooks

emerged from the meeting with the president's words of full support against racially motivated bomb attacks, but Hooks later criticized the Bush administration for its lack of action concerning inner city poverty and poor support for public education. Hooks and his family were targeted in a wave of bombings against civil rights officials in early 1990.

Since Hooks has been executive director, the NAACP has issued formal opinions on a wide range of topics, including the lack of black executives in Hollywood, the role of the black middle class in the improvement of life in the ghettos, and the 1991 nomination and confirmation of Judge Clarence Thomas to the U.S. Supreme Court.

Hooks has been a strong supporter of self-help in the black community. He urges wealthy and middle-class blacks to give their time and resources to those less fortunate. "It's time today ... to bring it out of the closet: No longer can we proffer polite, explicable, reasons why black America cannot do more for itself," he told delegates to the 1990 NAACP convention. "I'm calling for a moratorium on excuses. I challenge black America today—all of us—to set aside our alibis."

By 1991 some of the NAACP's younger members said Hooks was losing touch with black America and urged him to resign. Though Hooks countered by saying some young blacks have taken for granted the gains made during the civil rights movement of the 1950s and 1960s, in February 1992 Hooks announced his intention to resign by year's end, saying he could no longer keep up with the demands of the job.

Lena Horne

Entertainer, singer, actress
Born June 17, 1917, Brooklyn, New York

Combining a strong voice with good looks, Lena Horne became one of the most popular entertainers in the United States during the 1940s, '50s, and '60s. She used her talents to become a singer and actress for MGM, and eventually branched out to the Broadway stage, national television programs, and recording studios. Horne has traveled around the world and received numerous awards and accolades.

Grandmother had a major influence

Horne was born on June 17, 1917, in Brooklyn, New York, to Teddy, a numbers banker, and Edna Horne, an actress. The cou-

ple made a meager amount and were forced to live with Teddy's parents. When Horne was three, her father left the family, and a short time later her mother left to become an actress with the Lafayette Stock Company in Harlem. Horne was raised by her grandparents, and her grandmother, Cora Horne, was a domineering woman who had a strong influence on her. Cora was very active in the Urban League, the Women's Suffrage Movement, and the National Association for the Advancement of Colored People. She registered the two-year-old Horne as a member of the NAACP.

Around 1924 Horne moved in with her mother, who was chronically ill and moved from place to place in search of work. When her mother was away, she attended the Brooklyn public schools and the Girls High School until she was fourteen years old. Then her mother returned with a Cuban husband, Mike Roderiguez, and they moved to the Bronx area of New York City. At sixteen Horne quit school and went to work for the famous, for-whites-only Cotton Club in Harlem. The club's choreographer, Elida Webb, liked Horne because she was light-skinned, tall, slim, young, beautiful, and had long hair. Horne met and worked with some of the biggest names in black entertainment, such as Cab Calloway, Ethel Waters, Billie Holiday, Count Basie, and Duke Ellington. In her spare time she took music lessons.

In 1935 Horne left the Cotton Club to be a singer with Noble Sissle's Society Orchestra in Philadelphia. She received low wages and lived out of a suitcase, causing her to marry the first person she could find. In 1937 she married Louis Jones, a friend of her father, who was nine years older than she. Their four-year marriage produced two children—Gail and Teddy.

Recording with Charlie Barnett

Horne's tour with Noble Sissle's band led to a starring role in the short-lived revue *Blackbirds of 1939.* By the fall of 1940, Horne left her husband and children to return to New York to renew her career. Her intention was to find a suitable place for her children so they could live with her. Shortly before the year was out she received her big break. Charlie Barnett made her the chief vocalist with his all-white band, and they recorded, "You're My Thrill," "Haunted Town," and "Good For Nothing Joe," under the Bluebird label. The latter became a hit and she was able to provide a home for her children. Jones permitted her custody of Gail and they shared custody of Teddy.

In 1941 Horne was the featured singer at the Cafe Society Downtown, and with her fame rising, she began dating the world heavyweight champion, Joe Louis. In less than a few months of performing, she received an offer to perform at the Troncadero Club in Hollywood. In early 1942 she moved to Hollywood with her daughter and cousin, Edwina, who had been taking care of Gail.

After less than two months at the Little Troc Club, she was noticed by Robert Edens of Metro-Goldwyn-Mayer (MGM), who arranged for her to audition for producer Arthur Freed. In 1942 Horne was the second black American woman to sign a contract with a motion picture company in Hollywood. The seven-year contract provided her with an initial salary of two hundred dollars per week and clearly stipulated that Horne would not be asked to play any stereotypical roles.

Her first movie was *Panama Hattie,* which featured her in a role that was to be her mainstay at MGM. Her performance was limited to a guest-spot number that could be easily edited out during showings in Southern theaters. She was usually pictured in an elegant gown, leaning against a pillar. Other films in which she appeared in a guest role included: *As Thousands Cheer, Swing Fever, Broadway Rhythm, Two Girls and a Sailor, Ziegfeld Follies,* and *Till the Crowds Roll By.*

The only major film role she received from MGM was in the 1943, all-black film, *Cabin in the Sky* in which she portrayed the major temptress, Georgia Brown. Her last MGM film was *The Duchess of Idaho* in 1950.

During World War II Horne was the pinup girl for thousands of black American soldiers, and she performed on USO tours only when all soldiers were admitted to the auditorium.

With no new roles for Horne at MGM, she was loaned to Twentieth Century Fox, where she did another all-black film, *Stormy Weather.* This musical was based on the thinly disguised life of Bill "Bojangles" Robinson, and the title track of "Stormy Weather" is still her classic number. While she was filming *Stormy Weather,* Horne met composer-conductor Lennie George Hayton, who she secretly married in 1947.

One of the nation's top black entertainers

Horne was one of the nation's top black entertainers in the mid-1940s. Her nightclub and

Lena Horne

theater performances easily added up to $10,000 per week. Her record high was $60,000 per week in the fall of 1948 at Cibacabano in New York. When she returned in 1951 she grossed $175,000 in twenty weeks.

During the 1950s and 1960s, Horne was performing in movies, theaters, television, and recording studios. She made appearances, around the world and on national television programs. She lived a relatively quiet life in Santa Barbara in the early 1970s, but by 1974 she was performing on Broadway with Tony Bennett. In 1978 Horne played in the black movie version of the box-office failure *Wizard of Oz*.

Although Horne did a farewell tour between June and August 1980, she returned on April 30, 1980, to perform in *Lena Horne: The Lady and Her Music*. Since then she has won many awards in music and the Kennedy Center Award for Lifetime Contribution to the Arts. She currently lives in New York City.

Whitney Houston

Singer, actress, and model
Born August 9, 1963, Newark, New Jersey

"Gospel music was my greatest influence.... It gave me emotion and spiritual things.... Now, whatever I sing, whether it's gospel or pop or R & B, I feel it."

Whitney Houston burst on the scene in 1985 with her album *Whitney Houston*, which sold more than 13 million copies. Her next two albums also sold in the millions and firmly established her as a superstar of the American pop world.

Houston's bell-like voice and beautifully trained singing style have drawn rave reviews from most critics, though some complain that her approach is too mainstream. Yet it is this very quality that gives Houston such wide appeal. As *Time* magazine's Narada Michael Walden pointed out, "She can get the kids on the dance floor, then turn around and reach your grandmother." Houston invariably attracts a huge audience, whether singing pop, or rhythm and blues, or soul, or even gospel music.

Brought up in a musical household

The daughter of John Houston, who was head of the Newark Central Planning Board, and Cissy Houston, a noted gospel and soul singer, Whitney Houston grew up in East Orange, New Jersey, in a musically rich environment. From an early age she longed to be a professional singer, following the example not only

Whitney Houston

her mother but of her famous cousins, Dionne and Dee Dee Warwick.

Houston began by singing gospel music as a member of the choir her mother ran at New Hope Baptist Church. "I grew up in the church, and gospel music has always been the center of our lives," she told a *New York Times* interviewer. "At family celebrations, we always ended up sitting around the piano and singing. I couldn't get enough of gospel music when I was growing up."

During the 1960s her mother led a soul group called the Sweet Inspirations, which sang backup for "the queen of soul," Aretha Franklin. Houston was only five years old the first time she accompanied her mother to the recording studios to tape sessions with the Sweet Inspirations. From then on she was a devoted fan of Aretha Franklin. She would slip down to the basement, put on a Franklin record, hold one of her mother's microphones to her mouth, and sing for hour after hour,

happily imagining herself on a stage performing before a packed house.

Nevertheless, it was Houston's mother, not Franklin, who was her main role model. Houston told the *New York Times:* "My mom was my biggest influence. Everything she knows physically and mentally about singing she has passed on to me, and she taught me everything I know about the technology of the recording studio and about the business."

Although Houston's mother had hoped her daughter would become a teacher, she coached the girl assiduously when it became clear she had set her heart on being a singer. It was through her mother that Houston had her first engagements. At fifteen she began singing backup to her mother's nightclub act, and this led to backup singing for other artists, including Lou Rawls and Chaka Khan. Soon Houston was so busy that she wanted to drop out of school, but her parents insisted that she stay on at Mount St. Dominic Academy and complete her education.

Became a superstar overnight

Whitney Houston was still at high school when she launched what was to become her second career—that of model. On a visit to New York with her mother, her elegant beauty and slim figure attracted the attention of a passer-by, who told her that a modeling agency in a nearby building was looking for someone just like her. This sounded like a "come on," and Whitney and her mother were very cautious, but the stranger's statement turned out to be true.

Houston was taken on as a junior model, and over the next few years she appeared in such magazines as *Vogue* and *Seventeen*. On graduating from high school she was able to devote more time to modeling and to concentrate on her career as a singer. As well as singing backup for various performers, she did jingles for television commercials, and at the age of 19 she gave a special concert at a Manhattan nightclub before an audience of music industry executives.

Among those present was the president of Arista Records, Clive Davis, who offered her a contract with his studio. Houston had also been offered contracts by other recording studios, but she chose Arista because Davis had so succesfully promoted the careers of several well-known artists, including her cousin Dionne Warwick.

During the next two years Davis gradually built up Houston's reputation by having her perform at carefully selected places, and he spent an unheard-of $250,000 on the production of her first album. Titled *Whitney Houston,* it featured songs written by some of the top people in the business, and included duets with popular singers Jermaine Jackson and Teddy Pendergrass.

When the album was released in 1985 it rocketed Houston to fame. The album scored hit singles with the songs "You Give Good Love," "Saving All My Love for You," "How Will I Know," and "The Greatest Love of All," and it remained at the top of the charts for forty-six weeks. Although some critics complained that the choice of songs was unoriginal, Houston's singing was so polished and the tunes so catchy that the public flocked to buy the records. "This is infectious, can't-sit-down music," enthused Richard Corliss of

Time magazine. Millions of Americans agreed with him. Houston's first album sold more than 13 million copies.

Then Houston made videos of a number of the songs, including "You Give Good Love," "How Will I Know," and "Saving All My Love for You." She enjoyed doing the videos, saying that performing in them was like making silent movies—"No talking, just emotion on the screen." In 1986 Houston's performance in "How Will I Know" won her an MTV Video Music Award for best female video. That same year she also won two Grammy awards for best female pop performance for her songs "Saving All My Love for You" and "I Wanna Dance with Somebody (Who Loves Me)." To top if off, she also won an Emmy award.

Since the album and the videos continued to sell well, Arista president Clive Davis waited a year and a half before bringing out a second Houston album. Not until 1987, when sales were beginning to slow down, did he release *Whitney*. Like Houston's first album, *Whitney* was a phenomenal success. It was the first album by a female singer that had ever been such an instant hit, soaring to the top of *Billboard*'s charts immediately on its release. Its success was partly the result of its wide appeal. "I wanted to appeal to everybody— moms, kids, dads," explained Houston. "It's great we achieved that."

Houston's third album, *I'm Your Baby Tonight* (1990), sold a "mere" 6 million copies worldwide. For most recording artists such sales would be fantastically good, but they were considerably less than her first two albums. The public continued to rave over her music and play her records. She was undoubtedly one of the country's top superstars.

Subject of gossip and rumor mills

The outstanding success of Houston's albums brought her a multitude of engagements in clubs and concert halls, as well as guest appearances on talk shows and other television programs. She appeared on "The Merv Griffin Show" and performed in "Silver Spoons" and "Gimme a Break." In 1991 she was invited to sing "The Star-Spangled Banner" at the start of the Super Bowl, and she gave such a stirring rendition that she won even more fans across the country.

But along with the glamour and glory of being a superstar, Houston has had to put up with an unpleasant amount of criticism. Some rhythm and blues enthusiasts have said she is "too white" to be successful as a black performer. Others have attacked her stage performances as being stiff and uninspired, and the television show "Living Color" made fun of her dancing in a sketch called "Whitney Houston's Rhythmless Nation."

Worse still, Houston's private life has come under attack. In the early 1990s gossip writers spread the rumor that she was a lesbian and was having a love affair with her female assistant. At the same time other rumors suggested exactly the opposite—that she was involved in a relationship with actor Robert De Niro and with comedian Eddie Murphy. All these rumors were quelled for a time when in 1992 Houston married singer Bobby Brown in a much-publicized ceremony.

Nevertheless, the rumor mills have continued to plague Houston. In 1993 the *New York Post* printed a story that she had been treated in a hospital after taking too many diet pills. The *Post* said she was striving to get as thin as chart-topper Janet Jackson, who had once dated Houston's husband. The *Post*'s story was vigorously denied by Houston's lawyer, who pointed out that Houston had been rehearsing with a number of other people at the time she was reputed to be in hospital. "She has never taken a diet pill in her life," he asserted.

Despite these problems, Houston's career continues to expand. In 1992, at the age of twenty-nine, she had her first movie role in the feature film *The Bodyguard*. As Houston moves into her thirties, there are many directions she can take, and they all look promising. But it will be difficult for her to outmatch the astounding success she has had in her twenties.

Langston Hughes

Writer
Born February 1, 1902, Joplin, Missouri
Died May 22, 1967, New York, New York

"I felt that the masses of our people had as much in their lives to put into books as did those more fortunate ones who had been born with some means and the ability to work up to a master's degree at a Northern college."

L angston Hughes was one of the most talented writers of the Harlem Renaissance—that flowering of black literature in the 1920s—and he ranks among the major

American writers of the twentieth century. The author of poetry, plays, novels, short stories, and a variety of nonfiction, he produced more than fifty books during the course of his career. He was the first African American to earn his living entirely from his writing and his public lectures.

Most of Hughes's writings focused on "plain black people," whom he portrayed with gentle humor and compassion. For this he was criticized by black intellectuals, who accused him of betraying his race by concentrating on the least appealing side of black life. In his later years, he was also criticized by militant young blacks who felt that his writings should be more outspoken and aggressive.

Although Hughes wrote about ordinary black Americans, his own life was far from ordinary. By the age of twelve, he had lived in six American cities. When his first book was published in 1926, he had already been a cleaner, truck farmer, cook, waiter, college student, and sailor, as well as a dishwasher in a Paris nightclub. He also had visited Mexico, Africa, and Europe.

The young poet

Hughes's full name was James Langston Hughes after his father, James Hughes, and his mother, Carrie (Langston) Hughes. His father moved to Mexico soon after Hughes was born, but his mother stayed behind, and in the following years she was continually going from city to city looking for work. Sometimes she took her son with her, but for most of his early childhood Hughes lived with his grandmother, Mary Langston, in Lawrence, Kansas. A proud and gentle woman of

Langston Hughes

black and American Indian ancestry, grandmother Langston was a strong influence on the young boy.

When Hughes was a teenager, his mother married again, and in 1916 they settled in Cleveland, Ohio. For the next four years, Langston attended Cleveland's Central High School, where he took his first steps as a writer by editing the school yearbook and contributing poems to the school magazine. He also made numerous friends, many of whom were white; he found that the Jewish and foreign-born children were more democratic than other whites. He first became interested in socialism through them.

Hughes had visited his father in Mexico during his early childhood, and he stayed with him again when he was seventeen. The following year, having graduated from high school, he went for a longer visit, and it was while he was on his way there—on crossing the Mississippi River in the summer of 1920—

that he wrote his best-known poem, "The Negro Speaks of Rivers." The poem was published in *Crisis* magazine in 1921.

While staying with his father, Hughes had various pieces published, including a one-act play, but he spent much of his time arguing over where he should go to college. At length, he was allowed to attend Columbia University, and he enrolled there in the fall of 1921. But Hughes soon decided that he liked neither the curriculum nor the students. Within a year he had dropped out, preferring to live in Harlem, where he mingled with other writers and set his own schedule of reading and writing while supporting himself with odd jobs.

The young adventurer

In 1923, Hughes set out to see the world. First, he went to Africa, working as a cabin boy on a freighter and sending back articles that were published in *Crisis* magazine. Soon after he returned home, he set off for Paris, France, where he washed dishes in a nightclub until he had saved enough to travel through Europe.

Back in Harlem late in 1924, Hughes met Arna Bontemps, who was to become a close friend and co-author. When the two young men first met, both were just beginning to make their breakthrough as writers. Hughes's chance came in 1925 when he was working as a busboy in a Washington hotel. While the poet Vachel Lindsay was dining there, Hughes placed some of his poems alongside Lindsay's plate. This was even more effective than Hughes had hoped, for he read in the paper the next day that Lindsay had discovered a busboy poet! That same year, Hughes won a poetry competition in *Opportunity* magazine, and this led to the publication of his first book, *The Weary Blues* (1926).

The Weary Blues reflected Hughes's varied experience. It captured the sounds and rhythms of daily life in Harlem and included some poems relating to Mexico and Africa. The book was given several good reviews and was far better received than Hughes's next poetry collection, *Fine Clothes to the Jew* (1927), which aroused a storm of protest. With its colorful vignettes of life among the poor, the collection offended many black critics, who said that Hughes ought to concentrate on the positive aspects of African American culture, rather than exposing its faults.

The established writer

By 1926, Hughes had made enough money from his writings and other sources to enable him to enroll at Lincoln University, from which he graduated with a B.A. in 1929. While at college, he continued to write, and during the early 1930s he published several more poetry books as well as his first novel, *Not Without Laughter* (1930). He also brought out his first collection of short stories, *The Ways of White Folks* (1934), a book that reflected the bitterness he felt during those Depression years.

Hughes had become strongly left-wing in the previous few years, partly as of a result of travelling through the poverty-stricken South. He had also visited Cuba and Haiti, and in 1932 he set off to Russia with a film company to make a film about American race relations. Hughes was greatly impressed by the Soviet Union and did not hesitate to say so. Some of his most radical poetry was written during the year he spent there. The result of this trip was his nonfiction work, *A Negro Looks at Soviet Central Asia* (1934).

In 1937, Hughes's socialist enthusiasms took him to Spain, where he served as a correspondent for the *Baltimore Afro-American* during the Spanish Civil War. His sympathies were, of course, with the Spanish communists. Back home in New York the following year, he founded the leftist Harlem Suitcase Theater. One of his plays had been produced on Broadway previously, and in the next few years he concentrated mainly on writing for the theater, though he also wrote his autobiography, *The Big Sea* (1940).

With the outbreak of World War II, Hughes toned down his writing and became far less radical. This did not prevent him from being called before Senator Eugene McCarthy's Subcommittee on Un-American Activities during the Cold War hysteria of the 1950s. For a while Hughes was under a cloud, and some of his lecture tours were cancelled. However, he had a large and admiring public by this time, and before long his books were selling as well as ever.

Hughes published a number of books for children during the 1950s. These included *The First Book of Rhythms* (1954), *Famous American Negroes* (1954), and *The First Book of Jazz* (1955). He also published collections of short stories based on his popular fictional character, Jesse B. Semple (also known as Simple), whom Hughes had created some years earlier. Semple was a poor man who lived in Harlem and would talk about his troubles in return for a drink. Semple had plenty of troubles—money problems, problems with women, problems about life in general, and especially the problem of being a black man in a racist society. "White folks," he once said, "is the cause of a lot of inconvenience in my life."

Last years

As Hughes grew older, he continued to travel and write on a large scale. He revisited Europe and went to Africa several times. As well as producing his own works, he translated the works of others and edited a number of collections, such as *Poems from Black Africa* (1963) and *The Book of Negro Humor* (1966). His crowning achievement was his own collection of poems, *Ask Your Mama* (1961).

Hughes had long been interested in the theater, especially the musical theater, and during his last years he devoted increasing time to writing plays and scripts. The 1960s saw production of the highly acclaimed *Black Nativity* (1961) and *Jericho-Jim Crow* (1963), both of which involved gospel music. Hughes had always regarded music as an essential part of African American culture, especially the rhythms of jazz and blues (which are clearly echoed in his poetry), and increasingly he incorporated music into his works.

Whatever form Hughes's works took, all were imbued with a deep love of his race. Although he often treated his subject matter humorously, he did so with an underlying seriousness and with profound understanding and compassion. He once said that "there is no lack within the Negro people of beauty, strength, and power." He spent his life proving this fact in his writings.

Clementine Hunter

Folk artist
Born December 1886, near Cloutierville,
  Louisiana
Died January 1, 1988, Natchitoches,
  Louisiana

*"Like many other folk artists, she has done
most of her work for the people in her own
area—and at prices they can afford. They love
her for it."—Allen Rankin*

C lementine Hunter's career as an artist
began when she was in her fifties and
ended a few weeks before her death at the age
of l02. During that period, she produced several thousand paintings and other artworks,
which have been much sought after by collectors. With her bold colors and faultless sense
of design, she is considered one of the major
"primitive" artists of the twentieth century.

Hunter's paintings fall into three categories. First and foremost are the memory paintings. Some of these are flower paintings or
pictures of birds and other animals, but most
are scenes of people doing everyday things—
cooking, dancing, washing, going to school,
or attending weddings and funerals. The second category consists of scenes from the Bible, often with black people and black angels.
One of the best known is a Crucifixion scene
in which Jesus is black but the two thieves
crucified with him are white, while at the foot
of the cross there are black fieldhands working in a cotton field. The third category consists mainly of abstracts and other paintings
whose subjects were suggested to Hunter
rather than coming spontaneously from her
own ideas.

Growing up in Louisiana

Born on a Louisiana cotton plantation, Clem-
entine Hunter was the daughter of Antoinette
Adams and John Reuben. Her father was part
French, and she was originally given the
French name Clemence, though it was soon
changed to Clementine (pronounced
Clementeen).

Like her parents, Hunter was a Roman
Catholic, and the only school she ever attended was a small Catholic elementary school
in nearby Cloutierville. She had not been there
long when her family moved to Melrose Plantation near the town of Natchitoches. As a
result, Hunter did not continue her education,
and she never learned to read, remaining illiterate throughout her long life.

As soon as she was old enough, she went
to work in the fields, and in due course grew
up and had seven children—two by Charlie
Dupree, who died around 1914, and five by
Emanuel Hunter, whom she married in 1924.
Toward the end of the 1920s, Hunter became
a full time domestic servant for the white
family who owned the plantation. As well as
cooking and sewing and doing other house-
hold duties, she developed a talent for
quiltmaking and basketmaking.

These crafts were encouraged by the mis-
tress of the plantation, Carmelite Henry, who
was attempting to revive the local arts and
crafts. Henry had a large collection of
artworks, and in 1939 she hired a Frenchman,
François Mignon, to be the curator of her

collection. This proved to be a highly significant event for Clementine Hunter, because Mignon became her first patron—the first to recognize the exceptional quality of her work and the first to promote it.

The folk artist of Melrose Plantation

It was through Hunter's own initiative that Mignon became her patron. One night in the early 1940s, when she was about fifty-four years old, she called on Mignon, holding in her hand some half-used tubes of oil paint that had been left behind by a visiting artist. She told Mignon that she could "mark" a picture of her own, just like the artist, if she set her mind to it. Mignon gave her an old window shade to use as a canvas, and at five o'clock the next day, Hunter presented him with a completed picture. This is thought to be the first painting she ever showed to anyone outside her family.

Mignon was delighted with the painting and encouraged Hunter do more, providing her with paint and materials. She painted on whatever she could get hold of—cardboard boxes, paper bags, used bottles, gourds, old iron pots, even an old chest. Later, when she could afford it, she took to painting on canvas. From the beginning she used oil paint, layering it on in solid primary colors—the same bold colors she liked to use in her quiltmaking.

By the early 1950s, Hunter had gained a considerable reputation. In 1955, the Delgado Museum (now the New Orleans Museum of Art) gave an exhibition of Hunter's work, the first it had ever given for a black artist. At the same time, the Northwestern State College in

Clementine Hunter

Natchitoches held its first exhibition of her work. It was typical of those segregated times that Hunter was not allowed to view her work along with the whites who came to see it; she had to be slipped in by the back door when the gallery was closed.

The following year, she created one of her most important works: the murals that were installed in African House, a traditional African-style building at Melrose, dating from about 1800. Mignon had suggested that she paint these murals, which consisted of nine eight-foot-high panels and several smaller connecting ones. On them, Hunter painted scenes from plantation life.

In the 1960s, Hunter's style of painting changed markedly, focusing on abstracts. This was the result of the influence of writer and artist James Register, who settled in Natchitoches in 1962. Register had long been interested in Hunter's work, and in 1944 he had obtained a Julius Rosenwald Foundation

367

grant for her. He also had helped pay the funeral expenses when Hunter's husband, Emanuel, died.

Like Mignon, Register provided Hunter with paints and acted as an agent in selling her work. He regarded her as "almost a genius" and after moving to Natchitoches he decided to experiment with her talents. Cutting advertisements from old magazines, he pasted them onto boards and then offered them to Hunter to see what she would do with them. The result was a series of abstracts—about one hundred altogether—that Hunter painted in the mid-1960s.

Hunter's first paintings had sold for just a few dollars, but by the 1970s her pictures were selling at such good prices that some artists had begun to paint forgeries in her style, trying to sell them as Hunter originals. Almost every year, Hunter's work was shown in galleries, either in solo exhibitions like those at Fisk University (1974) or as part of larger shows, such as the "Black Women Artists" exhibition at the Smithsonian Institution (1984).

Hunter's success enabled her to buy a house trailer. She also bought herself space in a mausoleum, where she was buried when she died. Although she never traveled far from her home in Louisiana, her works have been shown across the country. Some are on permanent display in some of the nation's most prestigious galleries, including those at Illinois State University, Radcliffe College, the Dallas Museum of Fine Art, and the New York Historical Association. The woman who spent her entire life in a small community in the rural South is now honored from coast to coast.

Zora Neale Hurston

Writer, folklorist
Born January 7, 1891, Eatonville, Florida
Died January 28, 1960, Fort Pierce, Florida

"I was glad when somebody told me: 'You may go and collect Negro folklore.' In a way it would not be a new experience for me."

Zora Neale Hurston had an unusual career for a black woman early in this century. She studied folklore by traveling around the American South and the West Indies, asking about local myths, legends, and traditional practices. She is considered one of the most important collectors ever of African American folklore.

Hurston was also remarkable in that she was the most widely published black woman of her day—the author of more than fifty articles and short stories as well as four novels, two books on folklore, an autobiography, and some plays. At the height of her success she was known as the "Queen of the Harlem Renaissance." Yet all this did not bring financial security. Hurston was so desperately poor toward the end of her life that she died in a welfare home and was buried in an unmarked grave.

Grew up in Eatonville, America's first black-governed city

Although Zora Hurston was born at a time of strong racial discrimination, she never felt bitter about being black, nor did she even feel disadvantaged. This was partly because she recognized the richness of black culture, but it was also because she spent her early childhood in Eatonville. Situated in central Florida, Eatonville was the first self-governing all-black city, and it was a happy place for a child to grow up in. According to Hurston, it had "five lakes, three croquet courts, three hundred brown skins, three hundred good swimmers, plenty guavas, two schools, and no jail house."

Hurston's father, Reverend John Hurston, built a home on a large piece of lush land, and there he and his wife Lucy reared a family of eight children. Zora was a lively child, taking in all that was going on around her. She particularly loved to listen to the stories the neighbors told as they gathered on a shady porch, though she did not at the time realize the stories were folk tales.

This happy stage of Hurston's life ended at the age of nine, when her mother died. Within two weeks, her father had sent her away to school in Jacksonville. Zora had never been close to her father and when, within a short time, he remarried, their relationship became so bad that he tried to get the school to adopt his daughter.

No adoption took place, but Zora remained out of favor. When she was thirteen she was pulled out of school and sent to care for her brother's children. After similar work in other homes, she landed a job at the age of sixteen as personal maid to a white woman who was a member of a Gilbert and Sullivan theatrical troupe. The next eighteen months were among the happiest of Hurston's life as she traveled with the actors, feeling like part of their family. But she was determined to go back to school and get a thorough education, and with the help of her actress employer, she enrolled at Morgan Academy in Baltimore, Maryland.

Enjoyed her role in the Harlem Renaissance

When Hurston graduated from high school, her great ambition was to study at Howard University, and she enrolled there in 1918, having earned the money for her tuition by working as a waitress and manicurist. Money was to be a major problem during the next few years, since no one was supporting her, and after taking a course she would work for a while until she had enough to take the next one.

Hurston thoroughly enjoyed college life and began to write stories and articles. In 1921 she had her first success when one of her stories was published in Howard University's

Zora Neale Hurston

literary magazine. Like so many of Hurston's later writings, this piece was inspired by her memories of Eatonville. That was also the subject of a story and play which won her prizes from *Opportunity* magazine in 1925.

The *Opportunity* prizes brought Hurston to the attention of other young black writers, especially those in the group that became known as the Harlem Renaissance. On moving to New York in 1925, Hurston settled in easily among these intellectuals, making friends with such writers as Langston Hughes. She was particularly welcome because she came from a rural background with its own rich folk culture, and one of the aims of the Renaissance writers was to stress the richness of black culture. Hurston did so in her writings, to glorious effect, with homespun tales and humorous anecdotes about the Eatonville world she had so loved as a child.

Hurston had the satisfaction of seeing her stories published in magazines and of knowing that they delighted many people, both black and white. Nevertheless, they did not please everyone. Some of the writers of the Harlem Renaissance criticized her for portraying only the upbeat side of black life and of ignoring all the poverty and misery brought on by racism. To them Hurston replied, "I do not belong to the sobbing school of Negrohood who hold that nature somehow has given them a lowdown dirty deal." On the contrary, she looked around her and saw a rich heritage of black culture. It was there in everyday life—in people's habits, in the way they spoke and sang, in the things they laughed at—it was all there, to be enjoyed, celebrated, and made into literature.

During this period, as well as writing stories, Hurston earned her living by working as personal assistant to the successful writer Fannie Hurst, and it was with Hurst's assistance that she enrolled at Barnard College on a scholarship. Hurston was Barnard's first black student, but as usual she settled in happily, graduating with a B.A. in 1928. Meanwhile, in 1927, she married Dr. Herbert Sheen, an old flame from Howard University, but their careers soon came into conflict and they divorced in 1931. That year also saw the breakup of her friendship with Langston Hughes because of a misunderstanding over a play they had written together.

Lived as a talented anthropologist, died an unknown

After graduating from Barnard, Hurston entered Columbia University, where she studied under Franz Boas, the leading anthropologist in North America. Boas quickly realized that Hurston's passion for black folklore and her personal knowledge of it made her the ideal person to collect material on African American culture. This led to the first of her collecting trips, which took her to the South.

The 1930s were a wonderful time for Hurston as she wandered around, making friends in towns and villages, asking questions, noting the results, and learning—always learning—about the ways of the people she met. Although she was a scholarly expert, she did not look like one, and this was the secret of her success as a collector. People accepted her as one of them and therefore chatted to her freely, even about secret religious rituals. In Haiti and Jamaica she learned far more about the voodoo religion than any previous anthropologist had done.

Hurston discussed voodoo in *Tell My Horse* (1938). This was her fourth book. She had already published another book on folklore, *Mules and Men* (1935), as well as two novels, *Jonah's Gourd Vine* (1934) and her masterpiece, *The Eyes Were Watching God* (1937). Most of her books were published in the 1930s and early 1940s, and this was also the period in which she embarked on a second marriage, though it did not last, partly because she was away traveling so much.

In the 1940s her mentor, Franz Boas, was dead, Hurston's books were no longer bringing in large royalties, and she was finding it increasingly difficult to get her work published. Although she continued to write, the few articles she published did not bring in enough to live on. Never one to give in to despair, Hurston moved to Fort Pierce, Florida, in the 1950s. For a brief time she supported herself by going back to work as a maid, though she soon managed to get better jobs, working as a librarian and then as a substitute teacher. When in 1959 she suffered a stroke that made further work impossible, she moved into a welfare home, and there she died the following year, unnoticed by the world at large.

Nevertheless, neither Hurston nor her works have been forgotten, and a later generation has honored her memory. In 1973 the novelist and poet Alice Walker placed a marker in Fort Pierce at the place believed to be Hurston's burial plot. The stone reads "Zora Neale Hurston, A Genius of the South."

Ice-T

Rapper, actor
Born late 1950s, Newark, New Jersey

"Parents are scared because my record is Number One on the campus charts of Harvard for three months. These kids are being trained to grow up and become Supreme Court justices and politicians."

Mixing poverty with life in inner city Los Angeles can be the recipe for a life of crime. Ice-T managed to pull himself out of that life to become a successful rap artist. His songs are based on what he knows: robbery, murder, pimps, hustlers, gangs, and prison. His style has been emulated by several other rappers, including Ice Cube and N.W.A. Besides his music career, Ice-T has also appeared in several movies, receiving excellent reviews for his performances.

Incarcerated friends recommend rapping

Ice-T was born Tracey Marrow (some sources spell his surname Morrow) in the late 1950s. His parents were both dead by the time he reached the seventh grade, so he lived with his aunt in Los Angeles. At Crenshaw High School he wrote rhymes for local gangs and was slowly drawn into petty crime. When he was seventeen he left his aunt's home to hang out with his friends, and by the early 1980s Ice-T was drawn to rap music, influenced by the success of such rappers as Kurtis Blow.

He earned his first income from the medium in 1982, when he received twenty dollars from an independent producer for recording "The Coldest Rap."

This money was nothing compared to what he and his friends could make as criminals, and though Ice-T says that he was never truly a gang member, he had many friends who convinced him that crime truly did not pay. As more and more of his friends were sent to prison, they urged him to stick with rap music to stay away from jail. Ice-T continued to practice and relied heavily on the advice of his girlfriend, Darlene. In an interview with *Details* Ice said, "Even though we were broke, she knew that I could take five minutes out and go scam $20,000. I needed a girl who was ready to say, 'Don't do it, Ice. It's O.K.'" For a long time the two were too broke to even go to the movies. They simply lived in a little room and paid rent. They didn't even have a car for two years.

In 1984, Ice-T landed a part as a rapper in the movie *Breakin'*. By this time, rap had grown from a small urban phenomenon to a national one. Most of the successful rappers were from New York City, and it was difficult for Californian rappers to break into the market. California was known for its surf-lovin' Beach Boys and its psychedelic rock bands such as the Grateful Dead; it hardly seemed the place for rap artists—who produce rhymes about urban strife—to develop. But Ice-T broke through this barrier in 1987 with his debut, *Rhyme Pays,* with songs about Los Angeles inner city warfare. The rap "6 in the Morning," about a handful of gang members escaping the police, became especially popular. His songs contained gangster slang and strong language that provoked anxiety in many listeners.

Stuck with first warning sticker

Due to his controversial subject material, Ice-T's music caught the attention of several watchdog organizations, including the Parents' Music Resource Center. He caught fire from the political left and right for glorifying violence, theft, and sexism. His record received the first parental advisory sticker, which Ice-T reckons was due to the album's profanity. Ice-T responded to the warning label: "No one has yet been able to explain to me the definition of profanity anyhow.... I can think of ways to say stuff—saying things using legitimate words but in a context—that makes a more profane comment than any bullshit swear words."

Ice-T didn't soften his stance with his next album, the 1988 release titled *Power*. The cover featured a bikini-clad Darlene pointing a gun at the camera. "High Rollers" and "I'm Your Pusher" were well received, and Ice-T's video began appearing regularly on MTV. He also contributed to the soundtrack of the 1988 gang film *Colors*. His tough image came under attack from various camps, and in 1989 he toned his music down with the release of *The Iceberg/Freedom of Speech ... Just Watch What You Say.*

The cover featured Ice-T with guns pointed at both temples and the barrel of another in his mouth. Jello Biafra, former lead singer of the Dead Kennedys, delivered a right-wing martial law speech over a sampled piece of deathmetal guitar, which served as a counterattack on conservative thinking. Sales were good for the album, but some people accused Ice-T of going soft. "I just got caught up in messages—about freedom of speech. People at the record company wanted me to do that and I'm sorry that I listened to them," Ice-T told the *Los Angeles Times*. While spurning criticism that he had gone soft, Ice-T also faced competition from several new rappers duplicating his original style.

Acted in *New Jack City*

Ice-T reasserted his ascendancy by landing the role of an undercover cop in the smash 1991 film *New Jack City,* which also featured his new song, "New Jack Hustler." Acting was still a new experience for Ice-T, and he readily admitted to the media that he was scared about how the public would react. However, he received excellent reviews and accepted a role to play a drug dealer in the film *Ricochet,* released in 1993.

Ice-T released the album *O.G.—Original Gangster* in 1991. With twenty-four raps about life on the street, the album's themes can be summed up by titles, including "Straight Up Nigga," "Prepared to Die," and "Home of the Bodybag." It seemed Ice-T was ready to take on any of the new rap artists that were on his "turf." The album also contained a rock and roll song, "Body Count," named for the hardcore band he had assembled. Four different producers assisted with the album, and DJ Evil E. provided the mix of beats and samples.

Ice-T received many favorable reviews for *O.G.. Entertainment Weekly* gave it an "A," while the *New York Times* stated it "works

to balance the thrills of action and the demands of conscience." *Musician* commented, "It's his candor that really draws blood," and *Stereo Review* stated, "Ice-T raps in lighting-quick, no-nonsense rhymes that cut to the bone with lack of pretense or apology." *Rolling Stone* noted that "*O.G.* can be heard as a careening, open-minded discussion. Of course Ice-T does tend to follow his sharpest points with defiant kiss-offs.... But get past his bluster and this guy is full of forthright, inspiring perceptions."

O.G. received a parental advisory sticker because of its language and content. Ice-T's response to the sticker received a great deal of publicity: "I have a sticker on my record that says 'Parental Guidance is Suggested.' In my book, parental guidance is always suggested. If you need a sticker to tell you that you need to guide your child, you're a dumb f—in' parent anyhow."

Ice-T

Ice-T joined Lollapalooza, a traveling rock show organized by Perry Farrell, in 1991. The headline act was Farrell's band, Jane's Addiction, and included a diverse number of groups such as Black Rock Coalition founders Living Colours, the industrial dance outfit Nine Inch Nails, and British postpunk veterans Siouxie and the Banshees. Ice-T is the only rapper in the show, but he is looking forward to bringing rap to a white audience. "All I want them to do is come out and say 'I like him.' Not get the message, not understand a word I'm saying. Just think, 'Those black guys on the stage I used to be scared of, I like 'em.' I want to come out and say, 'Peace.' If I can do that, that's cool."

Roy Innis

Civil rights activist
Born June 6, 1934, St. Croix, Virgin Islands

"What black power is all about is that we have to demand that we be accepted for what we are."

A controversial and aggressive figure, who believes passionately in achieving equal opportunity for blacks in all areas of life, Roy Innis was national director of the Congress of Racial Equality (CORE) from 1968 to 1981. He then became the organization's national chairman.

Innis was one of the first civil rights activists to turn away from the efforts to integrate blacks into white society. He felt this was not the solution to American racism. "What black power is all about," he said, "is that we have to demand that we be accepted for what we are, and insist that we don't conform or blend with the rest of society." His solution was to build up the strength of the black community, to promote black businesses, banks, and schools, so that African Americans could gain a full share of economic and political power.

First experiences of racism

Roy Emile Alfredo Innis spent his early childhood in the Virgin Islands, where the people took great pride in their African origins. Innis's father was a policeman who died during the boy's childhood, and when Innis was twelve his mother brought him to Harlem. There he was shocked to find that black people were not proud of being black. "Black was almost like a cuss word," he said.

Innis attended Stuyvesant High School in Manhattan. Despite his good grades, he dropped out of school when he was sixteen, saying that he wanted to get away from home. He had heard that the U.S. Army would give him the chance to see the world and managed to get accepted by saying that he was eighteen. The army was a disappointment. It was totally segregated—the black soldiers even had a separate PX (post exchange or general store)—and instead of seeing the world, Innis was assigned to an all-black company at a Massachusetts army base.

Back in civilian life two years later, he finished high school and then enrolled at the City College of New York, where he studied chemistry. On leaving college, he worked as a chemical technician for Vick Chemical Company until 1963. He then moved to Montefiore

Hospital in New York City, where he was employed as a research assistant in the cardiovascular research laboratory. Innis stayed at Montefiore until 1967, and during this time he took on a union leadership role, representing Local 1199 of the Hospital Workers' Union. Meanwhile, he was playing an increasingly active role in the civil rights movement.

The Congress of Racial Equality (CORE)

Innis joined the New York–Harlem chapter of CORE in 1963. At the time, CORE was a multiracial organization whose aim was to integrate blacks into white society. Many of the members viewed Innis with suspicion, as dangerously extremist because he objected to the nonviolent approach of CORE. He believed that if blacks were attacked by white racists, they should defend themselves and fight back. He also began to question CORE's aims and methods, and this too worried some members. As he explained, "They would say that they wanted to break down the barriers one by one, and then finally people would intermarry and that would solve all racial problems. And I would tell them that they had found the solution all right, the 'ultimate solution'—like Hitler.... They were telling me about my genetic destruction. In other words, through intermarriage, the black race would gradually die out."

Innis was a convincing talker, and before long many in the group began to share his opinions, especially as the civil rights movement seemed to be making so little progress. Attempts at busing had not desegregated the New York schools, and the Civil Rights Act of 1964 had certainly not solved all the prob-

Roy Innis

lems. Clearly, it was time to try different tactics. So, despite some opposition from the pacifist members of CORE's Harlem chapter, Innis was elected chairman of its education committee in 1964, and the following year he was elected chairman of the Harlem chapter itself.

At CORE's national convention in 1967, Innis managed to get the word *multiracial* removed from CORE's constitution. He envisioned the organization as a black power movement, serving the needs of African Americans. The year 1967 also saw Innis's appointment as executive director of the Harlem Commonwealth Council. This was a federal project aimed at combatting poverty by starting small businesses in Harlem and training people to work in them.

In December 1963, Innis was named associate national director of CORE, and he stood in as director the following summer when Floyd McKissick, was not well enough to carry the load. It seemed logical that Innis would take over permanently from McKissick, but some members of CORE considered him far too radical, and it was not until 1968 that he was at length confirmed as national director. One of the first things he did was to bring in a new constitution, which specifically committed the organization to black power. He also centralized the organization, allowing the local branches far less power. "For the first time, CORE is one team working together," he said.

National director of CORE

Soon after becoming national director, Innis explained to *Life* magazine that black power involved having control of banks, businesses, newspapers, and so on. "We must control the institutions in our area," he said. He immediately took steps in this direction by getting a brokerage house to set up a branch in Harlem that would be mainly black owned and black staffed. He also started a newspaper, the *Manhattan Tribune,* which he co-published with William Haddad. It was a joint white and black effort, with Haddad giving the white liberal viewpoint while Innis and other black journalists presented the black power point of view.

Over the next several years, Innis continued to encourage black businesses and to push for more educational and political opportunities for blacks. Yet, he was never far from controversy. CORE had a stormy time under his leadership, and many members left. Innis's assertive character caused some members to accuse him of running a one-man show. Others queried the way he was raising funds and spending the organization's money. In the late

1970s, he had to fight a lawsuit over his handling of CORE funds—he was accused of appropriating some of the money for his personal use. When the matter was settled in 1981, Innis was required to contribute $35,000 to CORE over a period of three years, though he did not have to admit that he had misspent the funds.

James Farmer, who had founded CORE in 1942, watched these events with dismay, and in the 1980s he and other former CORE members tried to remove Innis from the leadership. Innis fought back and remained head of CORE—though it was no longer the vigorous organization it had been in the 1960s. By the end of the 1980s, most CORE groups had become inactive. This was partly because Innis himself had turned to other interests. In 1986, he ran for Congress as a Republican candidate. Although he did not win a seat, he remained interested in holding public office.

As Innis has grown older, his fervor has not mellowed. He can still get into shouting matches on television. Twice married, he has eight children, two of whom have died. His eldest son was killed while still a child—shot in the back by a man in a nearby apartment building. This may be one of the reasons why Innis views crime as even more destructive than racism. "We don't need more civil rights laws," he has said, "We need to clear our neighborhoods of drugs and crime."

Janet Jackson

Singer
Born May 16, 1966, Gary, Indiana

The Jacksons could be considered America's first family of music. Joseph, the father, played the guitar with the Falcons, and Katherine, the mother, played the clarinet. Brothers Michael, Jackie, Tito, Jermaine, and Marlon formed the Jackson Five, which soared to the top of the music charts during the 1970s. Michael went on to produce the biggest selling album in history, and several others have produced memorable recordings. Now there's Janet Jackson, who has managed to step out of the shadow of her famous musical family and stand out on her own. She has recorded two successful albums and acted in several television shows. Jackson was primarily regarded as Michael's little sister until her two hits, "What Have You Done for Me Lately" and "Nasty" hit the airwaves. Her first album, *Control*, soared to the top of *Billboard*'s album charts, and she followed it with the critically-acclaimed *Rhythm Nation 1814*, which featured the popular "Miss You Much."

Growing up with the Jackson Five

Jackson was born in 1966 (although some sources say 1967) in Gary, Indiana. By the time she was four, her five brothers were part of the singing-entertainment group, the Jackson Five. They reached nationwide popularity, which eventually led the family to move to a suburb of Los Angeles.

Originally, Jackson wanted to become a horse-racing jockey, but after her father heard her voice on tape, he began pushing her toward a career in music. When she was nine, she appeared on one of her brothers' variety specials. Jackson was spotted by producer

Janet Jackson

Norman Lear during this performance, and he recruited her for his situation comedy, *Good Times*. She played Penny, an abused child who was adopted by one of the regular characters. Later she portrayed Charlene, the girlfriend of Willis, on *Diff'rent Strokes*. While still in her teens, she joined the cast of *Fame*, a syndicated television series. Aldore Collier described her in *Ebony* magazine as growing up "before the television-viewing public, almost like a slowly blooming rose."

Jackson was also interested in music and produced two albums that were poorly received. The albums were aimed at teenagers and were co-produced by other members of the wholesome-image Jackson family. Jackson broke away from that image in 1984 and surprised her family by eloping with James DeBarge. A member of another family singing group, DeBarge, he had been Jackson's friend since she was ten years old. The marriage, however, ended in less than a year. There were several rumors about why the marriage broke up, including Jackson's age, but she denied that had anything to do with it. Suzanne Stevens, a reporter with *People* magazine, claimed that John McClain, an executive at A&M records, "hounded" her for eight months to annul the marriage for fear that it would hurt her career. Jackson said the reason for the split was due to the heavy demands placed on both her and her husband. She told *Ebony*, "It was really hard and it just couldn't go that way. You have to really have that free time together."

Control breaks loose

Shortly after her break with DeBarge, she began work on a new album, *Control*. She went on a diet, took voice and dance lessons for three months, and went to Minneapolis to record under Jimmy Jam and Terry Lewis, protégés of the singer/songwriter formerly known as Prince. The hard work quickly paid off. *Control* sold more than one million copies with "What Have You Done For Me Lately" and "Nasty" being the two biggest hits. *Rolling Stone* reviewer Rob Hoerburger stated it was "a better album than Diana Ross has made in five years." Ralph Novak, a reviewer with *People*, said the album contained too much instrumentation, but Jackson could "sing with such sweet clarity that it's a puzzle why anyone would insist on burying her." He also stated she was "clearly making a strident declaration of independence" with this album.

Although it may have seemed like a declaration from her parents, she still moved in with her parents after her marriage ended. Jackson's close relationship with her mother made the decision to return home easier, although her mother sometimes has some misgivings about Jackson's sexy image. One of *Control*'s songs, "Funny How Time Flies," once provoked Mrs. Jackson to comment, "I don't like that moaning at the end. I don't like it when my baby does that." Jackson said in *Ebony* magazine that she enjoyed living at home because she could have early-morning conversations with her brother Michael. The two have a common interest in exotic pets. In 1990, Jackson moved in with her boyfriend, Rene Elizondo.

In 1989 Jackson released another album, *Rhythm Nation 1814*, which featured the popular hit, "Miss You Much." The album sold well and *Rolling Stone* critic Vince Aletti gave it an excellent rating. The album deals with the issues of illiteracy, prejudice, homelessness, and other social problems interspersed with dance tunes. Her music and themes on *Rhythm Nation* have brought comparisons with Sly and the Family Stone and the late Marvin Gaye. Aletti praised the record's "simplicity and directness" and concluded that "nothing sounds slight and everything clicks."

Jackson supports the causes she sings about through a variety of charities including the Make-a-Wish Foundation and the United Negro College Fund. She currently resides in Los Angeles.

Jesse Jackson

Civil rights leader, politician, minister
Born October 8, 1941, Greenville,
    South Carolina

"These hands that picked cotton can pick the next president of the United States."

A Baptist minister and longtime political activist, the Rev. Jesse Jackson is one of the most dynamic black leaders the United States has known. Millions of Americans, black and white, have been inspired by his pulpit-style oratory, rallying behind his campaigns for civil rights and economic justice.

Jackson has pursued his aims by working within the system rather than against it, and in the 1980s he gained widespread support when he twice ran as a candidate for the Democratic presidential nomination. He has also taken on the role of diplomat, negotiating with foreign leaders, which has brought him great prestige abroad. At home his stature is such that public opinion polls have shown him to be the most important black leader and also the third most admired man in the United States.

The ambitious student

Jesse Louis Jackson is descended from African slaves, Cherokee Indians, and an Irish plantation owner. Like so many African Americans who have achieved success, he had to overcome major obstacles—in his case, the fact that he was illegitimate. He has said that his ambitious nature, his will to succeed, is the result of being teased as a child. He was determined to do better than the kids who taunted him.

Jesse Jackson's mother, Helen Burns, was an unwed high school student, and his father was a middle-class neighbor, a married man named Noah Robinson. When Jesse was two,

his mother married Charles Jackson, a postal worker and janitor, so the boy did have a father figure in his life. He was not formally adopted by his stepfather until he was sixteen. In the meantime, he grew up alongside half brothers who were legitimate and who were the favored children in the family.

Jackson hid his insecurity by assuming an air of superiority and by trying hard to be superior. Fiercely competitive, he felt the need to win at everything and quite often did. At Sterling High School in Greenville, he was president of his class, the honor society, and the student council. He did well in his schoolwork and excelled in football, baseball, and basketball. On graduating from high school in 1959, he won a football scholarship to the University of Illinois.

Jackson stayed only a year at Illinois. He had hoped to become a starting quarterback but was told that blacks were expected to be linesmen. There were numerous other slights too, so in 1960 he transferred to the all-black North Carolina Agricultural and Technical (A&T) College in Greensboro. There he became a star quarterback—as well as being elected president of the student body. On graduating with a B.A. in sociology in 1964, Jackson gained a Rockefeller grant to study at Chicago Theological Seminary with the aim of becoming a minister. He was ordained in 1968, having left the college two years earlier, just before completing the course, in order to work full time for the civil rights movement.

The civil rights activist

Jackson first became active in the civil rights movement in 1963, while a student at North

Jesse Jackson

Carolina A & T. It was because of his efforts that Greensboro became less segregated, for he led marches and sit-ins against hotels and restaurants that would not admit blacks. In 1964, he became southeastern field director of the Council on Racial Equality (CORE), and that same year he was also a delegate to the Young Democrats National Convention.

Before long, Jackson took on a larger leadership role. He was already a member of the Atlanta-based Southern Christian Leadership Conference (SCLC) organized by Martin Luther King, Jr., and in 1966 King chose him to head the Chicago branch of the SCLS's Operation Breadbasket. The aim of this project was to promote black-owned companies and to get more jobs for blacks in white-owned businesses, largely by boycotting those where there was blatant discrimination.

Under Jackson's leadership, Operation Breadbasket ran a highly successful campaign. Soon, many members of the black community were simply not shopping in stores where blacks had only menial jobs. One of the most successful efforts was against the A&P supermarket chain, which was subjected to four months of picketing and boycotts and at length agreed to hire over 250 new black employees, including managers and supervisors.

Other large firms did not wait for Operation Breadbasket to focus on them. They saw the way the wind was blowing and hired more black workers before they were forced to do so. Meanwhile black-owned businesses gained more customers, goods made in black-owned factories were bought by more retailers, and black-owned banks and other companies were given various forms of assistance by the government. These activities attracted widespread attention, and in 1967 Jackson was promoted to national director of Operation Breadbasket.

The charismatic leader

In 1968 Jackson was with Martin Luther King, Jr., when King was assassinated, and he later claimed that he held the dying leader's hand and heard his last words. Others who were present say this was not so. Jackson clearly hoped to succeed King as leader of the SCLC, and in fact he did gain considerable support, but the SCLC chose Ralph Abernathy instead.

During the next few years, Jackson continued to push for civil rights, organizing marches in Illinois and even running unsuccessfully for mayor of Chicago. Jackson's vigorous activity contrasted with Abernathy's less notable efforts, and Jackson made it plain that he was not impressed with Abernathy's leadership. On the other hand, Abernathy and his supporters were critical of Jackson, feuding with him over funding and accusing him of overstepping his authority, of being impatient and overly ambitious.

In 1971, Jackson resigned from the SCLC and formed his own organization, People United to Save Humanity (PUSH). Its aim was to get more political and economic power for black Americans and to inspire a sense of racial pride. As well as taking steps to protect black homeowners and workers, Jackson organized awards to honor prominent blacks. He gave radio broadcasts and speeches, spreading a message of hope and dignity: "I may be poor, but I am somebody," he had the crowds chant. "I may be uneducated, but I am somebody. I may be on welfare, but I am somebody."

Jackson's next effort, launched in 1976, was PUSH-Excel, a program that encouraged the young to take their education seriously and turn away from drugs and crime. As part of this crusade, Jackson toured schools, encouraging students to sign a pledge promising to study for two hours each night. The program had a notable effect in a number of states, though it also attracted criticism— largely because of the million-dollar grant it received from the Carter administration.

An international figure

In 1979, Jackson broadened his activities to include international politics. He went to South Africa, where he led protests against the system of racial segregation known as apartheid. He then visited the Middle East to try to improve relations between Israel and the Palestinians. This brought bitter criticism from the American Jewish community, for Jackson was photographed embracing Yasir Arafat, leader of the Palestine Liberation Organization. Nevertheless, Jackson had proved that he could function on the world stage—an essential for anyone hoping to be president of the United States.

In 1983, when Jackson announced his intention to run for the presidency in 1984, he said that he wanted to represent the poor and dispossessed, and he called on all disadvantaged Americans—women, Hispanics, blacks, Indians, Chinese, Europeans—to come together and form a "rainbow coalition." Although Walter Mondale won the Democratic nomination that year by a large majority, Jackson's candidacy caused Americans to think seriously about having a black president.

Meanwhile, during the 1984 campaign, Jackson twice proved his skill in foreign affairs. In January, after negotiations with the president of Syria, he obtained the release of a U.S. Navy pilot who had been held captive, and in June he persuaded President Fidel Castro of Cuba to release twenty-two Americans and twenty-six Cuban political prisoners. However, Jackson suffered a setback when it was made known that in a private conversation he had referred to Jews as "Hymies"— though he made a point of apologizing for doing so.

Jackson continued to take part in international affairs in the early years of the Reagan administration, making highly publicized tours of Europe and Africa. His position was thus far stronger when he tried to gain the Democratic presidential nomination in the 1988 campaign. This time, the media and the American public viewed him as a serious contender, and for a while he replaced Michael Dukakis as the front runner. Although Dukakis later recaptured the lead and became the Democratic candidate, Jackson gained 92 percent of the black vote and 20 percent of the white vote in the Democratic primaries—a total of 6.6 million votes.

After the 1988 elections, Jackson moved his family to Washington, where he continued to campaign on behalf of the poor and needy. In 1990, he was elected to the newly established position of senator for the District of Columbia.

A message of hope

Since 1964, Jackson has been married to Jaqueline Lavinia (Davis) Jackson, with whom he has had five children. He suffers from the chronic blood disease, sickle cell anemia, yet has never let this prevent him from committing himself totally to the causes he believes in. During his candidacy for the Democratic nomination, he told the black people of America, "these hands that picked cotton can pick the next president of the United States." Although Jackson did not run for the presidency in 1992, his message remains strong: the power is with the people, and it is possible for an African American to be president.

Mahalia Jackson

Singer
Born October 26, 1911 (or 1912), New
  Orleans, Louisiana
Died 1972

"I don't work for money. I sing because I love to sing."

W ith her compelling contralto voice, Mahalia Jackson earned the respect and admiration of people of all races and has etched her name in the history books as one of the finest gospel singers in the world. In her early days she leaned heavily on her Baptist upbringing, but as she grew older, her repertoire expanded, much to the delight of her fans. She appeared on radio, television, and in countless newspaper articles, and produced many best-selling albums.

The New Orleans music scene

Jackson was the daughter Johnny and Charity Jackson. Her father was a Baptist preacher, barber, and longshoreman; and her mother was a laundress and maid. Jackson was five when her mother died, so she was raised by an extended family of one brother, six aunts, and several half-brothers and -sisters. The musical life of New Orleans in the early 1900s had a big impact on Jackson as she was growing up. She lived beside a Holiness church whose rhythms and instruments gave her an appreciation of music. She was also surrounded by the music of Mardi Gras, street vendors, and the bars and dance halls of the city's black community.

To help support her family, Jackson worked part-time while attending grammar school. It is difficult to say exactly when Jackson quit school, but some accounts state she moved to Chicago when she was sixteen to join the Greater Salem Baptist Church and its choir. At Salem she also began a career in gospel singing as a member of the Johnson Gospel Singers.

Jackson had hoped to become a nurse when she arrived in Chicago, but she ended up working as a laundress and studied beauty culture at Madame C.J. Walker's and at the Scott Institute of Beauty Culture. She used her training to open a beauty shop.

Auditions for *Hot Mikado*

In 1936, Jackson married Isaac Hockenhull, a college-educated entrepeneur. Hockenhull realized that Jackson had great potential as a singer. He persuaded her to audition for the Works Projects Administration (WPA) Federal Theater production of *Hot Mikado* by Gilbert and Sullivan. It's been suggested that Hockenhull told Jackson that "nobody can touch your voice. You've got a future in singing. It's not right for you to throw it away hollering in churches. Woman, you want to nickle and dime all your life?" Jackson auditioned by singing "Sometimes I Feel Like a Motherless Child." She won the audition, but turned down an offer from Decca records to sing the blues since she felt she was a gospel singer. Hockenhull tried to convince her to sing the blues, as did legendary blues artist Louis Armstrong. Jackson refused to give in.

In 1929, Jackson met Thomas A. Dorsey, known as "the Father of Gospel Music," in Chicago. From 1937 to 1946 he became her musical adviser and accompanist. Their years together were highly successful, and by 1947 Jackson had become the official soloist of the National Baptist Convention. Besides traditional Baptist hymns and Dorsey-composed

songs, she became nationally recognized for her songs that were composed by the Rev. W. Herbert Brewster of Memphis. She recorded "Move On Up A Little Higher" with Apollo Records, which sold more than 2 million copies. She received the French Grand Prix du Disque in 1949 for her recordings of "I Can't Put My Trust in Jesus" and "Let the Power of the Holy Ghost Fall on Me." During the 1950s, she was featured on author Studs Terkel's popular Chicago television show. By 1954 she had her own radio and television show, owned a flower shop, and traveled to perform concerts.

Signs with Columbia Records

Jackson signed her highest-paying contract in 1954 with Columbia Records. Some of her hits with Columbia included "Down By the Riverside," "Didn't It Rain," "Joshua Fought the Battle of Jericho," and "He's Got the

Mahalia Jackson

Whole World in His Hands." She began singing less in churches and more often in concert halls. She was the first gospel singer to appear in concert at Carnegie Hall in 1950 and at the Newport Jazz Festival in 1958.

Jackson was also a strong believer in civil rights. When Martin Luther King, Jr. delivered his famous "I Have A Dream" speech at the Lincoln Memorial in August 1963, she thrilled thousands with her song, "How I Got Over." Jackson was a strong supporter of King and his Southern Christian Leadership Conference (SCLC). She also supported Chicago's Mayor Richard Daley and sang at the 1961 inauguration of President John F. Kennedy.

In 1952, Jackson conducted her first tour of Europe. She was credited as being the world's greatest gospel singer and received a lot of air play on French and English radio stations. In Paris she was called "the Angel of Peace" and became widely celebrated throughout the continent, singing to sold-out and standing-room-only concerts. Jackson loved singing so much, she used to give seventeen to twenty selections at a concert, even when she had to sing on successive nights. She returned to Europe in 1962 and 1963–64. She also toured Africa, Japan, and India in 1970. She met political leaders and royalty, including Prime Minister Indira Gandhi and members of the Japanese royal family.

Jackson was well known for her generosity, and she established a scholarship foundation in her name for young people who wanted to attend college. She received the Silver Dove Award "for work of quality doing the most good for international understanding."

Friends in the industry

Most of Jackson's friends were members of the gospel music field, such as Roberta Martin, Sallie Martin, Wille Mae Ford Smith, J. Robert Bradley, and Robert Anderson. She also had friends scattered throughout the entertainment industry including: Ed Sullivan, Dinah Shore, Duke Ellington, Louis Armstrong, Percy Faith, Harry Belafonte, and Albertina Walker.

In the book, *The Gospel Sound,* Tony Heilbut praises Jackson as the queen of gospel music. He called her "the vocal, physical, spiritual sympbol of gospel music. Her large (260 pounds), noble proportions, her face, contorted into something resembling the Mad Duchess, her soft speaking voice and hugh, rich contralto, all made her gospel's one superstar." Henry Pleasants, author of *The Great American Popular Singers,* says Jackson "would land on a note or a word she particularly liked, or wished to emphasize, and mouth it, or repeat it, or repeat parts of it, or shake it, or bite into it in a manner which often reminded me of a terrier puppy playing tug-o'-war with an old sock or shoe."

Michael Jackson

Singer
Born August 29, 1958, Gary, Indiana

Even when he was only five years old, it was apparent that Michael Jackson would one day become a legendary singer and dancer. He began his career with his brothers in the group The Jackson Five. They roared to success with several hit singles and their own television specials. As a solo artist, Jackson has had the unique ability to translate tunes from almost any genre—rhythm and blues, pop, rock, and soul—into success. Jackson has produced the largest-selling album in recording history, garnered a truckload of awards and honors, and thrilled millions with his videos and on-stage performances.

Born into a musical family

Jackson's father, Joe, was a crane-operator who moonlighted as a singer and guitarist for a small-time group known as the Falcons. His mother, Katherine, played the clarinet. They encouraged their children to become interested in music as a way of staying out of trouble. By the time he was five, Jackson and his four older brothers formed a rhythm-and-blues act known as the Jackson Five. The group won their first talent competition in 1963, received their first paying gig in 1964, and were thrilling local audiences by 1967. Steeltown Records, an Indiana label, thought they were good enough to produce a few singles.

The group's fortunes really took off after an appearance at the prestigious Apollo Theater in Harlem, New York. They received so many requests for appearances that their father quit his job to manage their career full time. They signed a recording contract with Motown Records and moved to California when Motown relocated its offices there. With the marketing strength of Motown behind them, the Jackson Five produced "I Want You Back," which was released in November 1969 and climbed to number one on the charts early the next year. They followed this single with

several other hit singles and won a Grammy Award in 1970 for "ABC." They also made guest appearances on a number of television shows including *The Ed Sullivan Show, American Bandstand,* and the *Andy Williams Show.* By 1972 the group was riding a wave of popularity. Although he was barely a teenager, Jackson was not only a millionaire, but also an international sex symbol.

In 1972 Jackson premiered as a solo artist with the Grammy-Award-winning album *Got To Be There.* He followed this with the gold album *Ben.* He continued to produce a string of solo hits, but devoted much of his attention to the Jackson Five. As the group matured, they eventually outgrew the agenda Motown established for them. When their contract with Motown expired in 1976, they signed with Epic to gain greater control of their music. They were renamed the Jacksons with Jermaine dropping out of the group and Randy joining in. In the summer of 1976, the group starred in "The Jacksons," a CBS musical/variety television show. Michael Jackson appeared two years later in the Motown/Universal film, *The Wiz,* and then collaborated with the film's music director Quincy Jones on Jackson's debut album on Epic, *Off the Wall.* The album sold five million copies in the United States as well as two million more abroad.

Destiny marks songwriting debut

Jackson made his songwriting debut with *Destiny,* an album that went platinum in 1978 and spun off two hit singles. In 1980 the group duplicated the feat with *Triumph,* written and produced by Michael Jackson and his brothers, Jackie and Randy. The next summer they embarked on a thirty-six city tour that produced *The Jacksons Live,* the group's last album, which was narrated by Michael Jackson. At about the same time he also sang "Someone in the Dark" about the movie *E.T.: The Extra-Terrestrial.*

The Jacksons decided to disband to pursue individual interests, and Michael Jackson became the most successful. In 1982 he produced the enormously successful album *Thriller.* It was a sensation that appealed to almost every musical taste and established Jackson as one of the world's pre-eminent pop artists. *Thriller* went platinum in fifteen countries, gold in four, and garnered eight Grammys. Sales exceeded 38 million copies worldwide, earning it a place in the *Guinness Book of World Records* as the largest-selling album in history. It spun off seven hit singles and Jackson became the first recording artist to simultaneously head both the singles and albums charts for both rhythm-and-blues and pop.

Jackson was riding a wave of popularity known as "Michaelmania." Critics called him "brilliant," a "rock phenomenon," and a "megastar." With this stardom came an ever-increasing lust for information from the public and the press. Although he has been in the limelight since he was five, Jackson has managed to carefully avoid making his private life public. *Maclean's* once stated that Jackson "has astonished his fans by shedding his lively, button-cute image and transformed himself into a mysterious, otherwordly creature perpetually posing behind a mask."

Since Jackson rarely gives interviews, he is often the subject of speculation in the super-

Michael Jackson

market tabloids. Stories have circulated that he has lightened his skin with chemicals and taken female hormones to maintain his falsetto voice quality. Other rumors question his sexual orientation and suggest that he has extensively remodelled his body with plastic surgery. Jackson has also been criticized in the press for his "weirdness" or "quirkiness." Producer and friend Quincy Jones rose to Jackson's defense in a *People* article by saying, "[Michael is] grounded and centered and focussed and connected to his creative soul. And he's one of the most normal people I've ever met."

The public and private sides

Many journalists have tried to delve into Jackson's private side without much success. Most view him as a paradox. He is a superstar and a devout Jehovah's Witness. He does not drink, smoke, or experiment with drugs. Some view him as a modern day Peter Pan—a man who refuses to grow up. *Newsweek* described him as "a stunning live performer, but also a notorious recluse.... He's utterly unlike you and me, with a streak of wildfire that unpredictably lights his eyes."

Regardless of how he has been described, most agree that his success has been based on his remarkable talents as a singer and dancer. His natural talent coupled with hard work and perfectionism has enabled Jackson to cross virtually every musical line ever drawn. Jackson has been credited with rescuing a moribund music industry and practically eliminating barriers barring blacks from mainstream music venues. Many critics have stated that Jackson has been able to be all things to all people. *People* magazine said his success is based on his ability to create "a portable dream." The writer explained that "in this dream world his androgyny does not threaten the virile, his youth does not threaten the old. His blackness does not threaten the white, for nothing seems quite real and all is softened by fragility and innocence."

Jackson's public image was brought under fire in the summer of 1993, when the father of a thirteen-year-old boy accused Jackson of molesting his son. Jackson was in Asia on a world tour at the time, but his spokespeople denied all charges of sexual misconduct on Jackson's part. They claimed that the child's father had attempted to extort $20 million from the performer before bringing the accusations to the police. Jackson told the media that a full investigation would clear his name.

Jackson has received a mass of music industry awards and has been honored for working with Lionel Ritchie to produce "We Are The World." It was recorded by a score of top artists to benefit the Ethiopian drought relief fund.

Jackson has continued to produce popular tunes and to work closely with top producers and directors in the music video industry. Some say his greatest work is on the stage, where critics and fans have called him one of the greatest performers of his generation. After so many record-breaking albums, many are wondering how he will be able to surpass his previous endeavors.

Shirley Ann Jackson

Physicist
Born August 5, 1946, Washington, D.C.

I n the complex world of physics, Shirley Ann Jackson is one of the America's leading young black scientists. She has made important contributions in several areas of this science, including the three-body scattering problem, charge density waves in layered compounds, polaronic aspects of electrons in the surface of liquid helium films, and the optical and electronic properties of semiconductor strained layer superlattices. Jackson has also served on numerous boards, received ten academic awards, and has published more than one hundred scientific articles and abstracts.

High school programs developed her career

Jackson was born on August 5, 1946, in Washington, D.C., to George and Beatrice Jackson.

Her parents firmly believed in an education, and her father fostered her interest in science by helping her build science projects. The excellent mathematics teachers and an accelerated science and mathematics program at Roosevelt High School provided her with the right tools to excel at university. Her home and secondary schools provided the basis necessary for the intellectual and psychological sharpness she would need to pursue a career in scientific research.

Jackson was valedictorian of her high school graduating class in 1964. She enrolled at the Massachusetts Institute of Technology, where she received a bachelor's degree in physics in 1968. Five years later she became the first black woman to earn a Ph.D. from MIT. Her research in theoretical elementary particle physics was directed by James Young, the first full-time tenured black professor in the physics department. Her activism on cam-

Shirley Ann Jackson

pus increased the black enrollment to almost 100 graduate students, many of whom have received their doctorates. She did volunteer work at Boston City Hospital and tutored at the Roxbury (Boston) YMCA.

After finishing her doctorate, Jackson became a research associate at the Fermi National Accelerator Laboratory in Batavia, Illinois. In 1974 she was named a visiting scientist at the European Center for Nuclear Research in Geneva, Switzerland. At both places she researched theories of strongly interacting elementary particles. Since 1976 she has been at AT&T Bell Laboratories in Murray Hill, New Jersey, where she has conducted research on a variety of topics dealing with theoretical material science.

Jackson's research has received critical acclaim within the science community, and she has been the recipient of ten scholarships, fellowships, and grants. They include: the Martin Marietta Aircraft Company Scholarship (1964–68) and Fellowship (1974–75); a Prince Hall Masons Scholarship (1964–68); a National Science Foundation Traineeship (1968–71); and Ford Foundation Advanced Study Fellowship (1971–73) and Individual Grant (1974–75). Jackson has also studied at the International School of Subnuclear Physics, "Ettore Majorana," in Erice, Sicily (August 1973) and the Ecole d'ete de Physique Theorique, Les Houches, France, (July–August 1978).

Besides the academic awards, Jackson has also received numerous honors. She was elected a fellow of the American Physical Society (November 1986); selected as "Woman of the Year" by the Lenape (Monmouth

County, N.J.) Professional and Business Women (October 1985); the CIBA-GEIGY "Exceptional Black Scientists" Poster Series (1981); and the Karl Taylor Compton Award of MIT (1970). Her professional society memberships include the American Association for the Advancement of Science, Sigma Xi, and the National Society of Black Physicists, of which she is a past president (1980–82).

A member of many organizations

In 1985, Jackson was appointed to the New Jersey Commission on Science and Technology by Governor Thomas Kean. She was reappointed and confirmed for a five-year term in 1989. She has been busy with many other organizations including the National Academy of Sciences, American Association for the Advancement of Science, and the National Science Foundation, promoting science and research and women's roles in these fields. She is a trustee at MIT, Rutgers University, Lincoln University (Pa.), and the Barnes Foundation. Jackson is also a director for the Public Service Enterprise Group (Newark, N.J.), the New Jersey Resources Corporation (Wall, N.J.), and Core States/New Jersey National Bank (West Trenton, N.J.).

Jackson is an active member of the Delta Sigma Theta Sorority and was president of the Iowa Chapter in 1966–68. She was vice-president of the MIT Alumni Association from 1986–88.

Jackson is also a busy writer, publishing more than one hundred scientific articles and abstracts. Her articles have appeared in *Annuals of Physics, Nuovo Cimento, Physical Review, Solid State Communications, Applied Physics Letters,* and *Journal of Applied Physics.* A complete listing of her published scientific works can be found in *Physics Abstracts.*

Jackson is currently employed at Bell Labs in New Jersey, where she now specializes in solid or condensed state physics. She is studying and seeking to explain the behavior of physical systems at or below the molecular level.

John Jacob

President of the National Urban League
Born December 16, 1934, Trout, Louisiana

"Job discrimination is not only a civil rights issue—it's a form of economic suicide."

When President Reagan's administration began cutting social programs in the 1980s, John Jacob became one of its fiercest critics. As the president of the National Urban League, one of the country's largest black organizations, Jacob attacked what he viewed as an indifferent American political system. He called on government to withdraw billions of dollars from the military budget to train minorities to become skilled laborers, and Jacob maintained the National Urban League as a powerful voice despite an 80 percent cutback in federal funding.

Found work in Washington, D.C.

Jacob was born on December 16, 1934, in Trout, Louisiana, to Emory, a Baptist minister, and Claudia Jacob. The family moved to Houston, Texas, where his father worked as a

John Jacob

carpenter and construction worker to supplement his church income but there was still not enough. The family of seven were cramped into two rooms with no gas or electricity, and Jacob did his homework by the light of a kerosene lamp and bathed in a kitchen washtub. His father instilled upon him the value of working hard so that one day things would be better.

Jacob worked hard at school and received an E.E. Worthing Scholarship to attend Howard University in Washington, D.C. In 1957 he graduated with a bachelor's degree in economics, then he joined the army for a year and became second lieutenant. Once back in Washington, he found limited job opportunities. He worked for two years as a post office clerk, a job he got with assistance from the office of Senator Lyndon B. Johnson. Next he was with the Baltimore Department of Public Welfare for five years, first as a public assistance caseworker and later as a child welfare

supervisor. Jacob had the unpleasant responsibility of deciding whether or not to take a child from a parent. During this time he also earned a master's degree in social work at Howard University. In 1965 he was appointed director of education and youth incentives at the Washington Urban League.

Jacob oversaw the creation of Washington-based Project Alert after racial riots broke out across the country during the summer of 1967. In the nation's capitol rioting lasted one day, resulting in the arrest of thirty-four people. The Washington Urban League responded by recruiting youths from the ghetto to act as leaders to bring residents' problems to the league. The league would then direct families to the appropriate social services. Jacob established several programs, including the Ford Foundation-funded Operation Equality and the government-funded Project ENABLE (Education and Neighborhood Action for a Better Living Environment).

Saw civil rights gains eroded by Republican presidents

After ten years with the National Urban League, Jacob became president of the Washington Urban League in 1975. In 1979 he served as executive vice-president of the National Urban League. A year later the chief executive, Vernon Jordan, was seriously injured in an assassination attempt, leaving Jacob in charge. When Jordan retired in 1982, Jacob was officially elected to the presidency by a unanimous vote.

The league of the early 1980s experienced a series of cutbacks in federal funding. The Reagan administration opposed affirmative action programs and mandatory busing of school children to desegregate public schools. Jacob criticized the administration, especially its appointment of a conservative majority to the Civil Rights Commission. A Supreme Court ruling during this time, stating that seniority takes precedence over minority rights for employment opportunities, reduced the number of jobs for minorities. Jacob joined other civil rights leaders and boycotted the hearings on employment quotas by the Civil Rights Commission.

Jacob released the 1983 National Urban League's annual report entitled the "State of Black America." The report claimed that blacks ended 1982 in worse shape than in 1981. He expressed concern that economic recovery may bypass many minority Americans, and that blacks would be hurt by the severity of the current economic recession and by federal cutbacks in social service programs. Jacob said: "Vital survival programs were slashed at the same time that the black economy was plunged even deeper into depression. The result was to drive already disadvantaged people to the wall." Since most blacks were employed in automobile and other blue-collar jobs that were hit hardest by the recession, he predicted that those industries would never employ as many people as in the past.

Urged Washington to reallocate military money

With the National Urban League undergoing financial strain, Jacob sought aid from private-sector companies to organize entry-level job training programs. He also proposed giving direct assistance from the league's own resources to poverty-stricken minorities and whites, including housing and job placement. Jacob urged the federal government to institute a full employment policy through public works and job training programs. He joined other civil rights groups in supporting economic boycotts against private industry to induce corporate funding for developing markets and jobs for racial minorities.

Jacob is a big believer in the self-help approach to solving black problems. To break the cycle of black poverty, he has suggested tutoring and counseling to raise Scholastic Aptitude Test (SAT) scores, a comprehensive teenage pregnancy prevention plan, and a male responsibility program for fatherhood. He has also addressed the issues of voter registration, education, drug control, and single teenage mothers dropping out of school and living on welfare. "What has distinguished us organizationally, is that in addition to our civil rights portfolio, we have always been a direct service organization," Jacob told *Ebony* magazine.

When the Soviet Union broke apart and the Cold War came to an end, Jacob said $50 billion from the military's budget should be used to train minority workers. Hopeful that new president George Bush would be open to civil rights issues, Jacob was soon disappointed. When Bush vetoed the Civil Rights Act of 1990, any hope of a reconciliation between government and the National Urban League ended.

Although Jacob believes in a self-help approach to social reform, he says that is not enough to end racial discrimination against blacks and other minorities. Government funding is necessary, he says, to provide fair competition at work and school and that the costs can be justified since highly skilled laborers will be the result. "Job discrimination is not only a civil rights issue—it's a form of economic suicide," Jacob once said, and he continues to hope that the American work force will admit more Hispanics, women immigrants, and African Americans.

Daniel James, Jr.

Commander in Chief, North American Air
  Defense Command
Born February 11, 1920, Pensacola, Florida
Died February 26, 1978, Colorado Springs,
  Colorado

"If you're at the top, you don't have to plead the way you do if you're at the bottom. You can exert a hell of a lot more pressure from the top with that authority than you can from the bottom with that torch, sign or brick. My motto is build a nation, not tear it down."

Nicknamed "Chappie," General Daniel James, Jr., became the first black to attain the rank of four-star general and to be named commander of the North American Air Defense Command. As the man who was once responsible for providing air defense for the continent, James commanded 63,000 people and controlled some of the world's most sophisticated weapons. A highly decorated military man, James also helped end racism in the armed forces by participating in sit-ins and standing his ground in white officers clubs. Upon his retirement President Jimmy Carter said James was "a superb military officer in times of peace or war."

Lived near the United States Navy air base

James was born on February 11, 1920, in Pensacola, Florida, to Daniel and Lillie James. His father was a lamplighter and his mother ran an elementary school for black children in her home. James's mother taught him at home until grade seven, while his father taught him how to handle neighborhood bullies. Since James grew up near the United States Navy's air base in Pensacola, he wanted to become a navy pilot.

After graduating from Washington High School in Pensacola in 1937, James entered Tuskegee Institute in Tuskegee, Alabama, with the intention of becoming a mortician, because, in the South, that was one of the few jobs in which African Americans had a good chance to succeed. After the United States entered World War II, Tuskegee became the country's major center for training black pilots. Upon receiving his B.S. degree, James completed his training in the government-sponsored Civilian Pilot Project. In January, 1943, James was accepted into the Army Air Corps Aviation Cadet Program.

James completed his fighter pilot training at Selfridge Field, Michigan, and during the final two years of the war, he trained pilots for the all-black 99th Pursuit Squadron. He also piloted C-37 supply planes to fields in the United States. While on supply duty at Freeman Field in Seymour, Indiana, on April 5,

1945, he and 100 other black airmen staged a civil-rights sit-in at a white officers club. "We were under arrest for three or four days," James later recalled. "They selected three of the men and put them on trial as a test case. Thurgood Marshall came down, defended them, and won the case. They let the rest of us go and dropped the charges."

President Harry S. Truman racially integrated the United States Armed Forces in 1947. James was stationed at Lockbourne Air Force Base, Ohio, until 1949, when he went to Clark Field in the Philippines as flight leader of the 12th Fighter Bomber Squadron. The first time he went into the crowded officers' club, the all-white group turned away from him and the room fell silent. The episode ended when Claude (Spud) Taylor, a white officer, went over to James and welcomed him to the base. "Spud and I became real tight," James said in an interview, "and that's when the 'Black Panther' tag took hold. (James used a black figure insignia on his combat helmet.)

Flew 101 combat missions during the Korean War

During the Korean War James was promoted to captain and flew 101 combat missions. Upon his return to the United States, he commanded the 437th Fighter Interceptor Squadron and the 60th Fighter Interceptor Squadron at Otis Air Force Base, Massachusetts. He was promoted to major and received the Massachusetts Junior Chamber of Commerce 1954 Young Man of the Year award for his community relations work.

James attended the Air Command and Staff College at Maxwell Air Force Base and

Daniel James, Jr.

graduated in June 1957. For the next three years he was assigned to Air Force headquarters in Washington, D.C., as a staff officer. In July 1960, he was transferred to the Royal Air Force Station at Bentwaters, England, where he directed operations of the 81st Tactical Fighter Squadron. From 1964 to 1966 he directed operations of the 4453rd Combat Crew Training Wing at Davis-Monthan Air Force Base, Arizona.

In 1967 James flew seventy-eight combat missions over North Vietnam as a wing vice-commander. On January 2 of that year, his force destroyed seven Communist Mig 21s—the highest such figure of any mission during the Indochina war. After a short stay stateside, James was made commander of Wheelus Air Force Base in Libya, North Africa, the largest American air base outside of the United States, in August 1969. During his seven-month stay he received high praise for his handling of relations with the military junta that took over the government of Libya soon after his arrival.

In March, 1970, James was stationed at the Pentagon as Deputy Assistant Secretary of Defence for Public Affairs. During the height of the Vietnam War, James was sent to college campuses to talk to protesting students. "In the very first week I got hit with snowballs," he remembered. "Later I got spit on."

James rose in rank over the next few years from one-star to three-star general. On September 1, 1974, he became vice-commander of the Military Airlift Command at Scott Air Force Base in Illinois. A year later he was promoted to four-star general and became the commander-in-chief of the North American Air Defense Command (NORAD). He was responsible for the surveillance and air defense of North American aerospace and for providing warning and assessment of hostile attack on the continent by bombers or missiles.

Besides his military duties, James was in high demand as a public speaker. He addressed many groups ranging from the Daughters of the American Revolution to youths in the Upward Bound program. He told young blacks and Spanish-speaking audiences that racism had virtually been eliminated from the Armed Forces, and the military offers great opportunities for those willing to work. "I have to impress the kids that nothing worth a damn is free," he told the *New York Post*. "I don't have to tell them I did it and I'm black.... I just might be an inspiration to that kid on the ghetto sidewalk to pick up a degree instead of a brick."

In fall, 1977, James suffered a heart attack and retired from the Air Force in Febru-

ary, 1988. He died of a heart attack later that month in Colorado Springs. Harold Brown, the Secretary of Defense, said James "fought for equal rights as he fought for his country, even when doing so was not popular. We are wiser, more tolerant and stronger because of Chappie."

Mae C. Jemison

Astronaut and physician
Born October 17, 1956, Decatur, Alabama

"More women should demand to be involved. It's our right. This is one area where we can get in on the ground floor and possibly help to direct where space exploration will go in the future."

Many people dream of flying high, but few have flown as high as Mae Jemison. In September 1992, when the space shuttle *Endeavour* blasted off with Jemison aboard, she became the first African American woman astronaut.

Many months of training and many years of education led up to this achievement, though not all of these preparations had been in the sciences. Jemison specialized in the sciences, earning degrees in medicine and chemical engineering, but she had also set her mind on being a well-rounded person with wide interests and knowledge. She therefore earned a degree in African and African American studies and went off to experience the world, working among the poor in Cuba, Thailand, and Africa.

"Science is very important to me," she has said, "but … one's love for science doesn't get rid of all the other areas. I truly feel someone interested in science is interested in understanding what's going on in the world. That means you have to find out about social science, art, and politics."

Science student

Mae Jemison had been fascinated by science since she was four years old, when her uncle first sparked her interest in the subject. She was encouraged by her parents, Charlie and Dorothy Jemison. Charlie was a maintenance supervisor and Dorothy a schoolteacher, and both were determined to provide Mae and her brother and sister with as wide an education as possible. Since the opportunities seemed better farther north, the family moved to Chicago from Alabama when the children were small.

At school, Jemison was often to be found in the library, deep in books about evolution or astronomy. She especially enjoyed science fiction, though she did not at the time imagine she would ever be an astronaut. Her first choice of a career was more down to earth. While attending Morgan Park High School, she was taken around a local university, and as a result she decided to become a biomedical engineer.

To gain the necessary background for this profession, Jemison took courses in biology, physics, and chemistry, but she found time to have an enjoyable social life too. She took dancing classes and art lessons, and was an active team member in various school projects. Despite all these activities, Jemison was consistently an honor student at Morgan Park

Mae Jemison

High, and when she graduated in 1973, she won a National Achievement Scholarship to Stanford University. At Stanford, she threw herself wholeheartedly into university life. She was head of the Black Student Union and gave classes on racism and other relevant subjects. At the same time, she was involved with dance and theatrical groups, producing and directing shows as well as performing in them. This led to a trip abroad in 1976, when she visited Jamaica as a representative of Stanford University at the Caribbean festival there.

In 1977, Jemison graduated from Stanford with a B.Ch.E. in chemical engineering and a B.A. in African and African American studies. She then enrolled at Cornell University Medical School and graduated with an M.D. degree in 1981.

Social worker and doctor

During her years as a Cornell medical student, Jemison took every opportunity to do more traveling. As well as wanting to widen her experience, she was eager to help others, and she found that she could do both by serving as a medical volunteer in the summer months. The volunteer work took her to Cuba and to a Cambodian refugee camp in Thailand, where she treated desperately thin, half-starved people who were suffering from tuberculosis and dysentery. In 1979, she made her first trip to Africa—an experience she thoroughly enjoyed. Her work there involved doing health studies in rural Kenya.

At Cornell, Jemison was as active in student organizations as she had been at Stanford, and it was not long before she was elected president of the Cornell Medical Student Executive Council, a role that took up a lot of her time. Even so, in 1979, she found time to organize a citywide health and law fair in New York on behalf of the National Student Medical Association.

After Jemison completed her medical degree and internship, she worked for a year as a general practitioner in Los Angeles. But she longed to return to Africa, and in 1983 she joined the Peace Corps as a doctor. She spent the next two years in West Africa, where she served as medical officer for Sierra Leone and Liberia.

This was challenging work, partly because Jemison was so young. At twenty-six, she often found it hard to get people to take her seriously; but they soon found how competent she was. Her work in Africa not only involved being doctor to the volunteers and the embassy staff, but she also had a host of other duties. As medical officer, she was responsible for teaching medical courses, supervising the laboratories, writing health manuals for the local people, and generally overseeing public health and safety in the area. It kept her very busy, and she loved every minute of it.

Astronaut

When Jemison returned home in 1985, she joined CIGNA Health Plans as a general practitioner in Los Angeles. She also began to think seriously about space travel. Ever since she had become fascinated by astronomy as a child—and ever since she had read her first science fiction story—there had been a curiosity about space, the dream that she might one day explore the skies. Because of the U.S. space program, this was now a practical possibility, and she had a suitably wide background and appropriate qualifications. Just to add to them, she enrolled in night courses in engineering at the University of California, Los Angeles. Meanwhile, she sent in her application to NASA … and waited hopefully.

Not long after Jemison applied to NASA, the space program suffered a terrible tragedy. On January 28, 1986, minutes after the space shuttle *Challenger* was launched from Cape Canaveral in Florida, it exploded and blew apart, killing all the astronauts on board. What had gone wrong? Until the scientists at NASA could discover the answer, there would be no more space flights.

This tragedy did not put Jemison off the idea of becoming an astronaut. Neither did the thought that she might have been one of those killed. As soon as the space program started up again, she sent in a new application, and in 1987 she heard the great news. Of the two thousand people who had applied to NASA, she was one of fifteen who had been picked for special training. Providing she passed the course, there was every likelihood she would become a space traveller within a few years.

The training course was no picnic. It involved tough physical challenges as well as specialized scientific training. Jemison had to learn how to jump with a parachute, and she had to practice surviving in the wilderness and in water, in case of accidents. On the technical side, she had to know about the workings of the space shuttle. "We are the ones who are often called the scientist astronauts," she explained to *Ebony* magazine. "Our responsibilities are to be familiar with the shuttle and how it operates, to do the experiments once you get into orbit, to help launch the payloads or satellites, and also do extra-vehicular activities, which are the space walks." It was a lot to learn, but Jemison passed the course with flying colors and was duly qualified as a mission specialist. Now all she had to do was wait her turn.

Her chance came in September 1992, when she made history as a crew member on the eight-day space mission of the *Endeavour*. This was a cooperative venture between the United States and Japan, and Jemison's duties included fertilizing frog eggs in space and seeing how they developed into tadpoles. She also gathered data on various medical aspects of space travel, such as motion sickness, and like the other astronauts she did her share of the general duties connected with the shuttle.

Since returning to earth, Jemison has been honored by many groups and has had the Mae C. Jemison Public School in Detroit named

after her. She makes a point of visiting schools to talk to the students, hoping to inspire them with the same love of science that has made her own life so exciting. She hopes for more excitement in the future. She would love to go back up into space; she told *Ms.* magazine that she would "go to Mars at the drop of a hat."

Beverly Johnson

Model, actress, singer
Born 1952, Buffalo, New York

"I'm not booked anymore as a Black model. I'm booked as a model. This means breaking into a new area and hopefully leaving the door open for more Blacks to do the same."

In 1971, when nineteen-year-old Beverly Johnson was looking for a summer job in New York City, she applied at the offices of *Glamour* magazine, hoping to be taken on as a model. Although she had no modeling experience, her appearance so impressed the *Glamour* editors that they hired her immediately. This was a fateful step for both the magazine and Johnson, for in the next three years she became a superstar of the fashion world—the top black model in the United States and the first ever to appear on the cover of *Vogue* magazine.

Along with her stunning good looks, flawless skin, and straight black hair, Johnson has an assured manner and easy charm that have greatly enhanced her career as a model. She has also made her mark as a singer and as a television and movie actress. As well, Johnson has entered the business world, introducing a line of beauty products and her own line of Beverly Johnson dolls. The multi-talented Johnson has even written a book, *Guide to a Life of Beauty* (1981). Not the least of her qualities is her commitment to helping others. The charities she supports include Africare and the Atlanta Black Education Fund, and in 1987 she posed with her daughter in advertisements on behalf of the AIDS Awareness Campaign.

High fashion model

Beverly Johnson's striking beauty is the result of her unusual bloodline. Her father, a machine operator, is part Blackfoot Indian. Her mother, a surgical technician, is a Louisiana Creole. When Johnson was a child, she considered her younger sister to be the truly beautiful member of the family, for she herself was tall and lanky. She was also very athletic—she very nearly qualifed for the 1968 Olympics in the l00-yard freestyle swimming event.

On graduating from high school, Johnson won a scholarship to Northeastern University in Boston. Her aim was to become a lawyer, but her college friends persuaded her to try modeling. They pointed out that her outstanding beauty and tall, slim figure made her an obvious choice. So in the summer of 1971, Johnson and her mother went to New York City to find Johnson a modeling job until classes resumed in the fall. The first places they tried offered little encouragement, but at *Glamour* magazine Johnson struck it lucky. The editors were bowled over by her looks, and they hired her immediately. "You're just what we are looking for," they told her, and she was sent out on location the very next morning.

Within a few weeks Johnson was doing so well that she had given up all thought of becoming a lawyer. The magazine's readers liked her looks so much that *Glamour* featured her on the cover, a move that doubled the magazine's circulation and led to even more photographs of Johnson. She was *Glamour*'s covergirl six times during her first two years as a model.

To Johnson's surprise, it was not only black readers who became her fans. "When I started being on the cover," she recalled, "white Southern readers—for the first time—said they wanted to be me. Black models never had that positive reaction before." Johnson's popularity was partly the result of her "supergirl-next-door" image. She came across as appealingly wholesome as well as beautiful—a pleasant, charming, and thoroughly nice person. She is one of the few models who have consistently refused to pose in the nude.

Johnson was soon snapped up by the Ford Modeling Agency, one of the best in the business. During the five years she stayed with Ford she made history by being featured on the August 1974 cover of *Vogue* magazine—the first black woman ever chosen for a *Vogue* cover. The international celebrity resulting from this photograph led to another "first" for black women when Johnson appeared on the cover of the French magazine *Elle*. In June 1975 *Vogue* capitalized on Johnson's fame by picturing her on the cover of its "American Woman" issue. Meanwhile, the Ford Agency kept her busy with a range of assignments, which included working as a runway model

Beverly Johnson

for the fashion designer Halston and singing "Come Fly With Me" in a television advertisement for National Airlines.

By the age of twenty-three, Johnson was earning more than $100,000 a year. Switching to Ford's rival, the Elite Modeling Agency, she continued to make history, breaking previous modeling records. By 1977 she had appeared on twenty-five magazine covers, including fourteen for *Glamour*. She was the most sought-after fashion model in the United States. It pleased Johnson that she was booked as a model, not as a black model. "This means breaking into a new area and hopefully leaving the door open for more Blacks to do the same," she said.

Life beyond modeling

Between 1971 and 1973 Johnson was married to the real estate agent Billy Potter. After her divorce, she entered into a relationship with Danny Sims, the music publisher and theatri-

cal manager who owns the Hemisphere Agency. Their daughter Anansa was born in 1980.

Soon after meeting Sims, Johnson began to change the direction of her career, concentrating on other areas in addition to modeling. In 1975 she appeared in the documentary *Land of Negritude,* which was filmed on an island in Senegal. Since then she has acted in several feature films, the most notable being *Ashanti* (1979), which also was shot in Africa. In the movie, Johnson is the kidnapped wife of Michael Caine, who plays a missionary doctor.

Johnson has also entered the music business, making a number of recordings. She took voice lessons for several years and in 1977 teamed up with rock singer Phil Anastasia to make two singles. As well, she produced the album *Don't Lose the Feeling.*

Television is another medium in which Johnson has performed. She has made guest appearances on the "Oprah Winfrey Show," the "Arsenio Hall Show," and other programs. She was also in Freddy Jackson's video *Tasty Love.* Alongside all these activities Johnson has continued to do some modeling, both on television and in fashion magazines and catalogues.

Character and brains are obviously key elements in Johnson's success, though her striking appearance undoubtedly plays a large part. The president of Senegal said that Johnson reminded him of the Queen of Sheba; others see her as a typical American. But for many people throughout the world, she is simply someone very beautiful, charming, and lovely—someone they would like to be.

Earvin "Magic" Johnson

Basketball player
Born August 14, 1959, Lansing, Michigan

"I didn't wake up in the morning and think that I'm going to get AIDS. I don't dream bad dreams about it. If I did, I'd be giving in to the negativity. When I dream, it's usually a dream that I'm still playing basketball.... I've always been this way, thinking positive, with a bright outlook on life."

Magic seemed like a natural nickname for Earvin Johnson. Whenever he took to the basketball court, he seemed charmed. He had a great scoring touch, superb ball control, and deft passing skills. When Johnson was at the top of his game, he led the Los Angeles Lakers to five NBA championships and was one of the highest paid athletes in professional sports.

Johnson's life took an unexpected turn. At a November 7, 1991, press conference, he announced that he had contracted the human immunodeficiency virus (HIV), which leads to the incurable, fatal disease AIDS. Johnson redirected his energies as a celebrity spokesman for safe sex and served on the National AIDS Commission.

Learned basketball while watching TV

Johnson was born on August 14, 1959, in Lansing, Michigan, the sixth of ten children. His father, Earvin Sr., worked on an assembly line at General Motors, and his mother, Christine, was a cafeteria worker. Often his father worked two jobs to support his large family. In his free time, Earvin, Sr., would watch basketball on television with Johnson and give him tips on how to play the game.

Johnson took a keen interest in basketball and spent many hours on the court. The neighbors called him "June Bug," because he used to hop from one court to the next. "I just wanted to learn to do everything I could to win," he told the *Washington Post*. "In the schoolyard, the only way you can stay on the court when there are lots of people around is keep winning.... And I wanted to keep playing. All day and all night long." He added that he was "blessed" with everything he needed to become a top-notch player—size, supportive parents, and good coaching.

As a sophomore at Lansing's Everett High School, he led his team to the Class A quarterfinals. The next year the team reached the semifinals, and in Johnson's senior year, they won the championship. Three times he was named All-State, and after scoring 36 points in one game, a local sportswriter nicknamed him "Magic."

Led college team to championship

After graduating, Johnson attended Michigan State University and led the Spartans to the 1977–78 Big Ten championship as a freshman. As a sophomore Johnson shattered a school record with 269 assists, and the Spartans advanced to the 1979 NCAA semifinals. In the championship game, Johnson squared off against Indiana University, led by forward Larry Bird. The Indiana star had been named College Player of the Year, but Johnson won the Most Valuable Player (MVP) award in the championship. After the game Bird signed with the Boston Celtics, and Johnson accepted a $600,000 offer from the Los Angeles Lakers.

Johnson's personability charmed his teammates and the local media. He was always in a good mood and was always ready for an interview. He felt a bit out of place in the big city, but he was at home on the court. Johnson's rookie statistics broke many Lakers records, including a .530 shooting percentage, 563 assists, a free-throw percentage of .810, and an average of 18 points per game. The Lakers, who were never serious contenders before, finished first in their division and then brought home their first world championship since 1972.

The most memorable moment during Johnson's first year took place during the sixth game of the NBA finals. With teammate Kareem Abdul-Jabbar unable to play due to an injury, Johnson started at center. He scored 42 points, grabbed 15 rebounds, had 7 assists, 3 steals, and 1 blocked shot. He was named the series MVP.

Endured second season nightmare

While Johnson's rookie season was a dream, his next one was a nightmare. He suffered a serious knee injury and was forced to miss 46 games. When he returned, his teammates resented and envied his talents. The Lakers made the playoffs and were heavily favored to beat the Houston Rockets, but they were badly defeated. Johnson received the brunt of the criticism. The tension between him and his teammates further increased when he signed a $25 million, 25-year contract in June 1981. Fellow Lakers, including Jabbar, wondered if the deal would give Johnson a say in team management.

Johnson's problems were further complicated when he and head coach Paul Westhead argued over strategy. Johnson blasted Westhead in the media and asked to be traded. Westhead was fired the next day. It seemed to many outsiders that Johnson was calling the shots for the team. He was booed, even in Los Angeles, but new coach Pat Riley turned the team around. The Lakers won the NBA championship for the second year in a row, and Johnson was again named MVP.

The next year the Lakers advanced to the finals against Larry Bird and the Boston Celtics. After a hard-fought series, the Lakers won. During the next two seasons, the Lakers and Celtics would split the championship.

Earvin "Magic" Johnson

With the Lakers winning championships in 1985, 1987, and 1988, Johnson became a big star in Los Angeles. Many of Hollywood's biggest names—Jack Nicholson, Michael Douglas, and Michael Jackson—were known to seek out Johnson. He traveled with bodyguards; lived in a fenced, guarded estate; and was mobbed by fans wherever he went. Johnson once told the *Detroit Free Press:* "people see the glitter and say to themselves, 'If only I could be Magic for a day.' I doubt if they could handle it, even for only a day. The glitter is part of it, but so are the people with schemes, the thieves running scams; so are the people who want to get so close that it becomes scary. There is never a normal day."

Announced his HIV status

In September 1991 Johnson married his longtime friend, Earletha "Cookie" Kelly, who was in the early stages of pregnancy. A few weeks later his life turned upside down: During a routine physical examination for an insurance policy, Johnson tested positive for the virus that leads to AIDS, an incurable and terminal illness. Dr. Michael Mellman, the Lakers team physician, advised Johnson to quit basketball in order to protect his immune system. With rumors circulating in the media, Johnson held a press conference on November 7, 1991, to explain the situation, after telling the other players on the team. Johnson said it was the most emotional experience of the entire ordeal.

Johnson retired from the game and became a spokesman for AIDS awareness; he also served as a member of the the National AIDS Commission. On September 25, 1992, Johnson resigned from the commission, citing President George Bush's lack of interest in their work as the chief cause. But he couldn't resist playing in the 1992 NBA All-Star game. Johnson dominated the game, scoring 25 points, pulling down 5 rebounds and making 2 steals. He was named the game's MVP.

Johnson's number was retired in an emotional ceremony at the Los Angeles Forum early in 1992. He played with the U.S. Olympic team in the summer of 1992, winning the gold medal in Barcelona, Spain. He attempted to make a comeback with the Lakers for the 1993 season, but quit during training camp on the advice of friends and doctors.

Although Johnson is free of symptoms, he cannot ignore the implications of his diagnosis. In 1991 Johnson told *Jet* magazine that he doesn't have fears about his life being cut short by AIDS. "The only thing I regret about leaving this earth is the fact that I won't see my baby grow to be old," he said. "I won't be able to spend the rest of my life with my wife.... Those are the ... things I regret."

James Weldon Johnson

Writer, NAACP executive secretary
Born June 12, 1871, Jacksonville, Florida
Died June, 1938, Wiscasset, Maine

J ames Weldon Johnson was a highly acclaimed poet and novelist who brought a new standard of artistry and realism to black literature. He was also the head of the National Association for the Advancement of

James Weldon Johnson

Colored People during the 1920s, leading many civil rights campaigns in an effort to remove the legal, political, and social obstacles blacks faced.

Brought up in a stable home

Johnson was born in Jacksonville, Florida, on June 12, 1871. Raised in a broadly cultured and economically stable locale, he attended the segregated Stanton School, where his mother taught. Since high schools were closed to blacks in Jacksonville, Johnson left home to attend secondary school and Atlanta University, where he began to realize the extent of racism in the United States.

After earning his bachelor's degree in 1894, Johnson worked as teacher and principal of Stanton School in Jacksonville, where he expanded the curriculum to include high school-level classes. He also became a spokesman on black social and political issues and in 1895 founded the *Daily American,* the first

black-oriented daily newspaper in the United States. Although the venture was short-lived, the newspaper became a voice against racial injustice and encouraged blacks to seek advancement through individual efforts.

A local white lawyer encouraged Johnson to study law, and in 1898 he became the first black lawyer admitted to the Florida bar. He practiced law in Jacksonville for several years in partnership with a former Atlanta University classmate. Johnson also wrote poetry and worked with his brother, Rosamond, to produce several popular songs.

Wrote songs for Broadway musicals

The brothers abandoned Jacksonville for New York in 1901 to seek their fortune as songwriters. Together with Bob Cole they secured a publishing contract that paid them a monthly salary. Over the next five years they wrote over 200 Broadway songs, including such hits as "Under the Bamboo Tree," "The Old Flag Never Touched the Ground," and "Didn't He Ramble."

Worked abroad as consul

While in New York, Johnson studied creative literature for three years at Columbia University and became interested in Republican Party politics. In 1904 he became treasurer of New York's Colored Republican Club and helped write two songs for Theodore Roosevelt's presidential campaign. When the national civil rights leadership broke into a conservative camp led by Booker T. Washington and a radical camp led by W.E.B. Du Bois, Johnson backed Washington. He returned the support by convincing the Roosevelt administration to appoint Johnson as the U.S. consul in Puerto Cabello, Venezuela, in 1906. With few official duties, Johnson devoted most of his time to writing poetry and the book *The Autobiography of an Ex-Coloured Man*. Published anonymously in 1912, it received little attention until reissued under Johnson's own name a decade later.

The Autobiography of an Ex-Coloured Man is the story of a man who is light-skinned enough to pass for white but who indentifies more closely with the black race. Early criticism of the novel emphasized Johnson's frank and realistic look at black society and race relations in the United States. In the 1950s it was reappraised, and a new appreciation of Johnson as a fiction writer emerged.

Promoted in 1909 to the consular post in Corinto, Nicaragua, Johnson found it a much more demanding position and one that left little time for writing. His three-year term of service occurred during a period of intense political turmoil in the country, and feeling he would have few opportunities in President Woodrow Wilson's Democratic administration, he resigned from his position in 1913. He returned to New York to become an editorial writer for the *New York Age,* the city's oldest and most distinguished black newspaper. The articles Johnson wrote over the next decade combined a sense of racial pride with a belief that blacks could improve their lives through education and hard work.

At the same time Johnson continued his creative writing. He used the Spanish he learned in the diplomatic service to translate Fernando Periquet's grand opera "Goyescas" into English, and the Metropolitan Opera pro-duced his libretto version in 1915. Two years later he published his first verse collection, *Fifty Years and Other Poems*. The book contained selections from the work of twenty years, and it drew mixed reviews.

Worked for NAACP

At the urging of W.E.B. Du Bois, Johnson accepted the newly created post of national field secretary for the National Association for the Advancement of Colored People (NAACP). His duties included investigating racial incidents and organizing new NAACP branches around the country. He helped raise the organization's visibility and membership following World War I. In 1917 he organized and led a well-publicized silent march through New York City to protest lynchings. In 1920 he made headlines for his on-site investigation of abuses that were committed by American marines against Haiti's black citizens. Johnson's report was published in a four-part series by *Nation* magazine, and had a tremendous impact on public opinion towards the government.

Johnson was named the NAACP's executive secretary in 1920. This was a critical time for the organization, since they had to defend the social and economic gains blacks made during the war years, when many migrated to northern cities and found jobs. Despite rising feelings of racism, Johnson was able to increase the NAACP's membership and political influence. He also tried unsuccessfully to get a federal anti-lynching bill passed.

Since he was disappointed with the policies of Republican presidents, Johnson broke with the party in the early 1920s and briefly joined Robert LaFollette's Progressive Party. Johnson pulled his support in 1924 when LaFollette refused to include black demands in their party campaign platform. He rejected Marcus Garvey's separatist "Back to Africa" movement and urged new black communities in northern cities to use their voting strength to force racial concessions from politicians.

Wrote critically acclaimed books

Despite the heavy demands of his job, Johnson continued to publish. He received critical acclaim in 1922 for editing the collection of black verse *The Book of American Negro Poetry.* He also compiled two books on black religious songs, *The Book of American Negro Spirituals* and *The Second Book of Negro Spirituals.* These books set the stage for *God's Trombones,* a collection of verse versions of rural black folk that many regard as Johnson's best work. He also wrote several other books including *Black Manhattan,* an informal survey of black contributions to New York's cultural life.

In December 1930, wanting more time to write, Johnson resigned from the NAACP and accepted a part-time job teaching creative literature at Fisk University in Nashville, Tennessee. In 1933 he published his highly regarded autobiography, *Along This Way.* The book discussed his personal career in the context of the larger social, political, and cultural movements of the times. Johnson remained active in the civil rights movement and in 1934 he published a book-length argument in favor of racial integration called *Negro Americans: What Now?* The civil rights movement was also the theme in his last major verse

collection, *Saint Peter Relates an Incident: Selected Poems.*

Johnson died in June 1938 after the car he was riding in struck a train at an unguarded rail crossing in Wiscasset, Maine. People across the country paid tribute to him and over 2,000 mourners attended his funeral in Harlem.

John H. Johnson

Publisher
Born January 19, 1918, Arkansas City, Arkansas

"Dream small things, because small things can be achieved, and once you achieve a small dream and make a small success, it gives you confidence to go on to the next step."

John Harold Johnson is head of the most prosperous and powerful black publishing company in the United States. The founder of *Ebony, Jet,* and several other magazines, he built up a multimillion-dollar business empire that now includes radio and television as well as other enterprises.

As a leading African American, Johnson has often played a public role on behalf of his country. He accompanied the vice-president to Russia and Poland in 1959, and in the 1960s he represented the United States at independence ceremonies in the Ivory Coast and Kenya. He also took part in a vice-presidential tour in 1975 to nine African countries.

Johnson's activities have brought him many awards, including the Spingarn Medal

(1966) and Chicagoan of the Year award (1984). A member of the Chicago Business Hall of Fame, the Publishing Hall of Fame, and the Black Press Hall of Fame, he has come a long way since he was a teenager teased by his classmates for wearing shabby homemade clothes.

The determined schoolboy

Johnson has said it was the teasing by the other kids that made him determined to succeed. He decided to show them he could do better than they, even though his mother was too poor to buy him new clothes. Johnson was brought up mainly by his mother, Gertrude (Jenkins) Johnson, because his father, Leroy Johnson, was killed in an accident at the sawmill where he worked.

Johnson was six when his father died. He passed his early years in a totally segregated environment, attending the school for black

John H. Johnson

children in the small rural town of Arkansas City. There was no black high school in the town, so the best Johnson could do after receiving his elementary certificate was to repeat eighth grade.

When he was fifteen, his mother took him to the 1933 World's Fair in Chicago, and they decided to stay there. Chicago offered far more opportunities than their hometown. Johnson would be able to continue his education, and his mother thought she might get a job as a maid or cleaner. By this time, she had married again, and before long they were joined by Johnson's stepfather. But work proved hard to find during the Great Depression, and the family was on relief for more than a year. Then Johnson's stepfather landed a job and Johnson also managed to get part-time work.

In the meantime, Johnson was attending DuSable High School on Chicago's South Side. Despite his shabby clothes, he gradually gained the respect of the other kids and was made president of the student council and president of his class. He also became managing editor of the school paper and business manager of the school yearbook, and he was a leading member of the debating team.

Despite all these activities, Johnson made time for his studies, worked hard, and became an honor student. In 1936, he was invited to speak at an annual banquet of the Urban League to honor outstanding black high school seniors. The main speaker was Harry Pace, president of the Supreme Liberty Life Insurance Company, which at the time was the largest black-owned business in the United States. So impressed was Pace by Johnson's speech that he offered the eighteen-year-old a job with his company and a scholarship to attend college part-time.

First steps in publishing

Johnson began at Supreme Liberty as an office boy, but within two years he had been promoted to personal assistant to Harry Pace. As arranged, he studied part-time at the University of Chicago, but he gave up these classes in 1938 and continued his studies at Northwestern School of Commerce, where he took night classes until 1940.

One of Johnson's duties as personal assistant to Pace was to help publish the company newsletter. In addition to providing the usual business information, the newsletter reprinted general news articles that were likely to interest African Americans. It was Johnson's job to go through the national newspapers and magazines to find these articles and show them to Pace, who then decided which to include in the newsletter.

While clipping the articles week after week, it occurred to Johnson that many people outside the company would also be interested in reading the pieces. So why not print them in a magazine? It would be a type of *Reader's Digest* composed specifically for African Americans. The more Johnson thought over the idea, the more he liked it—but the banks and loan companies did not. Every organization he applied to for a loan to launch his project refused to lend him money. It was too much of a risk, they said. A magazine aimed solely at a black audience could not possibly succeed.

In the end, Johnson raised a $500 loan by using his mother's furniture as collateral. With this money, he sent twenty thousand letters to Supreme Liberty customers, offering each of them a two dollar subscription to the *Negro Digest*. Some three thousand people replied, and this brought in enough money to launch a first issue of five thousand copies in November 1942.

To sell the copies that were not sent to subscribers, Johnson had his friends ask for the magazine at newsstands. When some newsstands began to carry it, Johnson gave his friends the money to buy any leftover copies so that the news vendors would think there was a great demand for the magazine and would make a point of stocking it regularly. To sell the *Negro Digest* in other cities, Johnson teamed up with magazine distributor Joseph Levy, and within six months they were selling fifty thousand copies of each issue.

Each issue included two regular features: an article by a black American entitled "My Most Humiliating Jim Crow Experience," and an article by a white American entitled "If I Were a Negro." After Johnson persuaded First Lady Eleanor Roosevelt to write an "If I Were a Negro" article, the circulation soared to 150,000.

The growing business

In November 1945, Johnson launched a second magazine, *Ebony*. It was patterned on *Life* magazine and was largely pictorial. More entertainment oriented than *Negro Digest,* its early issues focused on rich and famous African Americans. As Johnson explained, his aim was "to show not only the Negroes but also the white people that Negroes got married, had beauty contests, gave parties, ran successful businesses, and did all the other normal things of life."

Ebony was a success from the beginning. It sold out its first issue of twenty-five thousand copies and quickly became regular reading for the black community. From time to time, it was criticized by black intellectuals and others for being too sensational, too conservative, or too preoccupied with the glamorous lifestyles of people in show business. Black activists attacked it for showing too little concern about important issues. In recent years, it has at times taken a more aggressive stand, though basically *Ebony* remains a middle-of-the-road family-style magazine. This is what makes it so popular.

Johnson went on to launch other successful periodicals. *Tan,* a woman's magazine, began publication in 1950 and developed into a homemaker's journal with recipes and beauty tips. Then there was *Jet,* a weekly news digest started in 1951; it is still extremely popular. *Hue,* which was launched the same year and contained features rather than news, proved less popular and was soon abandoned. The most recent addition is *Ebony Man,* launched in 1985. According to Johnson, it is "for young black men on the go, young black men who are conscious not only of their grooming and their appearance but who feel secure about their prospects."

In the early days, Johnson had great difficulty persuading advertisers to buy space in his magazines, since they did not feel it would be worth the expense. To fill the gap and bring in the necessary revenue, Johnson created a mail-order company called Beauty Star, which advertised its products in his magazines. Beauty Star evolved into the Fashion Fair Cosmetics Company. Once Johnson's magazines had built up a large circulation, a wide range of companies were eager to advertise their goods. *Ebony* was the first black magazine in which white companies advertised general products not specifically aimed at black consumers.

Since 1962, the Johnson Publishing Company has brought out books as well as magazines, concentrating on biographies of notable African Americans. It has also diversified into other areas. Today, the company produces the syndicated television program "Ebony/Jet Showcase," and owns WJPC-AM radio in Chicago, Mahogany Travel, and a large amount of real estate. It also has a 20 per cent stake in the popular black woman's magazine, *Essence.*

Johnson's family plays an active part in his business. His wife, Eunice, whom he married in 1941, is president of Fashion Fair Cosmetics Company, and he is training his daughter, Linda Johnson Rice, to take over the Johnson Publishing Company when he retires. His son, John Harold, Jr., is no longer alive. In 1989, together with Lerone Bennett, Jr., Johnson wrote his autobiography, *Succeeding Against the Odds.* It is a fascinating story of a determined and imaginative entrepreneur. As Johnson pointed out when celebrating the twentieth anniversary of *Ebony:* "Achievement in the old era was measured to a great extent by material things. Today, achievement is measured in terms of whatever a man sets out to do."

Robert Johnson

Singer, guitarist, composer
Born May 8, 1911, near Hazlehurst,
  Mississippi
Died August 16, 1938, near Greenwood,
  Mississippi

"He was a natural rambler. His home was where his hat was, and even then lots of times he didn't know where that was."—Johnny Shines

So little is known about the life of blues musician Robert Johnson that many legends have grown up around him. One of the most extraordinary is that he sold his soul to the devil in order to become a brilliant guitar player. Other stories involve his death—that he was stabbed by a jealous husband or an angry woman. The truth seems to be that he was poisoned by an angry man.

Johnson's fame rests on the two recording sessions he did in the 1930s. Many of the numbers he recorded then were incorporated in his first album, *King of the Delta Blues Singers,* which was released by Columbia Records in 1961, long after his death. Other numbers appeared in *King of the Delta Blues Singers: Volume 2* (1970) and in *Robert Johnson: The Complete Recordings* (1990).

Delta blues are songs from the Mississippi Delta, where this melancholy and haunting form of music emerged. Typically the songs were performed by a male blues musician who accompanied himself on an accoustic guitar. Johnson's songs are among the most evocative of this music. They include the 1940s hits "Terraplane Blues" and "Sweet Home Chicago," as well as such numbers as "Love in Vain" and "Crossroad Blues," which were made popular by rock musicians in the 1960s.

Few details known about Johnson's life

Most of what we know about the life of Robert Johnson has been pieced together from the recollection of his friends, especially the blues musicians Son House and Johnny Shines. Other details have been discovered by researchers, but there are still many gaps in the story.

One certainty is that Johnson was raised in the Mississippi Delta—the stretch of fertile lowlands between Vicksburg, Mississippi, and Memphis, Tennessee. His hometown was the small community of Hazleton, Mississippi. People who knew Johnson as a teenager recall that he was keen to play the guitar but did not have one of his own. Apparently he used to grab other people's guitars and strum the strings vigorously, making a terrible din.

Nobody knows how or even when Johnson learned to play. According to one story, he ran away from home for about two years because his stepfather tried to make him work in the fields. Another story has him escaping from an unsuccessful marriage and returning two years later with a second wife. At all events, Johnson went away and came back, and when he returned he had his own guitar—a Gibson Kalamazoo—which he

Robert Johnson

could play beautifully. He showed such unexpected skill on the instrument that people began to murmur that he must have sold his soul to the devil.

Johnson was about nineteen years old at the time, and for the next six years he lived the life of a traveling blues musician, as many others were doing in the early 1930s. "He was a natural rambler," recalled musician Johnny Shines, who traveled with him for a while. "His home was where his hat was, and even then lots of times he didn't know where that was." Johnson went as far north as Chicago and Detroit, hopping freight trains to get from city to city and playing wherever he could gather an audience. "Played for dances, in taverns, on sidewalks," said Shines. Johnson also played in the many black nightclubs throughout the Midwest.

During these years Johnson perfected his style. Although he was greatly influenced by earlier blues artists, he developed his own special approach, making each song a statement with carefully developed themes. The combination of his sensitive lyrics, brilliant guitar work, and unusual singing style made him stand out from other blues musicians. "Unlike other equally eloquent blues, this is not random folk art, hit or miss, but rather carefully selected and honed detail, carefully considered and achieved," commented author Peter Guralnick in his book *Searching for Robert Johnson* (1989).

Twenty-nine songs enabled his 1960s revival

In 1936, when Johnson was in Jackson, Mississippi, he played some of his songs to music store owner H. C. Speir, who was a talent scout for the American Record Company (ARC). Speir liked what he heard and passed Johnson on to an ARC salesman, who took him to San Antonio, Texas, for a recording session.

The recordings took place in November 1936 at the Gunter Hotel, where ARC had set up equipment to record a number of musicians. Johnson's sessions spread over three days, during which he performed sixteen songs, most of which were later released as singles. Among them was Johnson's signature tune, "Terraplane Blues," which became a regional hit, and "I Believe I'll Dust My Broom" and "Sweet Home Chicago," both of which were standard blues numbers during the 1940s.

Six months later, in June 1937, Johnson was called back for a two-day session in Dallas, Texas. This time ARC was using an old warehouse as a recording studio. Johnson recorded thirteen songs, ten of which were released as singles the following year. He never made another recording, and he lived only one more year.

Johnson met his death when playing at a house party in Three Forks, near Greenwood, Mississippi. There he became far too friendly with the girlfriend of the man who had hired him, and apparently the man got even and slipped poison into Johnson's whiskey. Johnson died three days later.

Although Johnson's total recordings amount to only twenty-nine songs recorded in those two sessions in 1936 and 1937, his music survived to gain immense popularity after his death. Like other blues music, his songs attracted a relatively small public in the 1940s and 1950s as blues dropped out of fashion. But even during those years, a few Johnson songs were national hits, most notably "I Believe I'll Dust My Broom," which singer Elmore James recorded in 1951.

The big revival came in the 1960s, when rock musicians discovered blues music and added their own slant to it. Folksinger Bob Dylan said that Robert Johnson was one of the two musicians who most influenced him (the other was folksinger Woodie Guthrie). The 1961 album of Johnson's songs, *King of Delta Blues Singers,* was so popular that Columbia reissued it in 1969. Meanwhile the Rolling Stones scored hits with Johnson's "Love in Vain" and "Stop Breakin' Down," and Eric Clapton with Cream did the same for "Crossroad Blues."

Johnson's music has survived for fifty years, bringing each new generation a superb example of blues at its best. As the years pass, perhaps a little more will be learned about the man himself—but until then, much of Johnson's life will continue to be a puzzling but fascinating mystery.

Bill T. Jones

Dancer, choreographer
Born 1952, raised in Florida and Wayland, New York

"Yeah, life hurts like hell, but this is how I keep going. I have a sense of humor. I've got my brothers and sisters. I've got this ability to make something out of nothing. I can clap my hands and make magic."

While it is never easy to overcome the loss of a loved one, for dancer and choreographer Bill T. Jones the best way to cope was through dance. When his longtime friend, Arnie Zane, died of AIDS, Jones created an extraordinary dance called *Absence.* The dance evoked the memory of his late partner and lover and addressed the feelings associated with mourning. Zane's death is only one of several difficult topics Jones and his dance troupe have undertaken in recent years. Jones's troupe has been called "one of the freshest and most innovative modern dance troupes in the world."

Found dance more liberating

Jones was born in 1952 and raised in Florida and in Wayland, New York. His parents were migrant laborers and moved their twelve children wherever they could find work. In New

York Jones became a star high school athlete and was an award-winning amateur actor. He studied drama at the State University of New York in Binghamton but found the department too conservative, so he turned his attention to dance, where he was allowed more creative freedom. While at the university Jones met Arnie Zane, and the two traveled to Amsterdam, where they lived for several years. They eventually returned to New York, where they formed the American Dance Asylum. The troupe performed—completely naked—to great local reviews.

In 1982 Jones and Zane formed another dance troupe. Most critics felt the troupe's progressiveness in subject and execution were well done. *Interview* called the troupe "one of the freshest and most innovative in the world" and said they "reinvented the language of movement" in their performance with jazz drummer Max Roach at the Brooklyn Academy of Music's Next Wave Festival in 1982.

The dance company was enjoying financial success, but in the mid-1980s Zane became ill and was diagnosed with Acquired Immune Deficiency Syndrome (AIDS). Jones feared the illness would generate negative publicity, but Zane insisted on going public in the hope of educating people about AIDS. The troupe began exploring the emotional and physical aspect of the disease in their dances.

In a 1987 interview on the "MacNeil/Lehrer Report" Jones said: "Living and dying is not the big issue. The big issue is what you're going to do with your time while you're here. I [am] determined to perform." Before Zane died in 1988, the troupe performed dances of loss, grieving, anger, and ultimately

acceptance. That same year the company ran into financial difficulty, in part due to Zane's inability to dance. It was rescued from the brink of bankruptcy by a group of artist friends, who sold their works to raise $100,000.

Performed *Absence* in Zane's honor

To commemorate Zane's death, the troupe performed *Absence*. The piece was composed by Jones to depict the poignancy of a dancer who has lost a partner of many years. Jones performed as if missing a partner. He was out of balance on stage, lacking a counterpart and then pausing forgetfully for his partner's steps. His performance received rave reviews. *People* magazine felt the show had "a shimmering, ecstatic quality that was euphoric and almost unbearably moving." *New York* said the work took "its shape from Zane's special loves: still images and highly wrought, emo-

Bill T. Jones

tion-saturated vocal music." Soon afterwards another troupe member was sick with AIDS, and Jones choreographed *D-Man in the Waters*, which depicted dancers struggling with fateful tides.

Following these difficult episodes for the troupe was a time of triumph. They performed at the Houston Grand Opera in fall 1989 and debuted at the Munich Opera Festival in 1990. Their performance, *Last Supper at Uncle Tom's Cabin*, was in part inspired by Zane. Jones and Zane had been talking about Harriet Beecher Stowe's novel a few months before he died, and the idea for the dance began as a joke. After Zane died, Jones began to look more closely at the idea. He told the *New York Times*, "There is so much about people being torn from each other and people in pursuit of each other and with the kind of robust athletic partnering that we do, I think we'll produce something quite evocative."

The subjects in conflict are meant to be resolved during the course of *Last Supper at Uncle Tom's Cabin*. The dance begins with a quick summary of Stowe's book, about slavery, using nontraditional casting, mime, and masks to emphasize the role-playing and absurdity of slavery. The next section is a series of four solos by women presenting the troubles of a slave, a battered woman, a lesbian, and a prostitute. Jones then dances a solo portrait of Job, the biblical character ravaged by misfortune as a test of his faith in God, after which the biblical reference to Job becomes a tableau of the *Last Summer*. The final part of the dance is presented by an enlarged troupe in what *New York* termed "a sixties love-in." The magazine also stated that "it's

amazing how this sort of cheaply sentimental catharsis can still get to you."

New York took a broad view of Jones's choreography for *Last Supper at Uncle Tom's Cabin:* "Dance is not, primarily, what it's about. In genre, it's a multimedia extravaganza. Although there's plenty of movement—vibrant solos in an eclectic vocabulary, sternly patterned group work—someone's usually talking at the same time.... (It is a) work bristling with anger, energy, and provocative questions, but one apparently still 'in progress.'"

Jones told *New York,* "This piece must start as a fight and end as a huge song." The dance symbolizes his belief that life is full of jumbled and troubled experiences, but they can be made meaningful and beautiful through art.

James Earl Jones

Actor
Born January 17, 1931, Arkabutla,
  Mississippi

"Because I've had a varied career, and I've not typecast myself, nobody knows what I'm going to do next.... They don't know whether I'm ready to be a good guy or a bad guy."

When James Earl Jones was a child, he stammered so badly that he found it easier to write than speak. He not only overcame this problem and emerged as a skilled speaker, but he became a highly successful actor, the winner of Tony, Emmy, and Obie awards.

Jones has played every type of role, from medieval hero to science fiction villain. As the voice of the evil Darth Vader in the Star Wars films, his deep bass tones are familiar to millions of moviegoers. Less menacingly, his voice can be heard announcing "This is CNN" for Cable News Network. He has appeared as Jack Johnson in the 1970 movie about the champion boxer, as a spear carrier in the film *Henry V,* and even as a character in a TV ad.

Most of all, Jones is famed as a superb stage actor whose memorable performances in the plays of William Shakespeare and Eugene O'Neill have brought him wide acclaim. With his commanding presence, he can transform a role, playing with such strength and sensitivity that audiences spontaneously rise to their feet to give him a standing ovation.

Early years

James Earl Jones inherited his dramatic talents from his actor father, Robert Earl Jones, who played in the film *One Potato, Two Potato.* However, even before James was born, his father had left home to pursue his career, so James was fatherless throughout his childhood. He was often motherless too, since his mother, Ruth (Williams) Jones, was frequently away, working as a tailor. James saw her only on occasional weekends.

James tried not to blame his parents for deserting him; he knew that they had to earn money and that work was hard to get during the Depression, but he did feel hurt and abandoned. He was brought up by his grandparents, who eventually adopted him, and when

he was six they took him north to live on a farm near Manistee, Michigan.

It was around this time that the small boy developed a stammer, which eventually grew so bad that at his one-room grammar school he could only communicate with his teacher by writing. He still had the stammer when he became a student at Norman Dickson High School in nearby Brethren. One of the teachers there suggested that a possible cure would be to memorize speeches and go in for speaking contests. This Jones did, and by the time he graduated in 1949 he was not only speaking normally but was an eloquent member of the debating team.

Jones enrolled at the University of Michigan on a scholarship, intending to train to be a doctor, but after joining the drama group he realized that he would rather become an actor. Around this time, he visited New York and met up with his actor father, with whom he discussed his plans. His father was most encouraging and convinced him to make his career on the stage.

First, however, Jones had to do his military service. After graduating with a B.A. in drama in 1953, he joined the U.S. Army's Reserve Officers' Training Corps (ROTC). He spent most of the next two years in the Colorado mountains, involved in a course which he found so challenging and exciting that he changed his mind again and decided to stay on in the army. Fortunately for his future fans, his commanding officer persuaded him to try civilian life again before making his decision. Jones spent the next two years studying at the American Theater Wing, with the army pay-

James Earl Jones

ing for his tuition under the G.I. Bill. By the time he received his diploma in 1957, he was once again committed to a career in acting.

Success on the stage

Jones began his professional career in 1957 in a play called *Wedding in Japan*. From then on, he was seldom out of work, though he made only about $45 a week. When he was first in New York he lived with his father, who was also hard up, and to earn extra money they went out and polished the floors in some of the smaller theaters. Later Jones rented a scruffy apartment with no hot water, but it was cheap enough for him to afford without difficulty.

In these early years, Jones took any part and performed in any theater, however small, but in 1959 he had the excitement of appearing in two Broadway productions: *Sunrise at Campobello* and *The Cool World*. That year also saw his first appearance with the New

York Shakespeare Festival, though only as a spear carrier. His first major part in a box-office success came two years later, when he played Deodatus Village in Jean Genet's *The Blacks*. Jones's powerful performance in this part brought him glowing reviews, and when he rejoined the Shakespeare company in 1961 he was offered more important roles, such as Oberon in *Midsummer Night's Dream*. Then, in 1963, he was given the title role in *Othello,* in which he starred for over a year.

By this time, Jones's early perseverance was paying off and he was extremely busy. *Othello* was one of thirteen plays he appeared in during 1963, and in 1964, as well as continuing to play Othello, he appeared in the film *Dr. Strangelove* and in several television series. He was the first black actor to have a regular role in a daytime television serial when he played the doctor in "As the World Turns."

Star of stage and screen

The year 1967 saw Jones on a successful tour of Europe as the lead in Eugene O'Neill's *The Emperor Jones,* but it was the following year that he made his big breakthrough and became a celebrity. His sudden rise to stardom came through his portrayal of the world heavyweight champion Jack Johnson in the Broadway hit, *The Great White Hope*. In his eagerness to get the role, Jones trained to build up his muscles and had watched old movies of Johnson's fights. His efforts paid off with such effect that he was given a standing ovation at the premiere, which was repeated at almost every performance. The role won Jones a 1969 Tony Award as best actor, and when the play was made into a film in 1970 he was nominated for an Academy Award.

The 1970s and 1980s saw Jones winning more awards and also taking on roles normally played by whites, such as Shakespeare's King Lear and Lenny in John Steinbeck's *Of Mice and Men*. His most notable movie role during this period was the one in which only his voice was used as the malevolent Darth Vader in the Star Wars films. In 1982, Jones again played Othello—in a far more moving performance than his earlier one—and in 1988 he won a Tony Award for his portrayal of the baseball player in the play *Fences*.

Since turning sixty in 1991, Jones has cut down on his demanding stage performances so that he can have more time with his second wife, actress Cecilia Hart, and their son, Flynn Earl. He still appears regularly on film and television, taking a range of roles. He was the ex-convict private eye in the TV series "Gabriel's Fire," a writer in the movie *Field of Dreams* (1990), and a CIA chief in *Patriot Games* (1992).

Jones once said that he wanted to make his name as an actor, not as a black actor. This he has indeed done, with superb performances that rank him among the best in the business. As *Newsweek*'s Jack Kroll has said, "He's right in the room with you, but he's also in your mind, an electrifying double presence that only the strongest actors can create."

Leroi Jones

See **Baraka, Amiri**

Quincy Jones

Record producer, composer, arranger
Born March 14, 1933, Chicago, Illinois

"He's an enthusiast who thrives under a barrage of creative challenges and who exhibits uncanny emotional control as he moves from one high-minded hustle to another." —David Ritz

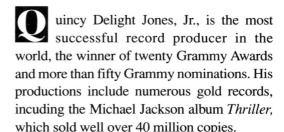

Quincy Delight Jones, Jr., is the most successful record producer in the world, the winner of twenty Grammy Awards and more than fifty Grammy nominations. His productions include numerous gold records, incuding the Michael Jackson album *Thriller,* which sold well over 40 million copies.

Jones has also made a name as a band leader, jazz trumpeter, and composer. His compositions include a large number of hit songs as well as theme music for television and movies. During his ten years as a composer in Hollywood, he wrote and arranged the music for more than thirty films and was four times nominated for an Oscar.

In recent years Jones has committed himself to a mammoth project—tracing and collecting all of black music from the year A.D. 500 to the present. "It is his range that distinguishes Jones," wrote David Breskin in *Life* magazine. "He has worked with everyone from Louis Armstrong to Eddie Van Halen, Billie Holiday to Diana Ross, Sinatra to Springsteen. No one in the history of contemporary American music has cut so wide a path."

First exposure to music was at age ten

Quincy Jones was not born into a home where music was part of everyday life. His father, a carpenter, did not play any instrument, and neither did most other members of his extended family. Jones's parents were divorced when he was a small child, and he was raised by his father and stepmother. He grew up in a large and diverse family that included three children from his stepmother's first marriage.

When Jones was ten the family moved to a suburb of Seattle, Washington. At his Seattle public school Jones learned the trumpet and quickly developed a passion for music. By the time he was a teenager he was writing his own arrangements and playing with a professional dance band.

In the small circle of Seattle musicians, it was inevitable that Jones would meet the young blind pianist Ray Charles, who performed at various nightculbs in town. Charles was just a few years older than Jones, and the two teenagers often stayed on after the clubs closed so that they could play bop together. During these jam sessions Jones picked up many valuable ideas of style and composition from the more experienced Charles. "A whole new world started," he said.

On graduating from high school, Jones won a scholarship to the Berklee College of Music in Boston, where he studied in the daytime while performing professionally in the evenings. He also studied at the Boston Conservatory of Music, but he soon left Boston to go on tour with the prestigious Lionel Hampton Orchestra. Jones had been hoping to land a spot with this big band ever since the age of

fifteen, when he had shown Hampton one of his compositions. Hampton played the piece and offered to employ the talented teenager, but the orchestra leader's wife insisted that Jones finish school first.

In 1956, when Jones was 23, he went to Europe with the State Department tour of jazz great Dizzy Gillespie. The following year he was back in Europe, touring with Lionel Hampton's band. When the tour ended, Jones stayed behind in France in order to study composition in Paris under the renowned Nadia Boulanger. Jones remained in France until 1960. During these years he formed his own big band and also gained first-hand experience of the recording industry. For three years he was music director of the Barchlay Disques record company.

Broke color bar in record industry

In 1961 Jones went to work for Mercury Records in New York as the company's music director. This involved writing songs as well as arranging and conducting the music. Over the years, Jones has written songs for some of the world's top musicians, including Louis Armstrong, Aretha Franklin, Sarah Vaughan, Peggy Lee, Frank Sinatra, and Michael Jackson.

In 1963 Jones produced his first hit record, Leslie Gore's *It's My Party.* The following year he was promoted vice-president of Mercury Records. This made Jones the first African American ever to hold such a position in a white-owned record company. He achieved another first in 1965 when he wrote the score for a Hollywood movie. Traditionally Hollywood employed only white musicians to write film music, but Jones had attracted the attention of a movie director with his score for a 1964 Swedish film, and the director then asked him to write the music for *The Pawnbroker* (1965).

Having broken through the Hollywood color bar, Jones took a little time to get established, but by the end of 1966 he had more offers than he could cope with. Until 1973 Jones wrote as many as nine film scores a year, including the scores for *Banning* (1967), *In Cold Blood* (1967), *In the Heat of the Night* (1967), *Cactus Flower* (1969), and *The Anderson Tapes* (1971). He also wrote for television, composing the signature tunes for "Ironside," "Sanford and Son," and "The Bill Cosby Show."

Meanwhile, Jones continued his work with the record industry as writer, arranger, and producer, recording his own performances as well as those of others. He stayed with

Quincy Jones

Mercury Records until 1969, when he moved to A & M Records. In 1981 he formed his own company, Qwest Records.

Produced album to aid famine victims

In 1974 Jones nearly died from a brain aneurysm—a burst blood vessel. The experience changed his outlook and gave a new impetus to his career. "Everything I do from now on has to be important to me, to have real meaning," he said. "It places a greater significance on everything I do, makes me do every album as if it's the last one I'll ever make."

Jones had made several successful albums in the past few years, including *Body Heat* (1973), which he said "was not a jazz album per se; it was a music album in which I tried to express the music that I feel." After his recovery he assembled a band of fifteen musicians and recorded yet another winner in this genre—*Mellow Madness,* which he dedicated to singer and songwriter Stevie Wonder.

In 1978 Jones's orchestration for the film *The Wiz* brought him together with Michael Jackson, and this led to their joint production of Jackson's first solo album, *Off the Wall* (1978). They followed up with *Thriller* (1983), which enjoyed record-breaking sales. Jones seemed to know all the big names in showbiz, and he was the obvious choice to produce *We Are the World*, the recording to aid victims of famine in Ethiopia. More than thirty top stars were to perform on this record, and handling them all could have been a difficult task. But Jones, with his customary aplomb, forestalled any problems by putting up a sign saying "Check your egos at the door."

Since the mid-1970s Jones's main preoccupation has been his project on the evolution of black music. The mammoth undertaking involves tracing, connecting, and bringing together the entire span of black musical history over the past 1,500 years. Jones has set up three timeline charts to cover the main elements: African music; European music as it relates to African music; and black music in America.

Jones's score for the movie *Roots* was part of this project. So was his recording *Back on the Block,* which was released in the late 1980s. The album portays several types of black music, including bepop and rap. *Interview* magazine described it as "more than jazz, more than hip-hop, more than documentary. Ultimately, it's Jones opening the blinds onto the vast panorama of African American tradition." This, in fact, is just what Jones hopes to achieve as he continues his mission of tracing black music and setting it on record in all its richness and variety.

Sissieretta Jones

Singer
Born January 5, 1869, Portsmouth, Virginia
Died June 24, 1933, Providence, Rhode
   Island

"I have a voice, and I am striving to win the favor of the public by honest merit and hard work."

ecause of her rich, mellow voice and accomplished singing, Sissieretta Jones was often compared to popular Italian soprano Adelina Patti. The press raved about Jones, calling her the "Black Patti," and she became one of the most famous concert performers of the 1890s.

Black Patti played to packed concert halls in Europe as well as North America, and she gave performances for American presidents and British royalty. Yet, because of her race, she never achieved her ambition to sing in opera. The musical world was not yet ready at the turn of the century to accept a black opera star—not even one with such a beautiful and highly trained voice as that of Sissieretta Jones.

Combined talent and educational opportunity

Black Patti was born Matilda Sissieretta Joyner, the daughter of Jeremiah and Henrietta Joyner. Her father, a former slave, was pastor of the Afro-American Methodist Church in Portsmouth, Virginia, but in 1876 he moved with his wife and daughter to Providence, Rhode Island, since it was a more comfortable city for blacks to live in and far less segregated than most.

White and black students attended the Meeting Street and Thayer Street schools where Jones was educated, and she also studied among whites when she signed on at the Providence Academy of Music in 1884. Music had been part of Jones's life since her earliest days, for both her parents were musical. Her father sang and conducted the choir, and her mother had a beautiful soprano voice. When they realized that their daughter, too, had a fine voice, they encouraged her to practice and arranged for professional training.

Sissieretta Jones

When Jones was eighteen, she enrolled at the New England Conservatory in Boston, and the following year, while still a student there, she gave her first professional performance. It was a benefit concert before an audience of 5,000 at Boston's Music Hall, and it was given ecstatic reviews by the press, who forecast a great future for the young singer. This not only delighted Jones, but it pleased her husband. Four years earlier, she had married Richard Jones, a young man who found it easier to spend than to make money. He had been a newsdealer before their marriage, and afterwards his main occupation seems to have been gambling.

Achieved phenomenal success

In 1888 Jones toured the cities of the East Coast—and took them by storm. She attracted large audiences in New York, Philadelphia, and Boston and was the first black artist ever to perform in Boston's Wallack's Theater. A

musical director who heard her telegraphed a colleague that he had found a "phenomenal singer," and this led to a tour of the West Indies. It is said that Jones was such a success on her West Indies tour that she was "showered with pearls, rubies, and diamonds" and was given five hundred dollars in gold by the president of Haiti.

Back in the United States the press had already begun to call Jones the Black Patti, and in 1892 she was the star attraction of the Grand Negro Jubilee at Madison Square Gardens. This proved to be a turning point in Jones's life, for it brought her to the attention of the public at large. Suddenly she was famous, sought after by concert managers, impresarios, and even presidents. That same year she was invited to sing in the Blue Room of the White House for President and Mrs. Harrison—the first of many such occasions.

Around this time, Jones signed a contract with businessman Major J.B. Pond, who managed several well-known musicians and writers. Pond promoted Jones vigorously, arranging for her to sing at Carnegie Hall and other prestigious locations. He teamed her up with black pianist Alberta Wilson, creating a most effective duo, and later added Paul Laurence Dunbar to the program, along with other celebrities. Pond made sure that his performers were well paid for their efforts, and he succeeded in getting Jones a fee of $2,000 for a week-long engagement at the Pittsburgh Exposition—more than any black artist had ever been paid before.

By 1893 Jones was at the peak of her career, a star attraction at the world's fair in Chicago, where music critics raved about the "surpassing beauty of her voice." It was at this point that her husband nearly ruined everything. He had acted as Jones's manager before she signed the contract with Pond, and now he began to do so again, booking her to sing at various places—without notifying Pond. The aim was to bring in extra money in addition to what Jones was earning through Pond, but the results were exactly the opposite. Pond was furious, and Jones's career was temporarily disrupted as she found herself involved in expensive lawsuits, which she could ill afford, since her husband had been spending her money almost as fast as she earned it. The resulting quarrels led to their divorce.

Despite these problems, Jones bounced back. She found a new manager and was soon on the concert circuit again, singing at such places as the New York Conservatory. She then set off on a tour of Europe, which ended in England with a command performance before the Prince of Wales at London's Royal Opera House, which she described as "one of the most exalted triumphs of my career."

Left concert circuit to sing vaudeville

Jones's frustration at not being allowed to perform in opera led her to leave the concert circuit in 1896 and sign on with new managers, who formed a vaudeville troupe called Black Patti's Troubadors. The Troubadors put on a type of minstrel show, offering "Mirth, Melody, Music and Darkey Fun." This was a distinct comedown after Jones's triumphant performances before royalty, but it gave her the chance to sing selections from her favorite operas.

The Troubadors were very popular, especially with black audiences, and they toured back and forth across the country until about 1908, when Jones reorganized them as The Black Patti Musical Comedy Company. This company was also popular at first, but it drew smaller and smaller audiences and finally disbanded in 1916.

Jones retired to Providence, Rhode Island, where for a while she looked after two homeless boys. Since she had no income, she supported herself by selling off her assets, including jewels she had been given, but she eventually became so poor that she had to go on relief.

Since no recording was ever made of Sissieretta Jones's songs, the "wonderful richness and fullness" of her voice which so thrilled the audiences who had the luck to hear her has been lost to the ages.

Scott Joplin

Composer, pianist
Born November 24, 1868, Texarkana, Arkansas
Died April 1, 1917, New York, New York

"One day the Maple Leaf will make me King of Ragtime Composers."

A round the turn of the century, ragtime music was all the rage, and the most popular ragtime melody was Scott Joplin's "Maple Leaf Rag." Ragtime evolved among the black community of the American South toward the end of the nineteenth century, and by the early twentieth century it was being played throughout the world. With its sprightly melodies and heavily syncopated rhythms, it was music that set one's feet tapping—the perfect dance music.

More than any other musician, Joplin shaped and popularized ragtime. He composed mainly for the piano, producing intricately crafted compositions that were beautifully melodic. Yet because he wrote popular music, he was not regarded as a serious musician, and when he attempted to break into the world of opera he met with no success.

After Joplin's death, as other forms of popular music replaced ragtime, Joplin was forgotten by all except jazz enthusiasts. But his music made a comeback in the 1970s, and during this revival it at last fulfilled his dreams of being appreciated by classical as well as popular music lovers.

Early years

Scott Joplin was born into a musical family. His mother, Florence (Givens) Joplin played the banjo, and his father, Giles Joplin, played the fiddle. All six of the Joplin children learned at least one instrument. Scott started on the guitar, but the piano soon became his favorite. This was partly his mother's doing. She took him along to the houses where she worked as a domestic and asked her employers if they would let him practice on their piano. The small boy showed such an instinct for improvising that he became the talk of Texarkana, and a number of music teachers offered to give him free lessons. The most helpful was a German musician, who taught Joplin harmony and composition as well as piano playing.

By the time Joplin was a teenager, he was making a modest living by playing at black churches and in honky-tonk saloons and bars. Although his father had long since deserted the family, he disapproved of the teenager's choice of career and tried to make him work for the railroad like himself. Their resulting quarrel caused Joplin to leave Texarkana, and he became a roving piano player, performing in the black clubs and bars throughout the Mississippi valley. By 1885 he was in St. Louis, Missouri, where he was employed as a pianist at the Silver Dollar Saloon, and in 1893 he was one of the many who flocked to Chicago to perform at the World's Columbian Exposition. Throughout these years, Joplin was constantly mixing with other musicians and absorbing their music as he evolved his own personal style.

In 1894, with the exposition over, Joplin settled in Sedalia, Missouri, which later be-

Scott Joplin

came known as the "Cradle of Classic Ragtime." Here he took the opportunity to get further training by attending music classes at the George R. Smith College for Negroes. At the same time, he led a full life as a performer. As well as being the pianist at the Maple Leaf Club, he played the cornet in the Queen City Concert Band, which is thought to have been the first band to play ragtime. He also did the occasional tour with the Texas Medley Quartette, a vaudeville group he had organized some years earlier (and which consisted of eight people, though it was still called a quartet).

King of Ragtime

In 1895, while touring with his Quartette, Joplin published two songs he had composed, "Please Say You Will" and "A Picture of Her Face." Both were sentimental and conventional pieces, a far cry from his ragtime style. Like the three piano pieces he published the following year, they were probably written for the vaudeville repertory of his group.

Joplin had already written some ragtime tunes, but he did not publish any until 1899, when he brought out *Original Rags.* Unlike his conventional vaudeville pieces, these were lively, beautifully crafted melodies that were clearly the creation of a master. That same year also saw the appearance of the sheet music of "Maple Leaf Rag," which Joplin had written two years earlier but had difficulty getting published. The rag was considered so difficult to play that it was rejected by two publishers before being accepted by the white Sedalia music dealer John Stark. To popularize a song in the 1890s one needed a music publisher, just as today one needs a record company. Although

the phonograph had recently been invented, it was not yet a common feature in American homes.

"Maple Leaf Rag" was such a hit that four hundred copies of the sheet music were sold in the first year, and by 1909 sales had reached half a million. Since Stark's contract with Joplin gave him one cent on every copy sold, Joplin was soon affluent enough to give up playing in the clubs and concentrate on writing music.

As "ragtime madness" swept the world, Joplin remained one of its leading exponents, turning out such pieces as "Peacherine Rage," "A Breeze from Alabama," "Elite Syncopations," and "The Entertainer." On his marriage to Belle Hayden in 1900, he moved to St. Louis, and during his five years there he produced nineteen superb piano pieces: rags, marches, and waltzes.

Meanwhile, Joplin was attempting longer, more ambitious works. Some years earlier he had written a ragtime ballet, *The Ragtime Dance,* which he at length persuaded Stark to publish in 1902. Stark was unhappy about risking his money on such experimental ventures, and Joplin could not persuade him to publish the ragtime opera, *A Guest of Honor,* which he completed in 1903. Although Joplin staged performances of both the ballet and the opera, neither was a commercial success.

Operatic composer

Joplin's marriage broke up in 1905, and four years later he married Lottie Stokes, who staunchly stood by him as his health gradually failed and his attempts to get accepted as a "serious" musician were consistently rejected.

Joplin spent most of the last ten years of his life in New York, desperately trying to break into the world of grand opera. He had written the opera *Treemonisha,* which he hoped to get published or performed, or at least taken seriously by classical musicians. As a black musician and a ragtime celebrity, he did not stand a chance. Not until much later in the century did African Americans at last break through the all-white barriers surrounding opera.

Treemonisha is not a ragtime opera. It is a complex work that includes arias and ensembles as well as an overture and instrumental preludes. Its plot centers on an educated orphan girl called Treemonisha who becomes the leader of recently freed slaves. The overall message is that African Americans should strive to get educated because by doing so they will find true freedom. With such a theme, the opera was far ahead of its time, and no publisher would take it. Joplin eventually published it at his own expense, and in 1915 he staged it in a small hall in Harlem. But it was a threadbare performance without any scenery and with a piano standing in for the full orchestra.

Joplin died believing his great opera had failed, but in 1972 it was given a full-scale performance by the Afro-American Music Workshop in Atlanta, and it has since been staged by major opera companies. The revival of interest in Scott Joplin began in 1970 when Nonesuch Records released a recording of some of his best pieces. Three years later his rags were included in the movie *The Sting.* So began a new "ragtime madness," which saw Joplin records and tapes selling by the millions. Meanwhile, the music world had at last recognized Joplin's genius. He is now ranked as a major American composer of great talent whose influence has been felt around the world.

Barbara Jordan

Politician, lawyer
Born February 21, 1936, Houston, Texas

"We are legislators, and we ought to remember that this is our role.... It is not a very sexy way to proceed in civil rights, but it is now an accepted, legitimate way to achieve gains for black people."

At the House Judiciary Committee hearings in 1974, one of the most articulate voices was that of Barbara Jordan. Her clear, firm statements and her precise assessments of the situation were watched with admiration by television viewers throughout the nation.

This was a difficult time for the United States and especially for the thirty-eight members of the committee. They had to decide whether or not President Richard Nixon had committed impeachable offenses in connection with the break-in of the Democratic National Committee headquarters at the Watergate Hotel. All were aware of the seriousness of the occasion and the importance of weighing every detail.

Although Jordan had not been long in Congress, she was already known for her clear thinking and straight talk—qualities that were evident in her speech to the committee. Summarizing her position, she staunchly declared

Barbara Jordan

her belief in the principles of the Constitution, and she roundly condemned Nixon's behavior as a breach of these principles. "My faith in the Constitution is whole.... I am not going to sit here and be an idle spectator in the diminution, the subversion, the destruction of the Constitution." With this speech, the black congresswoman from Texas became a national heroine.

Chose the law

As a child Barbara Charline Jordan never imagined that one day she would be a politician, let alone a national heroine. She did not even know what a politician was. Like so many African Americans of her generation, she was born into a very poor home, where she and her two sisters were brought up strictly. Their father, Benjamin Jordan, was a Baptist minister who demanded that they get top marks at school and would not allow them to go to dances or parties. Since they were also forbid-

den to go to the movies and did not have a television, Jordan assumed that all women spent their lives as her mother did.

Jordan's mother, Arlyne (Patten) Jordan, had been trained as an orator at the Baptist church, and Jordan showed a talent for public speaking too. She was the star of the debating team at Phillis Wheatley High School in Houston. By the time she entered high school, Jordan realized women could do other things besides keeping house, and she thought she might become a pharmacist. But she changed her mind when black lawyer Edith Sampson gave a talk to the school during Career Day. Although Jordan was not entirely sure what a lawyer did, she decided that she, too, would become one.

As a first step toward her career in law, Jordan enrolled at all-black Texas Southern University in Houston in 1952, majoring in political science and history. As usual, she shone as an orator, leading the university's debating team. After graduating with a B.A., magna cum laude, in 1956, she entered Boston University Law School. There she had a difficult time at first, for she found that her education in an all-black environment had put her behind the white students. "I was doing sixteen years of remedial work in thinking," she later noted.

Sought political office

On earning her LL.B. in 1959, Jordan returned to Houston to practice law, though at first she could not afford an office. She ran her practice out of her parents' home, using the dining room table as her desk. In addition Jordan worked as administrative assistant to the county judge and became involved in politics, working for Harris County's Democratic party.

In 1962 and again in 1964 Jordan ran for a seat in the Texas House of Representatives. Although she failed each time, she took heart from the number of people who had voted for her. Success eventually came in 1966, when she ran for a seat in the state senate and was elected by a huge majority. Jordan was the first black woman to serve in the Texas Senate, though she had not based her campaign on being a woman or on being black. "It feels good to know that people recognize a qualified candidate when they see one," she commented.

Jordan served for six years in the Texas Senate, and during those years she more than justified the voters' confidence in her abilities. Much of the legislation she supported was aimed at making conditions better for the poor. For instance, she helped create the state's first law establishing minimum wages. Her work brought her such respect that in 1972 the Senate honored her by choosing her as the traditional "governor for a day." As such, Jordan became the first black executive in the United States.

Served on House Judiciary Committee during Watergate

In 1971 Jordan turned her sights on the U.S. Congress, and the following year she was elected to the House of Representatives. On taking office in 1973 she disappointed some black politicians, because she did not take a militant position on civil rights. "We are legislators, and we ought to remember that this is our role.... It is not a very sexy way to proceed in civil rights, but it is now an accepted, legitimate way to achieve gains for black people." As she often said, she was "into brain power, not black power."

Shortly after taking her seat, Jordan was assigned to the House Judiciary Committee and thus found herself at the center of one of the major political dramas of this century. Although she did not like the idea of impeaching a president of the United States, she felt that the principles laid down in the Constitution must be upheld, and she said so fearlessly in her speech: "Has the President committed offenses and planned and directed and acquiesced in a course of conduct which the Constitution will not tolerate? That is the question. We know that. We should now forthwith proceed to answer the question. It is reason and not passion which must guide our decision."

Reason remained Jordan's watchword throughout her time in Congress as she worked to improve the conditions for the American people, and especially for those in need. She supported such social reforms as providing free legal aid for the poor, increasing minimum wage, and raising the amount of benefits received by the sick and elderly. As she said in her keynote speech at the 1976 Democratic Convention, she hoped to build a "national community" in which everyone would be able to share in the American dream.

This speech confirmed, yet once again, Jordan's brilliance as an orator, and it racked up another "first" for her, since it made her the first black woman to give a keynote speech at a party convention. Jordan had been the first African American woman in the Texas senate, the first black woman from the South to serve in Congress, and recently there had been talk that she might become the first black woman to be vice-president. However, she pushed the idea aside, saying, "It's not my turn." In 1978 she decided not to run for Congress again.

In 1979 Jordan launched a new career as a teacher, taking the post of professor at the Lyndon B. Johnson School of Public Affairs at the University of Texas. She felt the time had come to contribute in a different way, concentrating on the younger generation and instilling a set of sound principles in her students. "They are my future," she said, "and the future of this country." At the same time, she kept in touch with politics, and in 1992 she was again the keynote speaker at the Democratic National Convention.

Michael Jordan

Basketball player
Born February 17, 1963, Brooklyn, New
  York

"If things are going well, I don't have to score too much. I can stay in the background and get everyone else involved. If I sense we need that extra push, I can pick the time to explode."

K nown for his ability to fly through the air with the greatest of ease, Michael Jordan, the Chicago Bulls basketball star, is the most dominant player in the National Basketball Association. He can rebound, block shots, scoop up loose balls, and score almost at will. Jordan has been named the league's

Most Valuable Player on several occasions and was a member of the 1990–91 world championship team.

Has aptitude for sports at an early age

Jordan was born on February 17, 1963, in Brooklyn, New York, to James and Deloris Jordan. He was raised in Wilmington, North Carolina, where his father was an equipment supervisor in an electric plant and his mother was in charge of a bank's customer service department. Although the Jordans emphasized academics over athletics with their five children, they soon realized Michael had an aptitude for sports. They encouraged him to practice hard, set realistic goals, and to keep his grades high. When he was in ninth grade, he decided to become a professional basketball player. At 5 ft. 9 in. he was too short for the varsity squad, so he spent hours practicing his jump shot. By the time he was a junior, he had grown another six inches and improved his basketball skills to make the team. (He eventually reached 6 ft. 6 in.)

Between his junior and senior years Jordan was invited to spend the summer at the Five-Star Basketball Camp in Pittsburgh, Pennsylvania, a special session for the country's best high school players. Jordan displayed his outstanding skills. He was suddenly a hot prospect among college recruiters, and early in his senior year he accepted a basketball scholarship at the University of North Carolina at Chapel Hill (UNC).

Jordan made the starting team at UNC, which was an unusual feat for a freshman. He garnered national media attention on March

29, 1982, when he made a sixteen-foot jump shot with only seconds left on the clock to propel the UNC Tar Heels past the Georgetown University Hoyas 63–62 to win the National Collegiate Athletic Association (NCAA) championship. It was their first national championship in twenty-five years.

He continued to amaze basketball fans throughout his college career. He soared through the air, set a UNC scoring record, was a master rebounder, guarded two men at a time, scooped loose balls, blocked shots, and came through in key situations. Jordan was named All-American, and *Sporting News* called him the player of the year in 1983 and 1984. He also helped the U.S. team win gold medals at the 1983 Pan American games and the 1984 Summer Olympics.

Signed with the Chicago Bulls

With college no longer a challenge, Jordan left school after his junior year to sign with the Chicago Bulls of the National Basketball Association. He would later finish his degree in the off-season. The Bulls almost always finished at the bottom of the heap and were in desperate need of a superstar to keep the franchise afloat. Jordan didn't disappoint. He put on a one-man show wherever he went. Fans soon began turning out in droves to see "The Michael Jordan Air Show." They were treated with wild, whirling dunks in which he soared above players who were taller than himself, his tongue hanging out as testimony to his intense concentration. Fans were constantly amazed at his dazzling ball-handling skills, and he was a popular favorite during the league's slam-dunk competition. He finished

his first season with the second-best rookie season in NBA history, put the Bulls into the playoffs, and was named the league's 1985 Rookie of the Year.

Jordan missed most of the next season with a broken foot, and the Bulls were eliminated in the first playoff round by the Boston Celtics. They matched their playoff performance the next year, although Jordan became the second NBA player in history to score more than 3,000 points in a single season. He also set another record by scoring 18 consecutive points in a game against the New York Knicks. In 1988 the Bulls enjoyed their best season ever, and Jordan was named the league's Most Valuable Player, the Defensive Player of the Year, and was the Most Valuable Player at the annual All-Star Game. The Bulls defeated the Cleveland Cavaliers in the first round of the playoffs but lost to the Detroit Pistons in the second. Several key players, including Jordan, suffered injuries in 1989, but the Bulls continued to progress as a team. They beat the Cavaliers in the first playoff round and upset the New York Knicks in round two before falling to the Pistons in round three.

Despite the promise of better times ahead, the Bulls failed to live up to expectations in 1990. They made the playoffs but fell to the Pistons in the first round. Jordan was his usual one-man-show, but the rest of the team played poorly. At one frustrating point in the series, Jordan uncharacteristically lashed out at his teammates, accusing them of not playing up to their potential and expecting too much of him. A few responded by saying Jordan was a ball-hog, who never tried to help them improve their game.

Michael Jordan

Perhaps the team just needed to air its "dirty laundry," because in the next season everything seemed to come together. Jordan made an effort to restrain his own performance and began making plays to assist his teammates. Jordan remarked: "I try to be aware of when my team needs my creativity. If things are going well, I don't have to score too much. I can stay in the background and get everyone else involved. If I sense we need that extra push, I can pick the time to explode."

Unstoppable in the playoffs

The Bulls went on to finish first in their division that year and Jordan was named the league's Most Valuable Player. When it came to the playoffs, the Bulls were virtually unstoppable. They won fifteen of seventeen games, with Jordan unanimously voted the Most Valuable Player, and several other players enjoying an excellent playoff season. After the Bulls had finally won the championship,

Jordan told reporters; "I don't know if I'll ever have this same feeling again.... It's been a seven-year struggle for me and for the city of Chicago. And we did it as a team; all season long we did it as a team."

At a time when basketball popularity was sagging, Jordan almost single-handedly renewed interest in the sport. He is the most popular basketball player in the world and is in great demand as a spokesman for various products. Even before he played his first regular-season game with the Bulls, he signed with Nike to promote a special line of basketball shoes introduced in 1985 under the name "Air Jordan." The line eventually expanded to include tote bags, gym shorts, T-shirts, and sweatshirts. Soon other companies appeared at his doorstep—Wheaties, Coca-Cola, Gatorade, McDonald's, and the Illinois State Lottery. By 1991 Jordan was endorsing more products than any other athlete in the world.

One of the reasons Jordan has become so popular is due to his "good-guy" image. He is friendly and accessible, and he is active on behalf of various charities through the Michael Jordan Foundation. He regularly visits sick children in hospitals, lectures on drug abuse, holds summer camps for impoverished inner-city youths, and gives away game tickets to kids he meets in the rough neighborhood surrounding the stadium. Jordan appreciates the bouquets thrown his way, but he is also worried about having to live up to a certain image. "My biggest concern is that people view me as being some kind of god, but I'm not," he told *Esquire* magazine; "I try to live a positive life, love to live a positive life, but I do have negative things about me and I do make mistakes."

Nineteen-ninety-three was a difficult and tragic year for Jordan. His father was the victim of a random murder, and the media alleged that Jordan was involved in heavy gambling. On October 6 of that year the celebrated athlete shocked basketball fans everywhere by announcing his retirement from the game. "There's nothing left for me to prove," Jordan stated. "I can't step out on the court and know it's for no reason. It's not worth it for me. It's not worth it for my teammates." Jordan claimed that his father's death had nothing to do with his retirement. He will continue to act as spokesperson for Nike, with whom he holds a ten-year multimillion dollar contract. Fans began speculating about Jordan's comeback as soon as they learned of his retirement. "The word retire means you can do anything you want," he said. "So if I want to decide to play again, that's what I'll do. I'm not going to close that door."

Vernon E. Jordan, Jr.

Civil rights leader, lawyer
Born August 15, 1935, Atlanta, Georgia

"You knew there was colored water and there was white water, and you knew you sat upstairs in the theatre. It was a way of life, and you understood that. It never meant you accepted it."

With strong oratorical skills and a level head, Vernon E. Jordan, Jr., was one of the most visible and influential spokesmen for black civil rights. Using these skills, Jordan

soon held important positions with the National Association for the Advancement of Colored People and the Southern Regional Council. While still in his mid-thirties he became the executive director of the National Urban League, an organization dedicated to helping the black urban poor.

Attracted to the field of law

Jordan was born in Atlanta, Georgia, in 1935 to Vernon and Mary Belle Jordan. His father was a postal worker and his mother operated a catering business. The family lived in one of the first public housing projects built for blacks. Jordan had high grades in his segregated school and was an excellent basketball player and after high school graduation attended DePauw University in Greencastle, Indiana. The only black student in his class and one of only five in the university, Jordan fit in well with his classmates. He played basketball, wrote and acted in a play about racism in the South, and was vice-president of the school's Democratic club. He majored in political science and minored in history and speech. He also received several first prizes for oratory, including one at the Indiana Interstate Oratorical Contest.

After graduating in 1957, Jordan studied law at Howard University. He paid for his studies by working for two summers as a bus driver with the Chicago Transit Authority, making $2.45 an hour and sometimes working sixteen hours a day. While attending Howard he met and eventually married Shirley Yarbrough in 1959. The next year he graduated and received employment offers from several Washington-based corporate law firms, but he returned to Atlanta to join the civil rights movement.

Jordan worked as a clerk in the office of Donald Hollowell, a well-known civil rights attorney. Within a year Jordan's picture was in the newspapers for representing Charlayne Hunter, a black student, who successfully sued the University of Georgia to gain admittance. An angry crowd hoped to bar her from entering the campus, but Jordan used his six-foot four-inch body as a shield to protect her.

Directed Voter Education Project and United Negro College Fund

In 1962 Jordan was named the Georgia field secretary for the National Association for the Advancement of Colored People (NAACP). Jordan made speeches, organized new chapters, coordinated demonstrations, and boycotted industries that would not hire blacks. These boycotts were so successful that several Atlanta stores hired blacks that year.

Despite these successes, Jordan knew that blacks would have to use the vote to gain true power. He opened a private law firm in Arkansas in 1964 and also served as director of the Voter Education Project, run by the Southern Regional Council. This position took him across the South, coordinating voter registration drives and counseling black voters. As the number of black elected officials increased, so too, did Jordan's popularity. He became known among the black civil rights leadership as a level-headed mediator able to settle disputes whenever they arose within the ranks.

After announcing his intention to run for Congress in Atlanta in 1970, he was named executive director of the United Negro College Fund (UNCF), a fundraising organization to help finance black colleges. With Jordan in charge, the UNCF raised $8 million, which it gave to thirty-six member colleges.

Headed the National Urban League

In 1971 Jordan was asked to head the National Urban League (NUL) after the former executive director drowned while visiting Nigeria. The NUL was arguably the most important organization in the country for the cause of black empowerment. They hoped to obtain government and corporate assistance to fund job-training programs, early childhood intervention education, and other anti-poverty programs. Jordan was the first lawyer to head the organization, which had usually been run by social workers.

Jordan saw the NUL as a bridge between the white upper class and the urban poor. He sought funds from corporations and soon

Vernon E. Jordan, Jr.

found himself serving on the boards of several companies. Under his leadership, 17 new affiliates were added, giving the NUL a total of 117. During his ten-year leadership, he oversaw an annual budget of over $100 million, much of it supplied by the federal government. Combining his salary with the money made from serving on corporate boards gave him a six-figure income.

However, his taste in fine cigars and suits caused him trouble with other civil rights leaders. Jordan dismissed these criticisms. He told *Ebony* magazine: "If I do a good job here, the black people are not the only beneficiary; so is the country," he said. "The country has a vested interest in black people doing well. It is really true that the chain is as strong as its weakest link.... Those of us in leadership of the black community have an enormous burden of clarifying and defining the issues."

Shot in Fort Worth

Jordan traveled extensively for the NUL to promote social concern about urban poverty. In 1980, after speaking at the NUL's Fort Wayne local chapter, he visited for an hour with member Martha Coleman. When she was returning Jordan to his hotel, he was shot from a distance by a sniper using a powerful hunting rifle. Rushed to the hospital with a fist-sized hole in his back, he spent almost five hours in surgery and, over the next three months, underwent five more operations. Many people visited, including Jesse Jackson and then-President Jimmy Carter. Despite an investigation by the Federal Bureau of Investigation (FBI), no one was ever brought to trial.

After Jordan was released from the hospital, he vowed to return as NUL director as soon as he recovered. Then he retired from the organization in 1981, but he denied that the shooting had anything to do with it. He said his reason for retiring was that ten years in office was the limit for any one person. Jordan left the NUL shortly before it was hit by severe budget cuts to social services by the Reagan administration. It lost almost 80 percent of its federal funding during the 1980s.

When he retired from the NUL, Jordan said he would no longer be on the cutting edge of the civil rights movement, but he would still be involved as a lawyer. He joined the law firm Akim, Gump, Strauss, Hauer & Feld and has worked for the Dallas, Texas-based firm for more than a decade as a full partner.

Jackie Joyner-Kersee

Athlete, Olympic gold medalist
Born March 3, 1962, St. Louis, Illinois

"I remember where I came from, and I keep that in mind.... If the young female sees the environment I grew up in and sees my dreams and goals come true, they will realize their dreams and goals might [also] come true."

The heptathalon is one of the most gruelling sports in the Summer Olympic Games. This seven-event sport consists of the 200- and 800-meter dashes, the 100-meter hurdles, and four field events: the high jump, long jump, shot put, and javelin throw. Despite humble beginnings—she finished last in her first track competition—Jackie Joyner-Kersee has become a master of this sport.

She is the only woman to gain more than 7,000 points in the heptathalon four times. She also set a world record for the two-day event with 7,215 points at the Olympic trials, prior to the competition itself. Her superb performances have led her to receive numerous awards and accolades, and she is often touted as the world's greatest female athlete in the late 1980s.

Thrived despite tough early circumstances

Kersee was born on March 3, 1962, in East St. Louis, Illinois, to Alfred and Mary Joyner, both teenagers at the time. The city was economically depressed, and Kersee grew up in an area that was ravaged by street crime. Her family lived in a broken-down house and often slept in the kitchen to keep warm by the stove. With little food in the house, Kersee had to make do with mayonnaise sandwiches.

Despite her tough circumstances, she was determined to be a winner. At the age of nine Kersee entered her first track and field meet, but she finished dead last. She began training hard and by the end of the next week she could already feel improvement. She was soon winning meets, especially in the long jump, where it looked like she was most talented. When she was twelve years old, she jumped over 17 feet. Her family wanted to help her improve, and they installed a long jump pit at the end of their porch. They hauled sand in potato chip bags from a local playground to make the pit. The more she trained, the better she got. She became an inspiration to her brother, Alfred,

Jr., who would one day become an Olympic gold medalist in the triple jump.

Although Kersee spent much of her time practicing track, she did not let her academic studies slip. Her parents enticed her to study by grounding her for any Ds or failing grades. Kersee made excellent marks in high school and continued to develop her athletic skills. She won her first National Junior Pentathlon Championship when she was fourteen. She duplicated that feat for the next three years. In her junior year she set an Illinois state high school record of 20 feet, $7^1/_2$ inches in the long jump. Besides track, Kersee was involved in several other sports. She played volleyball and basketball and was part of the Lincoln High School girls basketball team that won sixty-two of sixty-four games during her last two years of school.

Earned place on U.S. Olympic team

In 1980 Kersee graduated in the top 10 percent of her class and accepted a basketball scholarship to the University of California at Los Angeles (UCLA). Before she began her freshman year she earned a spot on the U.S. Olympic team in the long jump. But instead of competing in the Olympics, Kersee and the rest of the American squad watched from the sidelines, due to the U.S.-instigated boycott of the 1980 Olympic Games in Moscow to protest the Soviet Union's invasion of Afghanistan. Kersee suffered another setback midway through her freshman year when her mother died of meningitis.

These setbacks only hardened her determination to become an Olympic athlete. She met Bob Kersee, whom she later married, and he convinced her to start competing in the heptathlon. Bob was a genius at recognizing raw talent and had the ability to mold athletes into contenders. With Bob acting as her coach, she qualified for the world track and field championships in Helsinki, Finland, in 1983, but she pulled a hamstring muscle and was unable to compete. She suffered from more bad luck the next year. During the Olympic Games in Los Angeles, California, she suffered another hamstring pull that caused her to fall 30 points behind the leader during her first day in the heptathlon. She fought back with an incredible throw in the javelin event, which set the stage for a showdown in the competition's final event, the 800-meter run. Kersee ran hard, but it was not enough to win the gold medal. She finished .06 seconds behind the time she needed to win, forcing her to settle for the silver.

The second-place finish boosted her confidence, and she knew that if she continued working hard she could eventually win the gold. In 1986 she participated in the Goodwill Games in Moscow and broke the world record in an amazing fashion. Kersee was the first athlete in history to break the 7,000 point mark in the heptathlon. Less than a month later she broke her own world record at the U.S. Olympic Festival in Houston, Texas. As a result of her outstanding performances she received the 1986 Sullivan Award, the 1986 Jesse Owens Award, and the *Track and Field News* Athlete of the Year Award.

These awards further encouraged her. In 1987 she won gold medals in heptathlon and long jump at the world track and field championships in Rome, Italy. Later that year she received the McDonald's Amateur Sportswoman of the Year Award and was named the 1987 Female Athlete of the Year by the Associated Press. She also grabbed newspaper headlines and magazine covers for her unorthodox and sexy racing outfits: fluorescent-colored bodysuits with one leg sheared off, covered by bikini bottoms, long hair, and three-inch multicolored fingernails.

Awarded Olympic gold medals

Her shining moment occurred at the 1988 Olympic Games in Seoul, South Korea. She won gold medals in the heptathlon and long jump, breaking her own heptathlon record in the process. She shared the spotlight with her sister-in-law, Florence Griffith Joyner, who won three gold medals. Since her superb performance, Kersee has received numerous accolades and honors. Kersee was again selected McDonald's Amateur Sportswoman of the

Jackie Joyner-Kersee

Year and the city of St. Louis named a day in her honor.

Kersee has sometimes been charged with using drugs to assist her performance, but she has always successfully defended her reputation by submitting to numerous tests that have found her drug free. She also suffers from asthma and cannot take the best medicine available to control the condition, since she would be ruled ineligible for competition.

Kersee has not forgotten where she came from. She raised $40,000 in her hometown of East St. Louis to reopen the Mary Brown Community Center, where she started her track and field career. During her visit she was introduced to 2,000 teenagers at the Kiel Opera House as "outstanding, beautiful, one of the fastest running and jumping and stomping women in history!" Kersee spoke about her goals and dreams and the importance of putting something back into the community that helped her along the way. When she is not in her hometown she tours the country, lecturing youth and civic groups and lending inspiration and insight.

And Kersee still has personal goals: "People look at my marks and say, 'you can't go any faster.' I don't believe that. I believe you can go faster in the hurdles and I believe I can throw farther and jump farther."

Index

Volume number appears in **bold**.

Art

Hunter, Clementine **2**
Lawrence, Jacob **3**
Parks, Gordon **3**
Tanner, Henry Ossawa **4**

Business

Bing, Dave **1**
Eldridge, Elleanor **2**
Gaston, Arthur **2**
Gordy, Berry, Jr. **2**
Johnson, John H. **2**
Owens, Jesse **3**
Proctor, Barbara Gardner **3**
Randall, Dudley **3**
Sims, Naomi **4**
Walker, Madame C.J. **4**
Walker, Maggie L. **4**
Winfrey, Oprah **4**

Dance

Ailey, Alvin **1**
Dunham, Katherine **1**
Hines, Gregory **2**
Jones, Bill T. **2**

Education

Asante, Molefi Kete **1**
Baker, Augusta **1**
Baraka, Amiri **1**
Barnett, Marguerite Ross **1**
Bethune, Mary McLeod **1**

Chisholm, Shirley **1**
Clark, Joe **1**
Cobb, Jewel Plummer **1**
Cole, Johnnetta Betsch **1**
Collins, Marva **1**
Cooper, Anna J. **1**
Craft, Ellen **1**
Davis, Angela **1**
Derricotte, Juliette **1**
Diggs, Irene **1**
Du Bois, William Edward
  Burghardt (W.E.B.) **1**
Futrell, Mary Hatwood **2**
Gates, Henry Louis, Jr. **2**
Hill, Anita **2**
Lewis, Elma **3**
Madgett, Naomi Long **3**
McClellan, George Marion **3**
Robeson, Elsanda Goode **3**
Rollins, Charlemae Hill **3**
Scott, Gloria **4**
Steele, Shelby **4**
Sudarkasa, Niara **4**
Terrell, Mary Church **4**
Washington, Booker T. **4**
Woodson, Carter G. **4**

Exploration and adventure

Coleman, Bessie **1**
Henson, Matthew **2**

Fashion

Campbell, Naomi **1**
Houston, Whitney **2**
Johnson, Beverly **2**
Keckley, Elizabeth **3**
Kelly, Patrick **3**

Malone, Annie Turnbo **3**
Sims, Naomi **4**

Film

Belafonte, Harry **1**
Berry, Halle **1**
Campbell, Naomi **1**
Davis, Ossie **1**
Davis, Sammy, Jr. **1**
Givens, Robin **2**
Glover, Danny **2**
Goldberg, Whoopi **2**
Gregory, Dick **2**
Hall, Arsenio **2**
Hines, Gregory **2**
Horne, Lena **2**
Houston, Whitney **2**
Ice-T **2**
Jackson, Janet **2**
Johnson, Beverly **2**
Jones, James Earl **2**
Lee, Spike **3**
McDaniel, Hattie **3**
McQueen, Thelma
  "Butterfly" **3**
Murphy, Eddie **3**
Parks, Gordon **3**
Poitier, Sidney **3**
Pryor, Richard **3**
Robeson, Paul **3**
Ross, Diana **3**
Singleton, John **4**
Snipes, Wesley **4**
Townsend, Robert **4**
Van Peebles, Mario **4**
Washington, Denzel **4**
Wayans, Keenen Ivory **4**
Winfrey, Oprah **4**